Teaching the Bilingual

New Methods and Old Traditions

Frank Pialorsi, editor

The University of Arizona Press

Tucson, Arizona

About the Editor . . .

Frank Pialorsi's interest in bilingual education began when, as a Fulbright lecturer at the University of Athens from 1963–65, he conducted classes in English as a second language. He later taught ESL methodology in Lebanon, Japan, and Korea under the Fulbright program. Since joining the faculty of the University of Arizona in 1967, he has received a Ph.D., headed the Center for English as a Second Language, directed the intensive summer programs for English for Spanish-speaking people, and taught English for foreign students. His publications are concerned with problems in bilingual education and ESL methodology.

THE UNIVERSITY OF ARIZONA PRESS

I.S.B.N. 8165-0372-9
L.C. No. 73-87717

For my father, who taught himself English

Contents

CHARTS AND TABLES

Preface

TAKEN AS A WHOLE, these readings represent an extremely varied mixture of subject matter and approaches, including a wide range of strongly held and often conflicting opinions and convictions with respect to the learning problems of bilingual and bidialectal students — notably the American Indian, the Spanish-speaking, and the urban black. This combination has been chosen to provide teachers who must now teach minority groups within a traditional system the opportunity to expand their scope of alternatives. In contrast to those who feel it would be best to allow the educational house to collapse to make way for rebuilding, I am simply offering material to repair the roof over the kitchen.

Three separate sections are headed up by the editor's general overview. The first part deals with a basic prerequisite to success in teaching the bilingual: bicultural understanding. Without personal and intimate understanding of and respect for the cultures of his minority-group students, the teacher cannot hope for meaningful communication in the classroom. The readings in the first part of this book will help him to assess his own role, whom he teaches, what he teaches, and what he *can* teach.

Part 2 is devoted to theories and experiments in multilingual communication and language learning. Readings range from general theoretical discussions to specific field surveys, all selected to provide the teacher with a view of possible applications and approaches.

The final section deals with practical application of theories and techniques in actual school programs. This last collection makes no claims of proving which techniques are best; instead it includes a variety of procedures which well-trained and experienced people are finding useful and which can serve as a base for further inquiry.

In his *Preface to Logic,* Morris R. Cohen writes, "Mixed studies, like mixed races and mixed constitutions, show the greatest vitality, and there could be no valid objection to the same textbook treating all . . .

important matters, provided the information given were accurate and the various points of view clearly distinguished." This has been the guideline for this volume.

I express my thanks to Keith H. Basso and Herbert B. Wilson, whose provocative courses concerning linguistic analysis and the culturally disadvantaged led to my gathering this collection of readings, and to Cecil Robinson for his helpful criticism. I also thank the staff of the University of Arizona Press for their skill and cooperation in projecting this book into published form.

FRANK PIALORSI

Introduction: An Overview of the Problems

The subject of how to make education more relevant for minority students, despite its broadness, does offer the chance to view various theories and procedures with a scope that specialization does not often permit. Our main obligation to minority-group young people is definitely twofold: one aspect is linguistic, the other cultural. The subtitle of this book, *New Methods and Old Traditions,* is not meant to imply contrast but complementarity.

To the responsible teacher, a sensible recognition of cultural and linguistic tradition should influence methods in the language class and in the overall education of ethnic groups. The proper degree of this recognition and influence is the question. The past has taught us that not enough produces a strong feeling of minority. But over-emphasis, in spite of what some fervent culturalists in the fields of anthropology, linguistics, politics, sociology, and education maintain, seems to bring about a not-so-splendid isolationism. Today various ethnic groups are making it clear that they do not wish to be tossed into that rather unstable equalizer, the American melting pot. Their minority roots, buried and sometimes trampled into the soil of the North American continent, are too old. They prefer instead to enhance the contents of the pot as a cultural side dish.

Not always trusting the statistics of academicians, we can hear testimony from the groups themselves. For example, in 1968, and appropriately on the Fourth of July, a three-column ad appeared in a Tucson, Arizona, daily newspaper. The relatively moderate Mexican-American position was never so clearly stated before or since. The ad was placed in direct response to an editorial which had urged the community to drop mentally, as well as graphically, its use of hyphenated Americanisms. We are all simply Americans, the editorial had claimed. Many in the Mexican-American community thought otherwise. Following are portions of their statement, which summarize the predominant moderate attitudes of the Mexican-American and, with few exceptions, of the other ethnic minorities:

[3]

The distortions and stereotypes contained in your editorial entitled "Hyphenated Americanism" was received with patient indignation by the Mexican-American community of Tucson. This city has the unique opportunity to gain strength and character through the conscious development of the three major minority groups represented in metropolitan Tucson — the American Indian, the Afro-American, and the Mexican-American. . . .

It is true that some of us have been fortunate enough to get an education. Statistics, however, prove that only a very few of us fall into the educated category. Throughout the Southwest, Mexican-Americans average 7.1 median years of schooling against 12.1 for Anglos and 9.0 for non-whites.

The Mexican-American takes pride in using the English language, which we accept as our national language. Nonetheless, we also enjoy the broader horizon of communication that comes from understanding Spanish, particularly in the Western hemisphere. The freedom to speak Spanish was, after all, guaranteed to us by the Treaty of Guadalupe Hidalgo.*

Now that a new philosophy is working in favor of minority groups in our pluralistic society, the dominant group is suddenly alarmed to find hyphenated Americans effectively working toward the establishment of social, economic, and political rights that have always been ours under the Constitution. The melting pot theory is based on the concept of wiping out the fundamental cultural distinctions of minority groups. The people who share these distinctive cultural attributes are therefore taught that the differences are a destructive force in the United States social framework to the extent that a stigma has been attached to them. We, however, view our cultural heritage as a source of pride and unity.

Mexican-American, the hyphenated term which we have accepted to identify the ethnic group that we represent, serves us well, for it recognizes our heritage as well as our nationality.

Both children and adults have been left so confused in regard to their position in the "American way of life" which stresses social and philosophical values for an Anglo-only society, that when these Americans are asked about their nationality, they respond with such answers as Spanish, Spanish-American, Latin, Latin-American, Mexican and Mexican-American. If an individual does not know who he is, how can he make an effective contribution to our ever-changing pluralistic society?[1]

Over one hundred Mexican-American citizens signed the above statement. They represented the Mexican-American Unity Council, the American Coordinating Council on Political Education, and the League of United Latin American Citizens.

To make education relevant for the children of these people, we must bear in mind their feelings. Too often our classes have done too little to improve the lot of minority-group students in a bilingual and bicultural society that tries to insist that it is not. Applied linguists, teachers of English as a second language, and teachers of English all would find it pleasant if their only worry was still a mere linguistic obligation — simply to "teach these people good English." But today it must be realized that

---

*The Treaty of Guadalupe Hidalgo contains no statement providing for the establishment of schools taught in the Spanish language.

the goal is to help every child become all that he can. To achieve this goal with minority children, no cultural or linguistic factor can be ignored.

Many of our schools must make great changes, especially those schools which fail to offer large numbers of non-native English speakers definite procedures for English language study. Many such schools are still giving minority-group children only a year or two of "special" English instruction. Afterward they are sent into the regular school programs. Some schools, influenced by structural-behaviorist methodology, limit English lessons to audio-lingual practice with no emphasis on reading or writing. The distinct disadvantage to the minority-group child when he rejoins his Anglo peers is obvious.

Today, too many, especially in the Mexican-Spanish communities, have had enough of these so-called "remedial" English classes and strictly Anglo-oriented school programs. They are tired of the accompanying sense of inferiority which automatically brings about poor performances by their children, who can speak and write neither good English nor good Spanish.

In response to their protests, many modern educators have come to the conclusion that English should be taught to non-native speakers as a second language for eight or even twelve years. For some students, this instruction should even be extended into the first year of college. What this program amounts to is a bilingual school in which the pupils are given primary instruction in their native language. Afterward they are taught through the use of both languages, except in the language classes. (In the Southwest, this notion is not so far-fetched, if we considered the area as having a pluralistic culture and a multilingual society.)

At this point we should distinguish between bilingual education and English as a second language (ESL). Bilingual education is the use of the native or home language as the medium for teaching a large part or even the whole of the curriculum. ESL is simply one aspect of this curriculum, however important. Bilingual exercises or the practice of alternately using two languages is still in the experimental stage as a classroom discipline, especially above the elementary levels. Another approach, relatively untried, which can be seen in recent Mexican-American literature, makes use of what Phillip Ortego calls "binary phenomenon at its best." This is a structured, creative mixing of the two languages, as can be seen in Alurista's poem quoted later in this chapter.

Language achievement tests, here and abroad, seem to indicate considerable superiority among bilingual pupils over monolinguals. An example of such test results, which shows that the problem is not indigenous to the United States only, concerns a bilingual school in South Africa:

> The English-speaking pupils, being the less bilingual to start with, gained more in Afrikaans than the Afrikaans-speaking pupils gained in English; in

fact, the gain was more than four times as big. As regards the first language or mother tongue, whether English or Afrikaans, there was no loss whatsoever on the part of those pupils attending the bilingual school. The highest degree of bilingualism, i.e. that obtained by adding the Afrikaans and English scores together, was obtained by bilingual children attending bilingual schools. Next came the bilinguals and Afrikaans home-language children attending English-medium schools, next bilinguals in Afrikaans-medium schools. The lowest on the list were the unilingual home language pupils attending unilingual-medium schools where the medium was the same as the home language, English and Afrikaans single-medium schools being about equally poor.[2]

Similar but less-detailed studies in the United States indicate the same results.[3]

But something else has been happening in the American Southwest. Emphasis has shifted from concern with merely language problems to an interest in reestablishing things Mexican as definitely inherent in the southwestern United States' experience. The purpose has been to give the Spanish-Mexican culture, as well as language, nearly the same emphasis that the English language and the historical English influence have over the rest of the country. This concern for the Spanish language and a reasonable propagation of the Spanish-Mexican heritage was shown prominently at the National Conference on Educational Opportunities for Mexican-Americans held in Austin, Texas, in 1968. The conferees were quite clear about their cultural objectives, which can be summarized thusly:

• Spanish and Mexican culture is as much a part of the American Southwest as any other aspect.

• In the states of California, Arizona, Texas, New Mexico, and Nevada, especially, we have a dual culture that in no way weakens the unity of the country except for prejudices and suspicions which have existed since the Anglos, Mexicans, and Spaniards first met to trade on the old Santa Fe Trail. The Mexican heritage should in no way be made secondary.

• The Spanish language, especially at the beginning grade levels, should serve with English as a means of communication in the classroom and among the students.

• Class content, especially history and literature, should include material from a vast bicultural storehouse which at present lies unused.

Those who feel these aims are too strong should remember that they are the reaction against an Anglo prejudice that for two hundred years could see no value in diversity.

⌐ As for the best methods of teaching English to non-native speakers and ethnic groups, we are not much beyond the planning stage. One paper at the 1968 Austin conference pinpointed the following needs in this area:

1. Diagnostic and performance tests need to be developed in order to determine the stage of bilinguality of students.
2. A wide variety of multi-level, well-articulated, programmed materials needs to be developed to meet both the group and individual needs of students.
3. The second language approach needs to be applied to the other language arts.
4. The teacher preparation implications of the above factors need considerable exploration and attention.[4]

Since this paper was presented, some progress toward these goals has been made. However, at more recent conferences on minority education, the conclusions have been just about the same. Aside from the few government-sponsored Title VII programs on the elementary level, little has been done. Predominantly Mexican-American schools in Arizona, for example, show English language programs in the planning state or as makeshift operations at most. By makeshift I mean inadequate scheduling and inexperienced and sometimes actually incompetent teaching, however well intentioned.

In government-sponsored programs for teaching English, oftentimes the money has come well before adequate planning. The fear of cutbacks, real and imaginary, has led project directors to the stance that, no matter what, there can be no failures. Reports of the success of various minority projects are bewildering to say the least. For example, I seriously felt that one such program went against just about everything I had ever learned in courses in English as a second language. At least two other linguists passed the same judgment. But, say the published reports, results show that "favorable attitudes toward [the project] . . . were consistent."

Beyond the cries for improvement in planning and implementation of such English language programs, another plea is repeatedly heard at conferences regarding the linguistic problems of minority groups. The majority of participants feel that the teacher of bilinguals, Anglo or Mexican-American, must be able to "feel" two cultures. But by being exposed only to strongly bicultural teachers (which to me means either Mexican-Americans or possibly Anglos fluent in Spanish who might have or think they might have a strong "feel" for the second culture), will the children have less interest in learning a second language for which they might "feel" no real need or affinity? It is true that the teacher must be free of any kind of ethnocentric nonsense. But if he is an Anglo in a predominantly Spanish-speaking society with a good contrastive analysis of the two languages always in mind, I maintain that an open cross-cultural attitude will open up more avenues between him and his students, and between his students and the Anglo majority known as the outside world, than will any hint of dual-centric pussyfooting.

No matter how English is looked upon by defensive minorities, it is a very real fact that a lack of usable English is one of the main reasons for the negative aspects of what Oscar Lewis has called the "culture of poverty." Before 1970, one had only to read the classified sections of any large city newspaper for evidence of this fact. In Los Angeles, for example, in the late 1960s, domestic servants could earn $125 per month with no English; $175 with a little English; and $200 to $300 with fluent English. This kind of blatant linguistic-economic discrimination has given way to simple announcements by employment agencies that they have "all kinds and all races." (Alleviating the plight of monolingual house-holders are printed aids such as *Learn How to Speak Spanish with Your Servant,*[5] a title which doubtlessly proves distasteful among the Spanish-speaking population.)

Even without considering socio-economic pressures, I don't think we have to apologize for requiring minorities to learn a language that is spoken by so many the world over. The possession of the skill to use English as a meaningful *second* language has very little to do with the damaging effects of acculturation and transculturation. The problems stem from attitudes and approaches within the schools. Anyone who has tried to learn a second language knows that the artificial classroom situa-tion requires a great deal of language practice. But outside the language class, in other areas of study, would practice achieved in a strongly bilin-gual situation, if implemented with better teaching techniques, allow us to take full advantage of the bicultural atmosphere and get even better results in both the cognitive and affective domains? I apologize for doing no more than raising the question, but perhaps it will encourage more research and innovation at all levels.

The matter of curriculum in the English class should certainly be a welcome challenge. We cannot forget the old axiom that language is a skill. Like any other skill, it must be practiced in order to be mastered or even used with minimum adequacy, especially at the primary level. Audio-lingual drill is in disrepute among some linguists, who are stressing the return to a rational or metalinguistic approach. People use language, they say, because they are rational. Intellect is more important than the mimic-memorization process.

But before we accept this wholesale premise, we might ask why a child acquires more competence faster than the more rational adult in learning a second language. And before deciding anything we should examine the objectives and results of the different approaches. The facts must be weighed carefully if our goal is to have our children move back and forth from one language to another. In speaking to Japanese teachers of English in Tokyo a few years ago, Charles Scott warned that because the audio-lingual approach to teaching language was so closely associated with developments in structural linguistics, it was a great temptation for the English teacher to look only to structural linguistics for the data and theoretical basis for his language teaching and ignore the less widely published material. Says Scott:

Such action will be of little benefit to the language teaching profession, since the very fact that there is more than one kind of "descriptive" linguistics being practiced today is not only a healthy indication of new vigor in linguistics itself, but also an indication of potentially new vigor in the entire English language teaching profession.[6]

Today, of course, there is good material on the transformational or generative approach, plus numerous eclectic procedures worth looking into.

An increasing number of recognized minority writers are telling us what a psychological jolt they experienced when they first understood the implications of being part of a minority in the United States. Teachers should make use of these writers, who can instruct the majority as well. This is especially true for the secondary level, at which there is an abundance of material explaining the ties and animosities of the different cultures. This vast storehouse could provide our language, literature, and history classes with a refreshingly different and truer view of this country today and yesterday. Our textbooks sadly need to include more writing pertinent to *all* those groups who have had a part in shaping America. Any classroom experience is more relevant if young learners can honestly feel they have some sort of cultural stake in the subject matter. In her short but penetrating book on Mexican-American youth, Celia Heller reports that the facts show that many of the Mexican-American dropouts know English well enough; the problem comes from "their so-called failure to assimilate."[7] She also points out that many second and third generation youths speak English with a foreign accent. If our task is to teach English, we should use English to instruct the student about himself and his world. This can be done through the simplest drill as well as the sophisticated essay. For example, efforts are finally being made to create material to which the Indian child can somehow relate. (Until recently American Indians were learning English from texts written for Spanish-speaking children in New York City.)

We should not be afraid of controversial material, for it is becoming obvious that it will be up to the schools to resolve so many of the cultural problems that plague us. One anthropologist has even suggested that non-English-speaking students start learning at an early age such situational statements as "Pay me"; "I want a raise"; "I quit"; and "Don't push me." Later they could struggle with something more sophisticated, such as, "Obviously you are not acquainted with the fair wage law of this country, you chiseling jackass."[8] But the problem, contrary to what some pragmatists think, is not simply one of finding the proper subject matter, for the complications of language represent different social realities.

The attempt to resolve what we might call the duo-cultural trauma is very much in evidence in the writing of the Mexican-American/Chicano intellectual. An extreme and intriguing example of treating two languages as "a single linguistic repertoire"[9] is found in the work of the Mexican-born poet, Alurista:[10]

> We Walk on Pebbled Streets
>
> we walk on pebbled streets
>   de orgullo pisoteado
> con placas (símbolos de la ley?)
>   the hassle
>   and the man:
> "hey . . .
>   punk; how old are you?
> —what are you doing"
>   —and he doesn't know
> we like to walk
>   mi gente a caminado mucho
> —desde el asia
>   through north amérika
> to the land of pulque y tunas
>   where the bean grows
> iron clad
>   tradición sagrada
> he hassles
>   and we walk
> like our forefathers
>
>   we walk
>   on calles empedradas
>   con sangre
>   orgullo lacerado
>   it bleeds
>   to freedom our wounds will heal
>   LA RAZA cicatriza
>   en la liberación
>   con voluntad propia
>   to dwell in the self determination
>   of our lives
>   and of our ambiente
>   of things and ideas
>   to design our streets
>   and pave our paths
>   self-willed eternamente
>   so that we may resume our walk
>   without a hassling badge
>   who knows not
>   porque camino.

Preceding Alurista's sophisticated form of a "binary phenomenon" (which some traditional detractors criticize as an inflated claim) are variations of so-called Border Spanish which, with more research, might have some useful implications in bilingual education. The following example from the Tijuana area is a combination of "low class" Spanish (so described by educated Spanish speakers from north and south of the border) and English borrowings shaped to fit Spanish morphology. Non-Spanish elements are italicized:

> Mi menda [mente?] es chicano, he pedaleado por los estaires bute de añales. Soy solano, no tengo cueva, ni *waifa* [wife], pero me *laican* [like] las gavachas, las huisas y las tintas. . . . [Mi padre] le *laicaban* [liked] *tu moch* [very much] las cebadas. . . . siempre estaba *wachado* [watched] por las chota o enjaulado en el tariz. Se pasondeo allí *gud taim* [a lot of time] porque medio apaño a un bolillo pá' tumbarle su jando.[11]

To the purists who object to such language disruption, we might reply that lexical borrowing by English speakers since the Norman invasion can be compared to nothing less than highway robbery. As for the Spanish-speaking objector, he should contemplate "pure" Castilian Spanish with its four thousand or so Arabic words.

* * *

Serious socio-linguistic problems among our children are not limited to non-native speakers. Among the twenty million blacks in the United States, non-standard dialects have proved to be a handicap to social and economic mobility. For example, one black student took a job as a receptionist for a Chicago television station, only to be dismissed after a one-week trial period filled with complaints by telephone callers from around the country who had found the girl's dialect totally incomprehensible. Today, demonstrable in the work of linguists and educators such as William Labov and Kenneth Johnson,[12] more and more attention is being paid to the treatment of bidialectalism. The approach of the past under predominantly Anglo authority, which might be summed up as "be or at least sound like us," is giving way to an understanding of the external as well as the internal forces that influence children in our educational systems. In other words, educators are reassessing the amount and value of the learning that actually goes on within the formal organizational compound known as the school, which for too long has unrealistically tried to place itself in a middle-class vacuum, apart from the overwhelming influences of our society.

Another promising note is the increasing number of college students interested in English as a second language and the related areas of bilingualism and bidialectalism. The Institute of International Education has listed over forty major colleges and universities that offer degree and certificate programs in the teaching of English as a second language. Several have Ph.D. programs. The institute also lists twenty-nine other schools which offer one or more courses in the area.[13]

English as a second language, along with bilingual and bidialectal education, is now a highly specialized field. It requires more than just the theoretical linguist, who sometimes comes dangerously close to overstepping his point of usefulness, frequently confirming Jespersen's observation that "breadth of vision is not conspicuous in modern linguistics." The supplements needed after the courses have been taken and the degrees have been received are the linguist's cool detachment from any pretensions about languages or language learning, the language teacher's love of language in and for itself, and the social anthropologist's keen insight into all aspects of life which influence the students.

Lack of such insight is common among some of our most dedicated teachers, as is repeatedly indicated by problems of motivation. A San Carlos Apache, Ned Anderson, outlines such problems as they affect American Indian students:

> Although competition has found a place in their lives in contact with the dominant society, the trait is less of a stimulus in the Indian society. Perhaps this is because few of the inhabitants of the Indian communities are motivated to strive for "success." The "successful" person, as pictured by the institution, is usually an outsider whose status is seemingly unattainable and *even undesirable in the eyes of the Indian.* [Italics mine][14]

Anderson, the first Apache from San Carlos to receive a college degree, continued his education in law school. He goes on to explain that this form of passivity on the part of the Indian student in our present educational system results in his failure to ask questions and seek clarification when needed. Under such a system there will no doubt continue to be a lack of achievement among Indian students as well as among students from other minority groups, due to their inability to relate themselves to the future.

Another problem besetting children from the reservation, the barrio, and the ghetto is a traditional lack of experiences which would benefit them when they enter higher education. Anyone who has visited a reservation boarding school knows that the students are exposed to the outside world through such elements as books, teachers, trips to town, and television. However, despite such exposures, so many young people who have grown up in the *midst* of our complicated society are finding it increasingly difficult to maintain with assurance any concept of self.

The remedying of such complex sociological situations is a great professional burden on the teacher, who originally simply wanted to teach language and literature. But it is a burden which must be taken up. With the help of linguistics and psychology, language teachers have had more than limited success in getting students to produce and comprehend English statements; the failure has been in giving them no "real sense of urgency" for using English or ways of reassessing their reasoning to make the philosophical switch that is necessary in going back and forth from one language to another.

In the field of language learning, the work of the teacher, the linguist, and the psychologist is by no means completed. We might say we haven't yet finished the first shift.

Through careful and imaginative language and cultural instruction, we must invest the teaching of our children — minority and majority — with pertinent inquiry, experiment, and reassessment. In doing this, we will establish and maintain the best possible method as a tradition.

Notes

1. *Arizona Daily Star,* July 4, 1968.
2. E.G. Malherbe, *Commentary: Description and Measurement of Bilingualism, An International Seminar,* ed. L.G. Kelly (Toronto: University of Toronto Press, 1969), p. 47.
3. See for example, the mimeographed report of the Conference on the Education of Spanish-Speaking Children and Youth (University of Texas, Austin, 1968). See also Nancy Modiano's study in Chapter 13 of this book for similar test results in a school in the central highlands of Mexico.
4. Frank Angel, "Program Content to Meet the Educational Needs of Mexican-Americans," in the mimeographed report of the Conference on the Education of Spanish-Speaking Children and Youth, 1968.
5. El Paso: Sandoval News Service, Inc., n.d.
6. Charles T. Scott, "Linguistic Science and the Teaching of English," in *Preliminaries to English Teaching* (Tokyo: English Language Exploratory Committee, 1966), p. 45.
7. Celia Heller, *Mexican-American Youth: Forgotten Youth at the Crossroads* (New York: Random House, 1966), p. 30.
8. Interview with Octavio Romano, *Druid Free Press* (Tucson), Nov. 5, 1969, p. 5.
9. John J. Gumperz, "Communication in Multilingual Societies," in *Cognitive Anthropology* ed. Stephen A. Tyler. (New York: Holt, Rinehart and Winston, 1969).
10. Reprinted from Alurista, *floricanto en aztlán* (Los Angeles: Aztlán Publications, Chicano Studies Center, University of California, 1971), poem 20.
11. Hernán Solís Garza, *Los Mexicanos del Norte* (Mexico City: Editorial Nuestro Tiempo, S.A., 1971), p. 90.
12. See for example Johnson's study of nonstandard Negro dialect in Chapter 16 of this book.
13. Association for Foreign Student Affairs, *English Language and Orientation Programs in the United States* (New York: Institute of International Education, 1969).
14. Ned Anderson, "I Broke the Barrier," *Indian Programs* 1 (Winter 1970): 1.

PART ONE

Prerequisite:
BICULTURAL UNDRSTANDING

There was a child went forth every day,
And the first object he look'd upon, that obt he became
And that object became part of him. . .
— Walt Whitman

1.

Just What Is "Equal Opportunity"?

ASHLEY MONTAGU

In a period when equality of opportunity is a principle which is at long last coming to be widely accepted, it is more than ever necessary to be alerted to certain problems which are bound to develop and which are likely to be with us for some time. Black children, and the children of Puerto Rican, Mexican, and American Indian descent, as well as others, will increasingly continue to find themselves in schools and in other situations in which they will not, on the whole, do as well as white children. Nor, on the whole, will members of these ethnic groups do as well in the open competitive market as whites.

In schools and colleges these non-white groups, though to a lesser extent than formerly, will continue to lag substantially behind in I.Q. tests and in school performance, as well as in general achievement. In view of these probabilities it is desirable for everyone concerned to understand what that lag almost certainly means, in order to guard against the danger of drawing the wrong conclusions.

Observe, it will be said by many, that they (especially blacks) now enjoy equal opportunities for education, and after years of it, where are their great scientists, their great inventors, their great abstract thinkers? A few writers, yes. Some athletes, yes. But, then, there has always been a sprinkling of those. Does not this lack of achievement, under conditions of equal opportunity, fully and at long last, remove all doubt that these people are of genetically inferior stuff compared to whites?

Reprinted from *Vista* 6 (Nov.-Dec. 1970): pp. 23–35, 56.

Ashley Montagu, formerly of Harvard University and of New York University, was chairman of the Department of Anthropology at Rutgers 1949–55. Through his books and lectures he has become a major influence in informing the public of the latest thinking in anthropology and social biology. His well-known works include *Man: His First Million Years, Man: His First Two Million Years,* and *Man's Most Dangerous Myth: The Fallacy of Race.*

The answer is that while it might seem so, the probabilities are that the failure to achieve equally under conditions of "equal opportunity" is due to environmental rather than to genetic deficiencies. For this conclusion there exists a considerable amount of evidence, some of which we shall consider in what follows. It is, however, much easier to attribute differences in achievement, especially scholastic achievement, to differences in innate factors, to heredity. But since the heredity of the individual represents the expression of the interaction between his genes and the environment in which those genes have undergone development, clearly the environment must always be considered as a major factor in attempting to assess the influences that have been operative in the expression of any trait. The meaning of this statement does not appear to have been always understood by those who have drawn the "obvious conclusions."

There is good reason to believe that what most of us have regarded as "equal opportunities," that is, the process of providing the young of different ethnic groups with the same conditions for learning and intellectual development, have, in fact, never existed. Never existed for the simple reason that those opportunities are unequally received. The unequal reception, the evidence suggests, is due not to group genetic differences, but to group cultural differences, to culturally produced impediments in the ability to learn and to think at comparatively equal levels of abstraction.

For high, even adequate, intellectual achievement certain prerequisite conditions are apparently necessary, quite unrelated to the quality of the genetic potentialities of the individual, assuming, of course, that these potentialities are normal. The necessary conditions are complex, but may be described as a stimulating cultural environment which encourages high aspiration levels.

A black child from the ghetto in the same classroom with a white child from the neighboring white slum areas is not enjoying equal opportunities in the classroom for the simple reason that he is not in a position to learn as relevant to himself much to which he is being exposed. The school generally offers him little that he can creatively incorporate into the background of his own ghetto culture. In that culture respect for learning has no place nor is there any high valuation of the ability for high abstract thought, so necessary for achievement in the sciences, philosophy, and the humanities, not to mention ordinary schoolwork.

The black ghetto child comes not only from a culture of poverty, but from a poverty of culture, parentally uninspired, rootless, barren, and aridly one-dimensional. He is altogether lacking in a framework in which to fit the ordinates to which he is being exposed, and which are for the most part meaningless to him because he has no means of putting them together into a meaningful co-ordinate system. The individual himself, it appears, must be rooted in a three- or four-dimensional cultural matrix through the ordinates of which he can meaningfully incorporate, learn, what he is being taught.

It is not sufficiently often pointed out that every individual must learn to learn, and that a great part of this is accomplished by the kind of stimulation he receives in the home, in relationships with parents and siblings, long before the child gets to school. The child, other things being more or less equal, will learn in the school in a manner very largely influenced by the kind of learning experiences he has undergone at home. Here the white child enjoys immense advantages over the black. By the time the black child arrives at school he has usually suffered massive deprivations which have resulted not only in a serious failure of development in his learning capacities, but also in his ability to assimilate what he does learn in anything like the meaningful context and manner with which the white child is able to learn.

The kind of changes that must occur in the black home and culture before the black child can enter the classroom on an equal footing with, and as prepared to learn as, the white child are complex. These changes probably belong in the same category as those that are and have been operative in many societies in which peoples of very different cultural backgrounds have come together without the more highly developed one, after many centuries, seeming to have had any significant effect in stimulating the creativity of the acculturated group. Let me give an example of this. The Romans occupied Britain for five hundred years, but insofar as any possible stimulus to creativity was concerned, the Britons seem largely to have escaped it. Invasions by Scandinavians, Celts, Angles, Jutes, Saxons, and Normans, extending over a period of more than a thousand years, similarly seem to have had little effect. It would, indeed, have been easy to conclude that the Britons were a genetically ill-endowed people. Following all that contact and stimulation by so many different peoples, what did the native population have to show for it? An Adam Bede, a Roger Bacon, and the author of *Everyman?* It wasn't much.

And then, all of a sudden, as it were, in the sixteenth century, there was such an explosion of bright stars as the world had not witnessed since the days of Periclean Athens. The appearance of so many major constellations that so unexpectedly illuminated the hitherto virtually empty English firmament: Shakespeare, John Donne, Thomas Heywood, George Chapman, Ben Jonson, Thomas Dekker, Philip Massinger, Christopher Marlowe, Francis Bacon, Gilbert of Colchester, as well as numerous other luminous spirits who followed in a continuous succession of new stellar births, would have been considered highly improbable by most of Britain's conquerors.

It is of interest to note that all these men, including the philosophers and scientists among them, were individuals of outstanding imaginative genius. It was during the second half of the following century, the seventeenth, that there was to develop that equally striking florescence of scientific genius.

From the Roman occupation to the appearance of the first men of genius and high achievement it took fifteen hundred years. This is, of course, a very crass and incomplete statement. A good deal of simmering had undoubtedly gone on for some centuries prior to what appears to have been a sudden explosion of genius. Nevertheless, the fact remains that it was only after fifteen hundred years of acculturative interaction, or whatever it was that was involved, that the English began popping.

It is to be observed that we are speaking here of "high achievement," of "genius." It is by the works of such individuals that we customarily evaluate a society's or an ethnic group's quality. Apparently certain specific conditions must develop in every culture before the latent potentialities for achievement in each population can be expressed.

What are these necessary specific conditions? These conditions are no longer a matter of conjecture, but on the basis of increasing evidence may be dependably deduced and indicated. The conditions necessary for achievement in any society are:

1. A cultural background of respect for achievement in the family in which the child has been raised.

2. Encouragements and rewards within the family and the culture which make it possible for the individual to acquire whatever is necessary in order for him to achieve in an achieving society.

3. A society in which the conditions of individual development have not physically affected his ability to learn. Nutritional deficiencies, for example, during fetal development may irreversibly damage large numbers of brain cells, and thus seriously affect the child's ability to learn. Nutritional deficiencies during infancy or childhood may produce similar damaging effects. The effects of some diseases during the early stages of development, prenatal and postnatal, can be equally damaging.

Nutritional deficiencies, especially protein deficiencies, as well as deficiencies induced by disease, are widespread throughout the world, and probably affected whole populations throughout the prehistoric period. This may, at least in part, account for the slow rate of cultural development during the greater portion of man's more than two million years of evolution. During that long period of secular time the struggle to survive constituted a virtually full-time occupation, and prolonged periods of undernourishment were probably the lot of every individual. Man suffered from protein and vitamin deficiencies, especially ascorbemia, that is, vitamin-C deficiency, a natural deficiency since man lacks the ability to produce this vitamin within his own body and must acquire it mainly from fruits of the citrus variety.

The combination of these factors: (1) the continuous and demanding struggle for existence, (2) the debilitating effects of disease, and (3) the neuronally damaging effects of malnutrition, would severely limit the members of any population in achievement of very much more than was necessary for bare survival. Add to this combination of factors those which continue to exist for many contemporary populations: (4) the absence of any cultural background, and (5) lack of encouragements, rewards, incentives, motivations, and aspirations for extraordinary achievement, and we have the necessary and sufficient conditions for ensuring the non-development of any and all potentialities for extraordinary or even ordinary accomplishment.

Potentialities require the proper environing conditions if they are to grow and develop and find appropriate expression. The expression of any capacity requires opportunities which stimulate the capacities to develop into abilities. Human development is not simply a matter of the unfolding of genetic potentialities but principally a matter of the cumulative, active process of utilizing environmental inputs. The adequate utilization of those inputs depends upon the environmental opportunities afforded the utilizing mechanisms, that is, the genetic potentials. The joker in that pack is, of course, the word "opportunities."

What are "opportunities"? What most culturally developed peoples with masses of nondeveloped people living in their midst have interpreted "opportunities" to mean is the hypocritically simplistic notion that political, legal, and educational rights somehow ensure the freedom to enjoy equal rights in everything else. This is, of course, utter nonsense. The laws on the books assuring equal political, legal, and educational rights to all citizens are, in practice, differentially applied and enforced. Equal laws do not in practice work out either as equality before the law or as equality of opportunity. Prejudice and discrimination operate to maintain impassable barriers against the subclasses who, as I pointed out many years ago, are treated as members of a lower caste.

In the deprived and depressed conditions under which the members of such subclasses or castes are forced to live, they are deprived of the greatest of all opportunities: *the opportunity to learn to respond with advantage to available opportunities.* The absence of this basic opportunity, by whatever means produced, seriously interferes with the ability to respond to the available opportunities.

The *basic opportunity* necessary for all human beings if they are to realize their potentialities is comprised of the obverse of those factors which I have described as principally responsible for the lack of high achievement in the members of certain populations. The necessary ingredients in *basic opportunity* then, necessary for achievement, are:

1. Some freedom from the continuous pressure to survive, that is, the enjoyment of a certain amount of leisure.

2. Good health or relative freedom from disease during fetal and childhood development.

3. Freedom from the effects of malnutrition during fetal, childhood, and adult development.

4. Growth and development in an environment with traditional roots in a cultural background providing the matrix and the context from and in which are derived those meanings which, in terms of those meanings, make the world intelligible and meaningful to the child and the person he becomes. If the traditional roots are deep and extensive, and his cultural background rich and multidimensional, he will have within him what used to be called "an apperceptive mass" which will enable him to respond with advantage to the environment in which he finds himself. If, on the other hand, his traditional roots are shallow or nonexistent and his cultural background arid, he will himself be unable to take root and develop in what remains an essentially inhospitable environment.

5. Finally, for creativity and achievement, the encouragement and nurturing of high aspiration levels, the fueling and development of incentives, the promise and experience of rewards are necessary.

Genius or high achievement remains an unexpressed potentiality in the absence of these conditions. In order to start its motors running not only is the fuel, the opportunities, necessary, but the fuel must be ignited, and that is accomplished not merely by turning the key in the ignition, but by ensuring the presence of an adequately charged battery, *the basic opportunity.* A healthy battery, adequately charged, properly connected to the spark plugs, will respond to the key being turned in the ignition, but not otherwise. All the necessary conditions must be fulfilled if the engine is to be started and to be kept running. It matters not how otherwise well we attend to the design of the car; it will not run unless the basic requirements of its motor are met. So it is with human beings. Unless the basic internal requirements for achievement are met, no matter what external opportunities they are exposed to, they will largely be unable to respond to them. The process of achievement is a creative one, creating power by a complex of relations which are only made possible in an environment of *basic opportunity.*

Most of us are not persons of great or extraordinary achievement, and it is desirable to recognize that in every human context it is not genius in some specific area that is of significance, but rather the generalized ability to make the appropriately successful responses to the ordinary challenges presented by the environment, to be plastic, malleable, and adaptable. And of such adaptive behavior all men everywhere, within the normal range of variation, are capable. Nevertheless, we tend to evaluate the status of societies by the measure of their extraordinary accomplishments. This is fair enough, but it is quite unfair to draw the conclusion from the differences in accomplishment that those societies which have fewer accomplishments to their credit than others are therefore genetically inferior to the others.

By this measure the Britons would have been held genetically inferior to the Romans. But the truth is they were *not* genetically inferior, but only culturally different, and apparently for the most part quite unmotivated for the very good reason that the conditions of life were such as to be all time-consuming in the struggle for survival. Basic opportunities were almost completely wanting, and it was not until such opportunities were afforded an increasingly large number of individuals in the population that a Shakespeare could make his appearance.

Until similar basic opportunities are afforded all populations compared, whether they be the aborigines of New Guinea or the blacks of New York, it is premature as well as wholly unjustifiable to attribute differences in achievement between populations to genetic factors.

It is, apparently, difficult to persuade those who are so ready to settle for a genetic explanation of differences in cultural achievement that it is only by equalizing basic opportunities for everyone that the conditions will be provided for making any sort of valid judgments concerning the possible role played by genetic factors in social and individual differences in cultural achievement. Until such basic opportunities are made available to everyone, all statements attributing differences in cultural achievement must be adjudged what they are: conjectures without any scientific basis or merit whatever.

Ultimately, of course, the whole question of "race" is a pseudo one, a system of pseudological rationalizations based on insufficiently analyzed evidence designed, usually, to bolster prejudices and defend indefensible positions; evidence which at once denies and rejects science, logic, and humanity. However unsound and unreal such beliefs may be, we know only too well how very real the unsound and the unreal can become. Be that as it may, it cannot be too often repeated that the issue at stake is not a scientific one, but a question of ethics. By virtue of the fact that he is a human being every individual has a right to his birthright, which is development. The greatest riches of the person, of his community, of humanity, lie in the uniqueness of the contribution that each individual has to make to his fellowman.

It is not a question of "superiority" or "inferiority" but the encouragement of individual fulfillment, whatever the individual's limitations, that society must consider among the first of the purposes for which it exists. The greatest of all talents, and the most important for man, is the talent for humanity. And what is talent? It is involvement. And the talent for being humane operationally means the involvement in the welfare of one's fellowman. All human beings have the capacity for such involvement. Racists commit the greatest of all crimes because they obstruct the development of this capacity and prevent the individual's fulfillment as a human being. To the extent that these crimes are committed, to that extent are the individual, society, and humanity impoverished.

The deprivation of any man's right to fulfillment diminishes each of us, for we, as well as he, have lost what he has been deprived of, for we are all involved in each other. Whether we wish it to be so or not, this involvement is inherent in the very nature of nature, and especially of human nature. The most basic of all opportunities is the right to growth and development as a humane being who has been deeply involved in the love of others, for the health and identity of the person consists in the meaningfulness of his interrelationships.

2.

The Encounter-Communication Workshop for Language Teachers

LEON A. JAKOBOVITS

This discussion outlines a program of in-service training for teachers and administrative school personnel which is designed to foster a better understanding of the problems involved in the education of children from minority groups within an educational system that is defined and administered by the cultural interests of the dominant social or national community. Most parts of the world are faced with this situation, to a lesser or major extent, inasmuch as linguistic and cultural pluralism is a more usual pattern of nationhood than uniculturalism. In the United States, the region which constitutes the sociocultural focus of this proposed training program, major viable and dynamic linguistic/cultural minorities exist, the most notable being the black ghetto of the inner city in large metropolitan areas, the Mexican-Americans in the Southwest, the Puerto Rican population in New York, the Cuban immigrants in Miami, and the various Amerindian groups throughout the North American continent.

In the last decade or so, we have witnessed a major upsurge of militant expression on the part of linguistic/cultural minority Americans — Afro-, Mexican-, Puerto Rican-, and Indian- — giving us such slogans as Black Power and Red Power. While there are many obvious differences that distinguish the history and context of these various movements, they all share the common characteristic of being attempts at cultural revival and assertion in the face of a long history of repression and assimilation on the part of the dominant middle-class, white, Anglo-Saxon culture.

Adapted from Chapter 8 in *The New Psycholinguistics and Foreign Language Teaching: Collected Essays,* edited by Leon A. Jakobovits (Rowley, Mass.: Newbury House Publishers, 1971). Reprinted by permission of the publisher and author.

Leon A. Jakobovits of the Psychology Department, University of Hawaii, has concentrated on the personal, psychological aspects of language teaching. He has done extensive fieldwork in this area and is known for his efforts with teachers in bilingual education in the Dade County School System, Miami, Florida.

One of the most important social devices used by a dominant culture in its attempt to acculturate and assimilate minority groups is, of course, the formal educational system represented by the schools. Teachers thus constitute primary agents, not only of socialization in the enculturation process of the children of the culturally dominant group, but also of the acculturation process of the children of the cultural minority groups. Teachers, therefore, given the role that society relegates them to, as the transmitters of the dominant cultural values, tend to be conservative, and, in the face of challenge by militants of minority groups, they become in effect reactionary agents, standing in the way of liberation from perceived cultural repression.

In the context of cultural conflict, the school becomes a battlefield reflecting the social reality of the community, and the teacher becomes the focus of opposing forces. To members of minority groups, the teacher has become a symbol of repression, an enemy to be feared and mistrusted, and the school, an alien place to be left as soon as the law permits. Small wonder, then, that a majority of minority-group children are high school dropouts. The vicious cycle of the economically underprivileged is thus perpetuated generation after generation, continuing to undermine the stability of society as a whole. The very institution that is supposed to establish and maintain stability and order in society thus becomes a barrier to these forces.

It is only recently that some awareness of the process just described has become widespread in American society, but it has already resulted in some very important changes in policy on the part of government and the educational establishment. Since 1967 the Bilingual Education Act under Title VII has fostered the development of dozens of experimental programs throughout the country, representing a new recognition of the necessity of legitimizing the aspirations of minority groups for the maintenance of their cultural heritage. The psychological climate in many schools in the Southwest that have large groups of Spanish-speaking children has changed from linguistic repression on the playground to, at least, linguistic tolerance, if not yet wholehearted approval.

Despite these visible signs of change, however, it cannot be said that the problems have been solved, or even, that the wheels have been set in motion for their eventual solution. For instance, graduates of the largest and oldest bilingual elementary school in the country, Coral Way School in Dade County, Miami, overwhelmingly choose not to continue bilingual education in junior high school, despite the availability of such a program. Furthermore, despite a burgeoning of research in the field of sociolinguistics, which is revealing the simplistic and uninformed character of many teachers' conceptions of black English, there remains an apparently unshakeable conviction that black English is an inferior mode of communication, unsuitable for the expression of ideas involved in school subjects.[1] I feel that there is taking place in educational circles a subtle but insidious shift from racial to ethnic prejudice, away from the black man's biological entity to his social entity, his language and culture. And I see prejudicial shifts of no less virulent form in the case of the Mexican-Americans and the Puerto Ricans; shifts from an outright linguistic repression to prejudices directed at cultural aspects of the individual's integrity, embodied by such platitudes as, "They are a good and simple people; they like flowers and dancing; they are not ambitious for making money."

We are dealing here with nothing less than outright ethnic prejudice in the traditional forms of American ethnocentrism. There is little evidence that a fundamental change has taken place in the melting-pot policy of promoting The American Way of Life. There is little evidence that the educational establishment is ready to abdicate its role as an agent of assimilation for the dominant middle-class, white Anglo-Saxon culture. The Bilingual Education Act, the very symbol of a new attitude of tolerance toward cultural minorities, may, within the context of the old climate of ethnocentrism, become one more tool in the arsenal of an assimilatory agency. The Title VII program explicitly affirms the primary importance of English, and its main justification is the hope that it might help to prevent retardation in school performance. Modern objectives of the American school system remain the same. Seldom is the possibility raised that the various cultural minorities in the United States may have different objectives for an educational system. The possibility of allowing these cultural groups to define and evolve their own educational objectives is seldom suggested. And yet, it is doubtful that anything short of this can sustain a viable, dynamic culture and restore dignity to millions of "aliens" and alienated people in this country. For, just as the survival and evolution of the dominant American culture depends in large measure on its educational institutions, so does the survival of the Afro-American, Mexican-American, and Amerindian cultures depend on educational institutions designed by them and for them within their cultural premises.

Until such time as the minority cultures gain sufficient political freedom to implement and evolve their own educational objectives, the concept of the bilingual school remains the least destructive alternative within the present sociopolitical reality. The problem that faces us in this endeavor is, how can we evolve the bilingual school into a bicultural school? Whatever Congress and educational administrators might say or do about this problem, its solution ultimately lies with the teacher and what he does in the classroom. A bicultural policy is a set of directives on pieces of paper, or something one makes speeches about, but it doesn't insure a bicultural school. A bicultural school that is so in fact, rather than in policy, is a place where certain forms of communication take place between teacher and pupil. The characteristics of these bicultural forms of communication are different from those propounded in a unilingual school or a unicultural bilingual school. To bring about the reality of a bicultural school, the teacher must know what these particular objectives are, understand them in a personal and intimate way, and, furthermore, must consider them intrinsically valuable for himself, as well as for his pupils. To know them intellectually is not sufficient; he must want them, desire them, as a personal goal in life, as an enrichment of his Self. To achieve bicultural communication, an individual must become as complete a bicultural person as possible. This goes for both the teacher and the pupil.

It should be noted at this point that bilingualism is not the issue in the encounter-communication workshop. Our conception of the ideal bilingual overlaps with biculturalism, true, but, which comes first, bilingualism or biculturalism? It isn't useful to phrase the problem in these divisive terms, for the two processes are interrelated in their etiology. Research in this area suggests that a *precondition* for the development of ideal bilingualism is an "integrative" orientation toward the second culture on the part of the learner.[2] Similarly, for bicultural communication to develop there must exist on the part of the interactants a prior attitude of mutual acceptance, respect, and a feeling that the other's culture is as worthwhile to acquire as one's own.

As is the case with bilingual performance, the end product, that of achieving truly bicultural status, is not the issue in the workshop. Rather we are concerned with inducing the psychological climate that is favorable for its development and occurrence, for bicultural communication can take place in the absence of either perfect bilingualism or perfect biculturalism. For instance, as the unilingual, unicultural, Spanish-speaking child enters first grade, taught by a bilingual or semi-bilingual American teacher, a cultural confrontation takes place in the classroom. For meaningful communication to develop between them, that confrontation must be transformed into an encounter. The pupil must want to become more "like the teacher," and the teacher must want to become more "like the pupil." As the weeks and months go by, they learn from each other and they grow together, each of them becoming more than what he was before. They now belong, in greater or lesser extent, to two cultures, even though neither of them may ever be perfectly bilingual or perfectly bicultural. This is the context of bicultural communication we must strive for in the bilingual school.

Cultural Confrontation vs. Encounter

Cultures in contact may be in a state of confrontation as in Canada, Belgium, or India, or they may be in a state of encounter, as was the case in ancient Rome after the conquest of Greece, or is today the case in Finland, Switzerland, Israel, or Japan. What is the difference?

Confrontation implies competition; encounter implies cooperation. In a competitive relationship, what one wins the other loses; in a cooperative relationship, both are winners and there are no losers. When two people interact, each of them must take certain personal risks: to address someone may mean a rebuff through the other's silence; to ask a favor may mean refusal; to reveal an attitude may mean condemnation; and so on. When the interlocutor isn't trusted, as is the case in confrontation or competition, one doesn't like to take many or significant risks; one must remain shielded and guarded. When the other is trusted, one can afford to take risks, to open up, to communicate, to encounter, to cooperate.

What leads to mutual trust?

The "safest" atmosphere is that in which the one values and admires the other, and proves it by wanting to become like the other, the culturally integrative orientation. There is no way of faking this process by paying lip service to the other's "right to be different"; the diplomatic subterfuge is quickly discovered; it can be felt like a brick wall. No significant risk-taking will be attempted; there will be no encounter and no real communication.

Most of us have experienced at some time or other in our lives the process of encountering someone, although in a competitive society such as ours, that wonderful experience is rare and the instances few and far between. We must search our memories way back, into early childhood, to recapture that taste of trust, safety, and freedom. As socialized adults, we have learned to be discreet, polite, cautious, self-reliant, strong, ambitious, successful, mature, outer-directed, task-involved, autonomous, dutiful, and of course repressed, guarded, secretive, isolated, and alienated from each other.

Though our memory of the encounter process be distant, our longing for it remains strong and immediate. People throughout the country, of all ages and walks of life, have begun to form small artificial groups in an attempt to get back together again. What distinguishes these basic encounter or sensitivity groups from natural groups such as family, social, neighborhood, or church groups, is the members' recognition of why they are there, and the agreement to attempt to interrelate by means of a new social contract: cooperation instead of competition, at the personal feeling level. Differences in feeling and attitude are not just tolerated or politely "respected" — in fact, they are frequently challenged, sometimes vigorously rejected, but the members commit themselves to protect each other's selfhood, to feel for each other, to make the other person's pain one's own, so that, should one make the other suffer, he will be causing his own suffering, and should he give pleasure to the other, he will contribute to his own delight; in short, to encounter rather than confront.

The Nature of the ECW

The encounter-communication workshop is a program of study conducted in small groups and is designed to give the individual a better understanding of himself within the context of interpersonal communication. In the bilingual school setting, it takes the form of in-service training for teachers and other administrative personnel, who meet regularly throughout the academic year, exploring under the guidance of a program director ways of transforming the bilingual school into a bicultural school, in which the emphasis shifts from bilingual education *per se* to bicultural communication.

The study program involves two types of activities: an objective analysis of role-dyadic interactions in the school in terms of a linguistic-communication model; and an analysis of the subjective aspects of interpersonal relations, including social contracts, trust, risk-taking, self image and its management, and personal metaphysics. Included in these activities are an initial diagnosis of the prevalent modes of personal interaction in the particular school setting, and action programs designed to introduce changes in them coupled with constant feedback and evaluation of the results.

The encounter-communication workshop is not slated to be either "psychotherapy" or a "how to" course in interpersonal communication. It is not slated to be either a sensitivity training laboratory or a basic encounter group. Neither is it a traditional academic training program. It does, however, have some affinity with all these types of undertakings. For instance, although much attention is spent on analyses of the communication process within the technical framework of academic disciplines such as linguistics, psychology, and anthropology, the interpersonal context and social climate of the study group is personal and intimate, mirroring certain aspects of the sensitivity training laboratory.

Because of this, special care must be taken on the part of the principal, not only to explicitly state the voluntary nature of such a program, but also to insure that school personnel do not feel in any way under pressure to participate. In some instances, individuals in a job setting may be hesitant to decline to participate in a "voluntary" program set up by their superiors "for their benefit." It is the responsibility of the principal and the program director to see to it that such subtle pressures do not in fact exist in connection with an encounter-communication workshop, both vis-à-vis initial participation and eventual completion. The lack of free and voluntary choice with full awareness of the nature of the workshop undermines its very goals, and, in addition, constitutes unethical duress and an infringement upon individual freedom.

Prior to making a decision about participation in an encounter-communication workshop, it is incumbent upon the individual to clearly understand "what it is all about" and "what he is getting himself into." This is achieved by reading a description of the program such as outlined in the following discussion, by familiarizing oneself to some degree with the readings suggested herein, and by an exploratory face-to-face interview with the program director. These cautions are expressed here both for the sake of the prospective participants and for the sake of the program's success.

The Social Contract and the ECW

Two different approaches have previously been used in the study of human communication. On the one hand, academic disciplines such as psychology, linguistics, and anthropology have given us a tradition of "objective analysis" and a formalized language of theory, within which hypotheses are formulated and checked against certain empirical consequences, using the "scientific" or experimental method. On the other hand, sensitivity training laboratories and basic encounter groups also deal with the problem of communication, both with the self and the other, but from a very different perspective; emphasis is placed on the subjective aspects of experiencing the communication as an interpersonal transaction of feelings, agreements and disagreements, sympathy, support, hostility, threat, trust, and the like.

Traditionally, these two approaches to communication not only remained distinct and separate, but were seen as mutually exclusive and incompatible. The "scientific" method did not admit concepts that had no objectively definable parameters and excluded from its input evidence that was not observable under "controlled" conditions. Those concerned with feeling and experiencing felt constrained and frustrated under the requirements imposed by the experimental method. "Two cultures" of discourse and activity thus developed, each viewing the other with mistrust and suspicion.

The encounter-communication workshop is conceived as a "third culture" activity, different from the other two, yet drawing upon both.

The three words in this expression encapsulize its focus and method: "encounter" reflects the fact that a different social contract defines the interpersonal behavior of the group participants; "communication" not only represents the main concern of the study program, its content and focus, but draws attention to the process itself, which includes a new way of being present to others, of communicating with them; "workshop" is intended as a distinguishing feature from "course" or "seminar," and is a way of emphasizing the self-exploratory and participatory nature of the activity.

Some explanation is in order as to the meaning of *social contract* as used here. All transactions between people are governed by some set of rules or regulations, either recognized or implicit, that may be called the social contract. Everyday commonplace conversation takes place within the context of such participatory rules that specify such things as what one may talk about, in what way, and under which circumstances. For instance, the extent to which one overtly renders internal verbalizations depends on the formality level of the interaction (how intimately the conversants know each other, whether other listeners are present, etc.) and the degree of risk-taking they are ready to engage in (how much they trust each other, whether they are engaged in cooperation or competition, etc.). In sensitivity and encounter groups, a "cultural island" is established, in which the social contract governing interactions is made explicitly different from "the outside" of everyday life: honesty is mandatory, feelings must be expressed, self-disclosure is encouraged, growth-producing confrontations are attempted, nonverbal physical contact is deliberately engaged in, and so forth. The success of the group experience is defined in terms of the extent to which the individual develops the capacity to relate to others in the group, in the ways specified by the "artificial" social contract.

In the encounter-communication workshop, no specific social contract is set forth as the "desirable" way of interacting and toward which the individual is supposed to aspire for his interpersonal growth. Instead, the participants are encouraged to explore interpersonal transactions under various social contract obligations as defined by role dyads. To do so, they must first learn how to identify in explicit terms the sets of rules that define a particular role-dyadic interaction as experienced in their daily lives. Once this is successfully accomplished, they can then experiment with changes in some of the specific rules. For instance, a teacher might wish at one time to decrease the formality level that characterizes his typical interaction with the principal and, at another time, he might wish to *increase* the formality level of his typical interaction with a teacher-aide. In the former case, greater expression of feelings will take place; in the latter case, less intimacy is wished. The success of the encounter-communication workshop is measured, not by the capacity to adhere to any specified social contract, but by the extent to which the individual comes to develop the ability to bring about desired changes in some specified aspect of an existing relationship outside the workshop. The special and artificial contract in the ECW derives from the fact that it makes possible such exploratory activity, without the usual social consequences that accompany such activities outside the group. It is for this reason that the participants in such a workshop should be made up of those individuals who are normally engaged in role-dyadic interactions on the outside (such as the school setting). Under normal circumstances, the risks involved in such exploration between co-workers would be too prohibitive.

The Structure of the ECW

An ECW program centers around two types of activities: (1) a communication analysis of the setting, coupled with an action program that introduces corrective measures in interpersonal behavior; and (2) basic encounter experiences that explore and monitor the subjective psychological concomitants of the action program. The first type of activity is objectively analytical and is oriented toward overt actions. The second type of activity is subjectively analytical (not necessarily in the psychoanalytical sense) and is oriented toward inner feelings and attitudes. This is not "psychotherapy" in that it is not designed to bring about psychological change or reprieve from anxiety and "psychological problems." Rather, it is "honest psychological talk among lay equals," the kind of interchange that may take place between intimate friends. It is both analytically explorative and mutually succoring.

Most of the interchange in an ECW program takes place in small group sessions (eight to twelve people) held periodically throughout the academic year, under the direction of the program leader. These special sessions, each of which may last for several hours of intensive interaction, are held in the context of the day-to-day routine of the teacher's work and the various on-going action programs attempted in connection with the ECW program. We shall now examine in greater detail the nature of these two activities.

The Communication Pattern of the Setting

A preliminary analysis of a communicative interaction leads one to specify certain abstract conceptual elements of the following sort: a *message* which constitutes the content of the communication, the *informa-*

tion that is being transmitted by the *sender* or *source;* the intended *receiver* of the message or the *destination;* and the *code* in which the message is contained (e.g. English). The message is *encoded* at or by the source, is transmitted through a *medium* or *channel* (e.g. sound waves) and is *decoded* at or by the receiver or destination. This *communication cycle* involves processes of *transformation* at various points: the encoding process transforms thoughts and intentions, which are mental phenomena, into physical manifestations such as speech sounds that are structured according to the system of rules of the code (language); similarly, the decoding process transforms the coded message back into mental phenomena, through a process of syntactic, semantic, and other kinds of analyses.

There are different types of transformation processes, each having different characteristics. We shall be concerned in this discussion mostly with functional transformations rather than physical; the latter focus on such things as the relation between brain-patterned discharge and articulatory speech movements and the relation between articulatory speech movements and spectographic electric patterns. Functional transformations focus on the equivalence-relation of patterns irrespective of their physical constituents, such as, for instance, the relation between thought and word, between intended meaning and received meaning, between abstract grammatical elements (noun, verb, morpheme, subject, object, etc.) and concrete phonological ones (sequence of words, sentences), and so on.

The essence of a communication analysis lies in a specification of the nature and character of its various transformation processes. All transformations can, in principle, be described and specified by a set of rules called a *generative system.* For instance, the transformation of the set of objects – flour, water, yeast, salt, etc. – into "bread" can be specified by a generative set of rules, a "recipe," which when applied or followed step by step, will yield the object in question. Similarly, the particular object known as a "sentence of English" can be generated by following a complex series of steps or rules specified by a "grammar," some of which will be transformational.

The analysis of a complex activity, such as human communication, into transformations is an abstraction, a convenient fiction designed to help us specify the activity in as much detail as possible. It allows us to make certain explicit hypotheses about how a process *might* take place so that we can test them against certain empirical consequences. Let us, to begin with, examine the following hypothetical interchange and see the kinds of processes that might be involved in ordinary, everyday communication:

Daughter: Jimmy is here!
Mother: You haven't cleaned up your room.
Daughter: We still have to pick up Donna.
Mother: Mother is coming. And I still have to shop for some groceries.
Daughter: She'll understand. Besides, she isn't that well organized herself.
Mother: But you promised!
Daughter: Oh, but you don't understand! Last time, he got very mad,
    because traffic is so heavy at this time of the day.
Mother: Oh, he is such a finicky! What's wrong with Steve, anyway? He
    is so much nicer.
Daughter: He doesn't like Bernie.
Mother: I thought Donna was going with Archie.
Daughter: The Redmen are playing at Queen's this weekend.
Mother: Mother will never understand. I'll have to speak to Dad again.
Daughter: Oh, all right! I'll make my bed, but you do the rest.
Mother: All right. Hurry up!

Ordinary conversation is highly elliptical. To understand this interchange, we must supply a great deal of information that is *implicit*. Some of this information is culturally available, and some of it is situation specific. For instance, Mother's concern is understandable only if we know the critical attitude which a mother-in-law can have vis-à-vis her son's wife, and the anxiety on the latter's part about making a good impression. Furthermore, we must be aware that granddaughters do not share this concern, but they in turn are much more anxious about how their boyfriends feel, a concern not generally reciprocated by mothers. In addition, we could guess that cleaning up one's room has been a chronic problem in this family and that Mother has some leverage on Daughter by threatening to complain to Dad, the disciplinarian with whom Daughter would rather avoid another clash. Other aspects of this interchange need situation-specific information to make them understandable. For instance, we must know that Steve is another boy with whom Daughter has gone out in the past; that Bernie is a substitute for Archie, the latter being Donna's regular boyfriend; that Archie is a football player with the Redmen, and so on. All this remains unstated and implicit, since Mother and Daughter share a common background experience and knowledge, and there is no need to state these facts. They are "understood."

In addition to sharing background knowledge, both cultural and situation specific, the interactants have in common certain background expectations, and engage in certain specific sorts of reasoning, largely inferential. For instance, Daughter knows that Mother expects her to help in house-cleaning chores, especially at a time of crisis (e.g. when mother-in-law shows up). Mother knows that Daughter expects her to ease up on her house-cleaning demands when Daughter finds herself in a crisis situation (e.g. grouchy Jimmy is waiting). These are some of the unstated background expectations that regulate this interaction and without which each person's appeal wouldn't make sense: "Jimmy is here!" (therefore you can't expect me to keep my promise to clean up the room); "Mother is coming!" (therefore you are supposed to drop everything to help me straighten up the house). Both interactants must in addition engage in inferential reasoning that is peculiar and appropriate to the nature of the particular communication act in progress. For instance, Daughter reasons that someone who isn't organized herself can't be critical of others for being like they are . . . so, "She'll understand." Note that this kind of "can't" isn't a physical impossibility, or even a logical one, but more like an injunction that she "ought not." On the other hand, the fact that Donna is going with Bernie rather than Archie ("The Redmen are playing at Queen's this weekend") is to be deduced on logical premises, given the knowledge that (a) Archie plays for the Redmen and (b) the Redmen are away at Queen's — *ergo* Archie can't take Donna out.

Thus, to understand the process of commonplace, everyday communication, our analysis will have to deal with implicit, unstated information of a cultural and situation-specific sort, with shared background expectations, and with several types of inferential reasoning. But this is just the beginning. Why do Mother and Daughter have a disagreement in the first place? How is the disagreement resolved, and why is the halfway solution acceptable to both parties? What else goes on between Mother and Daughter, besides the overt argument about cleaning up the room? ("But you promised!" and "What's wrong with Steve, anyway?")

To resolve these issues we must widen our circle of analysis to take in psychological factors such as Mother's and Daughter's personalities, their needs, ambitions, values, and conflicts: social-psychological factors such as the family's socio-economic status and religious affiliation, their conceptions of the roles of parent, boyfriend, and mother-in-law, their conceptions of social institutions such as the family and marriage, their conceptions of social practices such as dating; and, ultimately, the moral and philosophical premises within which all the previous factors are embedded.

Put in this context, a full analysis of even the simplest communication interchange is a quite formidable undertaking. And yet, it is difficult to escape the conclusion that some such analysis, of at least this complexity, is made by an individual in everyday life, in commonplace communicative acts, otherwise he could not engage in successful communication. But, of course, the analysis is done "unconsciously," automatically, effortlessly, and it becomes prohibitive only when we attempt to make explicit all the steps that make up this complex human activity. A child of four or five has developed and internalized an extremely complex system of rules we call "grammar" that enables him to produce and understand an infinite number of grammatical sentences. This knowledge is almost totally unconscious and is arrived at seemingly effortlessly, naturally. And yet, after many, many years of hard work, thousands of intelligent and technologically skilled linguists are unable to describe this knowledge in an explicit sense, and they may not ever be able to do so.

In that case, why bother with the attempt? Speaking from a practical point of view, there is a great deal to be gained from explicit descriptions of implicit or unconscious processes, even though these descriptions remain partial and incomplete. Consider the technological achievements made possible by an incomplete, partial, and even internally contradictory description of the physical universe. We do not need to have a complete description of communication processes in order to be able to either improve their quality or control them in some ways. It is likely, however, that the better, more valid, and more complete our description is, the better will be our chances to affect communication processes in ways we deem advantageous. This is the motivation and the anticipated pay-off for doing this kind of analytic activity in the ECW.

In such an undertaking, there are various strategies we can follow to maximize our chances of success in the solution of certain problems. Since in the ECW we are very much concerned with cross-cultural communication, we want to focus our attention on those factors that both facilitate and hinder the effectiveness of communication in the bicultural setting. No serious attempt at finding clearcut formulas can be made within the confines of this discussion, but it might be useful to sketch out a strategy.

The structure of the ECW, within which the analysis is to be made, has already been presented. Thus we shall be concerned, among other things, with identifying differences in background expectations and communicative inferential reasoning between the interactants that are both senders and receivers of messages, paying particular attention to the various transformations in which information is lost or intention misinterpreted.

Background expectations, particularly those that are culturally defined, tend to form clusters, such that given expectations r, s, t, it is more likely that expectations u, v, w will co-occur in that cluster, than would, say, a, b, c. For instance, an adult male is more likely than a teenage female to respond favorably to a request such as, "Pardon me, do you have a match?", when accosted by a stranger on the street. Similarly, a pupil in the lower grades may make of the teacher a request that he be allowed to go to the toilet, which he would not make of his parents at home or a stranger on the street. Or again, a school principal's comment on the teacher's behavior in the classroom has different import for her than a similar comment addressed to her by a pupil, fellow teacher, or assistant teacher. These clusters of expectations form what we call *role behavior* and this is to an extent culturally defined. Every communicative interaction between two people, which we shall call a *communicative dyad,* or simply a *dyad,* is conditioned to a greater or lesser degree by these socially defined role behaviors. In other words, every communicative act is to some extent a *role-dyadic interaction.*

One source of *noise* (misunderstanding, misinterpretation) in a role-dyadic interaction lies in differences in role expectations (or role conceptions) between the two members of the dyad. Consider the following interchange:

Teacher: Johnny doesn't seem to respond to any form of punishment I administer in the classroom.
Father: I can't understand that. At home, he doesn't dare disobey me.

Johnny happens to respond extremely well to physical punishment. Father's puzzlement comes about through the fact that he misunderstands the teacher's reference to "any form of punishment I administer," failing to realize that physical punishment is implicitly excluded from "any form" due to her own (or the school's) definition of her role behavior.

Similarly, differences in inferential reasoning may bring about exasperated misunderstanding. Consider this familiar situation:

Teacher: Blake, I told you there is to be *no talking* during the examination. Please, hand in your paper.
Pupil: But, sir, I only asked him for an eraser!
Teacher: I said there is going to be *no talking.*

Blake's reasoning could have gone something like this: the teacher said "no talking" because it is forbidden to exchange information during the test; but asking for an eraser is not cheating on the exam, hence that is permissible. The teacher's reasoning was, of course, something different: I don't want verbal interchange of any kind since I won't know whether they are asking for an eraser or exchanging information about the test. The older pupil who understands the teacher's reasoning would instead raise his hand and make the request of the teacher.

It would appear, then, that one strategy which might prove useful in an attempt to improve communication in a particular setting is to isolate the important role-dyadic interactions that occur in that setting and to proceed with a detailed specification of the expectations and inferential behavior that are typical for them. One way of doing this is through analysis of real or hypothetical interchanges. For instance, a teacher and a principal can tape-record some of their daily verbal interchanges and participate in the analysis done by the group as a whole. An additional method is to tape-record a dyadic interchange produced by "role-playing," in which one teacher, say, plays the role of a principal, and another that of a parent. "Role reversals" can point up sharply differences in background expectations such as, for instance, a teacher playing the role of a pupil and vice versa.

The number of role-dyadic interactions in a school setting can be quite large: teacher-teacher, teacher-assistant teacher, teacher-principal, teacher-pupil, parent-teacher, etc. It is not essential that every possible role dyad be analyzed. For one, some of these are less frequent and crucial than others, and their relative importance may vary for particular roles and individuals. For another, much of this kind of analytic activity can be done by the individual on his own, outside the group. What is important is to develop the analytic attitude toward communicative acts, so that it can be used by the individual *when he chooses to do so*. This may seem a very artificial, ponderous, and cumbersome way of engaging in communicative acts, but the intention is not to eliminate spontaneity from communication, but, rather, to develop sensitivity in detecting inefficiencies in it. To achieve the latter goal, the individual must develop methods of obtaining feedback from the interlocutor that will give him information about the other's assumptions, presuppositions, expectations, and inferences. Such information can then be used to clarify points of misunderstanding.

At this point, one may ask what one can do to improve communication when the problem is not one of misunderstanding, but, rather, genuine disagreement about means, methods, and ends. While this question is also quite pertinent to an objective communication analysis, it touches more intimately on such psychological factors as attitudes, conflicts, perceived threat and insecurity, trust, ego strength, maturity, and the like, to be discussed below.

The Encounter Process

An explanation of an event, process, or other phenomenon constitutes a set of statements or assertions arranged in some sequence whose structure follows certain rules. One important difference between a "good" and a "bad" explanation is that if we act upon the premises of the good one we are more likely to achieve some goal, such as change or control of other or similar events. To put it in reverse, an explanation that gives us that power of change and control is better than one that does not. There are numerous psychological explanations and theories about people, how and why they think and act in the way they do. We do not wish to get bogged down in polemics about which are the really "true" explanations. Let us simply agree that we shall accept as "working hypotheses" certain psychological accounts of communicative interactions as long as they seem to give us the capability of changing and affecting communicative acts in ways we deem desirable — their "truth" or ultimate validity is of no concern.

Here, then, is a series of statements of a psychological nature that purport to describe how people may think, feel, and act in a role-dyadic interaction. (Remember that here, as in previous analyses, it is not claimed that these are conscious, explicitly recognized processes.) Such interactions may be labeled the "Private-Public Dichotomy," and can be summarized as follows:

1. As a person, I consist of two parts: a private self which I feel consciously as the subject or actor of my thoughts and actions, and a public self, "me," of which others are aware.
2. In the eyes of others, my private self, the "I" or ego, is to be held responsible for the actions of my public self of which they are aware, the "me."
3. Society (parents, friends, neighbors, colleagues, employers, "the law," etc.) has established certain rules to which people ought to conform. When my public self, the "me," conforms to these rules, the private self, the "I" which is responsible, is rewarded in various ways (money, praise, friendship, etc.). Similarly, when the "me" departs from these rules, the "I" is punished in various ways (imprisonment, social isolation, disapproval, etc.).
4. If I am to maximize the rewards society has to offer, and minimize its punishments, "I" must put the best "me" forward.

Now, if these are indeed some major premises upon which an individual acts in his mental and interpersonal behavior, certain consequences will follow, which we will examine next.

A. *The Danger of Discovery.* Any policy or strategy which involves the "I" putting the best "me" forward confronts the "I" with the ever-present danger of being exposed as a fraud, with dire consequences (loss of acceptance and friendship, ostracism, retribution, etc.). The "I," therefore, labors under constant stress and fear. For instance, if the "me" is presented for others' benefit as religious, law-abiding, honest, genuine, friendly, loving, pure, compassionate, and charitable, while "deep down," the "I" knows that it isn't like that, it must always be watchful, be continually on its guard, lest others "see through" the "me" and withhold the rewards which the "I" craves. It follows from this that others become a source of threat; they are the "Inquisition." An impenetrable barrier is thus set up between oneself and others, whether the other be a stranger like the customs officer past whom one is trying to smuggle something, or an intimate like a spouse from whom one is trying to hide "selfish" thoughts and desires. True trust between two people can never develop as long as one is trying, through subterfuge, to "con" the other. In addition to the stress due to the danger of discovery, there is added the no lesser stress of loneliness; the feeling of being "by oneself," rather than "with another."

B. *The Cancer of Guilt.* If one looks more closely at the "I," one discovers that it, too, contains an internal barrier and is divided against itself. Freud popularized the three-way division of the "ego," "super-ego," and "id," standing respectively for the self, the authority representative, and the biologically given urges. Religious spokesmen emphasize the "good" and the "evil" within us. Some psychologists speak of the "real ego" image versus the "ideal ego" image. However one chooses to conceptualize the divisiveness of the self, one is faced by the sad ravages wrought by the opposing forces within us: guilt, self-hatred, ambivalence, conflict, self-punishment, self-denial, and others.

It is important to realize that so long as the individual acts consistently upon the premises outlined above as the "Private-Public Dichotomy," there is no solution to the impasse: it is a classic instance of what psychologists have come to call "the double bind." The argument can be stated this way: Society sets up a distinction between the "I" and the "me." It furthermore sets up rules which govern how the "me" ought to be. The individual internalizes this division along with the system of differential rewards and punishment that is designed to insure its continuance. Now the individual is caught in a double bind of "damned if you're right and damned if you're wrong," since if he plays society's game of putting the best "me" forward he is confronted with guilt and self-condemnation, even though he minimizes the danger of discovery by being a good con-artist; on the other hand, if he tries to avoid the guilt of duplicity by letting his true self show, society will punish him for not being as it prescribes one ought to be. The individual caught in this game-trap can never win. Is there no solution, then, to this impasse? There is; in fact there are essentially three "Ways of Liberation" from the double bind which men have offered over the ages. Let us examine each in turn.

A. *The Way of the Straight Path.* Man is born with "animal" instincts which, if allowed free expression, would destroy him. Society establishes rules of behavior designed to suppress, counteract, and keep in check these destructive tendencies. "Conscience" is the internal censor-watchdog (whether God-given or created by society), which punishes infractions not externally detected by society. Neuroses are symptoms of the internal conflict between the animal urges fighting for expression and the counteraction of conscience trying to keep them in check. Guilt feelings, unhappiness, and the extremes of depression are caused by wayward actions, feelings, and thoughts. Three methods are recognized for handling these negative consequences. One is atonement and restitution for wrongdoing which gives the individual a reprieve and a next chance; a second is the strengthening of the "voice of conscience," through discipline and dedication, which allows the individual to resist temptations; and the third, much more recent in history, is that proposed by Freud and the psychoanalytic movement, which consists of weakening the unreasonable demands of a stern conscience run wild with power, and the greater acceptance of the biological urges within us — a kind of midway solution, a practical compromise.

B. *The Way of Self-Actualization.* Man's instincts are not necessarily destructive and can be channeled into ways which would satisfy both the individual and society. Various lines of thought exist concerning which channel or channels would lead to this mutually acceptable *modus vivendi;* such as finding and constructing "meaning" in life, actualizing our inner potentials, and learning how to love oneself and others. The various existential philosophies and the motive-rationale behind the current "small group movement" (encounter, sensitivity, Gestalt therapy, etc.) concerned with ways of experiencing, can all be classified in this category. The emphasis has shifted from neurosis and guilt to "alienation" (from oneself, from human fellowship) or loneliness, which is attributed to the artificial creation by the socialized individual of a separation between how one really is and how one ought to be. The solution proposed is, then, abandoning notions of how one ought to be, and finding out how one really is, substituting the latter for the former as a goal of life. At the same time, it is asserted that being "how one really is" is not merely the only sane solution, but also that it is not inimical to a well-functioning society.

C. *The Awakening from the Illusion of the Social Game.* This solution to the double bind is found in Eastern philosophies, especially in Zen Buddhism and Taoism. It is only recently that these ideas have come to be popularized in the West. There are many interpretations and versions of the Eastern "Ways of Liberation," and we shall discuss only one of these, as interpreted in the writings of Alan Watts.[3]

The reality of the distinction between the "I" and the "me" is denied and viewed as a social fiction, an illusion encouraged by society as a means of controlling the individual. The assertion of the existence of "I" as a cognizant, responsible subject-actor makes it possible for society to maintain a system of differential rewards and punishments, both externally through social sanctions and internally through the "voice of the conscience." In fact, it is asserted, no such distinction exists, the "I" being an abstraction of the total "me," and indeed, of the environment and the world. The illusion of the "I" as an actor (and, hence, an agent to be held accountable and responsible for one's actions, feelings, and thoughts) is achieved by a deliberate repression of the total "me-environment" by ignoring it — an act of "ignore-ance" as well as ignorance. Loneliness and alienation are not caused by an *actual* separation — between the "I" and the "me," between the "me" and the "other," between life and death — but rather by the *illusion* of a separation, hence the way of liberation from this misery is to awaken to this subterfuge perpetrated by society, to realize it is illusory, not real. Unhappiness, the fear of death, the struggle between good and evil, the striving to be better, are paranoid constructions, and liberation from them comes about by realizing that they are illusions, not realities.

This philosophy, unlike the first two discussed, specifically denies the necessity of acting upon the major premises set forth here as the "Private-Public Dichotomy." There is no solution to the double bind, so long as the "I"-"me" fiction is retained. Guilt is not possible if there is no "I" to be held responsible for what the organism *is* (*does, thinks, feels,* are terms which necessarily retain the actor-action dichotomy).

There is a likely misinterpretation of this position which ought to be dispelled. The solution to the double bind here offered is not to be equated with the Western scientific premise of "determinism" or other Eastern philosophies of "fatalism." On the surface, there are points of similarity. Determinism views the organism as a machine (in the formal, mathematical sense) controlled ("programmed") by environmental contingencies interacting with biological structures and properties; it thus denies "free will," "consciousness," and the like, treating these as "mental" fictions. Fatalism is the mystical belief in a pre-ordained order, which individual choice and decision-making cannot affect or change. On the other hand, the Zen Buddhist and Taoist metaphysics denies the validity of such dichotomies as "determinism" versus "free will," "pre-ordained order" versus "individual choice." The concept of determinism makes sense only in conjunction with or in contradistinction to the concept of "free will": in effect, one must first accept the *possibility* of the actor-action model of the "free will" hypothesis before one can reject it in favor of the deterministic hypothesis. But in Zen Buddhism and Taoism, the actor-agent model is not accepted as meaningful, relevant, hence possible; it is seen as a pseudo-question, and consequently the determinism/free will issue never arises.

It is for this reason that if everyone became "liberated," the world and society wouldn't suddenly and drastically change, since the world and society already are the way they are, not by anyone's "doing," but because they cannot be what they are not. Society is not an "artificial" system set up against nature; it is part of nature. Sanctions that men "set up" to "control" each other are not "artificial" rules to thwart "natural" urges; they are part of man's environment, and they will, of course, continue that way; otherwise, they wouldn't exist in the first place. The only essential difference between the "liberated one" and those who are not, is their *attitude* — toward the self/environment dichotomy, the paranoia "against" death, the illusion of alienation, the fiction of the "I" as the house divided against itself. This difference in attitude will certainly make a difference, since men who labor under the illusion that they are unhappy and alienated *have* neurotic symptoms and *are* at war with themselves, their fellow men and the world. Men who do not have this fiction *cannot have* neurotic symptoms, and *cannot be* at war. It is, thus, not a question of choice, but a statement of what is. This third interpretation of the "Ways of Liberation" from the double bind is more abstract and general than the first two, which are subsumed under it.

For practical purposes, it would seem better for the individual to adopt one of these three "Ways of Liberation," or some version of it, as a working hypothesis upon which he can act consistently, than to wait for a theoretical resolution. Whichever interpretation is adopted, it will enable the individual to become more analytic about his interpersonal interactions. Even if we wish to assume that if one interpretation is correct, the others must be wrong, it is still possible that acting consistently on any one of the interpretations may lead to improvement in one's relationship with others; and, in addition, it provides the individual with further evidence upon which to make future choices.

What does it mean to "act consistently and analytically" on some premise or interpretation? Another way of putting it is to say that the individual must be explicitly aware of his situation, physical as well as interpersonal. For instance, he must determine the nature of the social game he is playing with others, or with a particular individual. What kind of a contractual arrangement does he have? What are the rules that govern his interactions? This kind of analysis can reveal the self-contradictory nature of many of his activities, and while such revelation does not necessarily enable one to change, it would seem to be a precondition for it, and in addition, such a realization may reduce the distress that accompanies the feeling of being moved by blind forces.

Let us take a concrete illustration of a problem suggested at the beginning of this discussion. A teacher may genuinely and firmly believe that bilingual education should be used as a means of acculturation. She bases this belief on the premise that given the fact that her Spanish-speaking pupils are going to grow up in the American scene, they must adopt white, middle-class standards if they are going to be successful in life. She is encountering a great deal of trouble in her task: the pupils show no real desire to learn English beyond certain rudiments of everyday commonplace communication; they show no real progress in reading and writing; their interest in history and arithmetic is slight; they do spotty homework; they are unenthusiastic and unfriendly; they show no real ambition to achieve and get ahead. She has tried being friendly and "understanding"; she has learned to be fluent in Spanish and even has paid a few goodwill visits to the homes of some of her pupils. But year after year the fruits of her teaching remain very modest and unsatisfactory. She has reached a frustrating and incomprehensible impasse. What can she do?

The first step in any analytic approach is to examine objectively the premises upon which she is acting. She may begin with the background assumptions and presuppositions of three of her central concepts — the American scene, middle-class standards, being successful in life — and the inferential reasoning that links them into a proposition: (a) the students are going to grow up in the American scene; (b) given the fact that one is going to grow up in the American scene, it follows that he must adopt middle-class values; (c) to be successful in life, one must adopt middle-class values.

Having made this analysis (which we will not do here), the next step is to get feedback from her pupils to see what their premises about these issues might be. Two possibilities now arise: (a) her pupils share the same premises, or (b) her pupils do not share the same premises and presumably she can now identify the important differences.

If the case is (a), she now must examine whether her interactions with the pupils are interpreted by them in the same way as she interprets them, namely if what she does in the classroom and outside is designed to and does contribute to the objectives of the shared premises. If her pupils' interpretation is different, or if in fact (b) is the case, then she is going to realize in a more profound way than she has before why it is that her teaching has remained unsuccessful. On the basis of this knowledge, she can introduce some changes into her activities, specifically designed as corrective measures.

Suppose, for instance, that José Valdez figures it this way: "I cannot become a true North American unless I think and act like one. If I do, my family and friends will consider me strange, and I am going to lose them. OK. But, now, if I try to really become a North American like my cousin Pedro, and maybe even marry an American girl and live in an American neighborhood, they're not going to accept me, 'cause my name is Spanish, my skin is dark, my family lives in the slums, and all that. So, where will I be? Nowhere! That's not for me! Teach is not going to make an American out of me. The hell with school! I'm gonna go work and have fun with the boys."

And suppose Roberto Ramírez figures it this way: "It would be a good idea to do well in school, graduate, get a good job, make more money than José, live in a bigger house, and have a new car. But, why do I need to know all that stuff about American history and that poetry stuff, and write all those compositions in English? Ugh! And Teach isn't interested in us anyway. She pretends to talk like us; her Spanish is pretty good, actually, but then she wouldn't even give Rogelio a good strapping for coming late every day. She doesn't give a damn! If I could only graduate without having to do all that homework, and get a good job, and. . . . "

Writing hypothetical accounts such as these is itself a good exercise for showing up one's misunderstandings or ignorance of the other. In this case, the present writer's own misconceptions would be shown up by having "Valdez" and "Ramírez" and "Rogelio" comment on them.

Continuing in this vein, the teacher would now set up new and clarified contractual arrangements between herself and her pupils, with her Spanish-American assistant teacher, teacher colleague, principal, or pupils' parents. The content of these new "contracts" would depend on her needs, values, and wishes, as well as those of the other party. She may not wish to or be able to become bicultural herself, in which case, she cannot make her pupils bicultural and achieve complete bicultural communication with them, but as long as her relationship with the other is clarified and does not masquerade under false pretenses, the two parties can still perceive each other as being of mutual benefit, within the limits of the contract. People can tolerate differences for the sake of mutual interest, so long as the arrangement is clearly recognized and entered into *voluntarily*. In the absence of both explicitness and voluntary participation, such interaction is tainted by mistrust and perceived as manipulation or subversion.

The setting up of new, explicit, and voluntary contracts requires honesty and equality. The two are preconditions for building trust. Honesty involves analytic self-examination as well as risk-taking, for if one isn't honest with oneself, the other person, not knowing which of your actions and feelings are deliberate and which are "unconscious," will interpret contradictions as dishonest intent and dissimulation. Equality presupposes respect and acceptance, and the realization that most of the values we so dearly cherish are culturally given, not immutable truths of nature. This realization, in turn, presupposes an analytic understanding of our concept of the self, our knowledge of the nature of guilt, our definition of what constitutes responsibility, and the ultimate metaphysics to which we unconsciously subscribe. And, here, we have come full circle, back to the "Ways of Liberation" and the double bind in which we find ourselves. From the objective methods and language of the communication model, we are led back to a highly subjective metaphysics, which, in turn, leads us to an examination of our everyday actions and feelings, and back again to the underlying philosophy, within which we embed our analysis of contractual arrangements and interpersonal behavior. The ECW is a program that takes the individual and the group repeatedly through this cyclical loop.

Notes

1. Carl Bereiter and Siegfried Engelmann, *Teaching Disadvantaged Children in the Preschool* (Englewood Cliffs, N. J.: Prentice-Hall, 1966). Thomas Kochman, "Black English in the Classroom," mimeographed (Chicago: Department of Linguistics, Northeastern Illinois State College, Oct., 1969).
2. For example W.E. Lambert, "A Social Psychology of Bilingualism," *Journal of Social Issues* 23 (1967): 91–109.
3. A good source is Alan Watts, *Psychotherapy East and West* (New York: Ballantine Books, 1969).

READINGS

The following sources are suggested for background reading in preparation for, and in conjunction with, an ECW program dealing with bicultural communication in the school setting:

Bales, R.F. *Personality and Interpersonal Behavior.* New York: Holt, Rinehart, and Winston, 1970.

Egan, Gerald. *Encounter: Group Processes for Interpersonal Growth.* Belmont, Calif.: Brooks/Cole (Wadsworth), 1970.

Ellis, Albert and Harper, R.A. *A Guide to Rational Living.* Hollywood, Calif.: Wilshire Book Co., 1961.

Fromm, Erich. *The Art of Loving.* New York: Harper & Row, 1962.

Garfinkel, Harold. *Studies in Ethnomethodology.* Englewood Cliffs, N.J.: Prentice-Hall, 1968.

Goffman, Erving. *Interaction Ritual.* Garden City, N.Y.: Doubleday Anchor Books, 1967.

Jakobovits, Leon A. *Foreign Language Learning.* Rowley, Mass.: Newbury House Publishers, 1970.

————. *A Psycholinguist Speaks to the Language Teacher.* Rowley, Mass.: Newbury House Publishers, 1973.

————. "The Dynamics of Integrity Groups: A Subjective Account." (Unpublished; available from L.A. Jakobovits.)

Kochman, Thomas. "Black English in the Classroom." Chicago: Department of Linguistics, Northeastern Illinois State College, Oct. 1969. (Mimeo.)

Lambert, W.E. "A Social Psychology of Bilingualism." *The Journal of Social Issues* 23 (1967): 91–109. Also other articles in that issue.

Rogers, C.R. *Freedom to Learn.* Columbus, Ohio: Charles E. Merrill, 1969.

Schutz, W.C. *Joy.* New York: Grove Press, 1967.

Searle, J.R. *Speech Acts.* Cambridge, England, and New York: Cambridge University Press, 1969.

Shuy, R.W., general ed. The Urban Language Series. Washington, D.C.: Center for Applied Linguistics. Several books of interest.

Smith, A.G., ed. *Communication and Culture.* New York: Holt, Rinehart, and Winston, 1966.

Tyler, S.A., ed. *Cognitive Anthropology.* New York: Holt, Rinehart, and Winston, 1969.

Watts, A.W. *Psychotherapy East & West.* New York: Ballantine Books, 1969.

3

Myth Out of Mexico:
The Conquest in American Literature

CECIL ROBINSON

The peoples of Post-Columbian America, North and South, have a common experience in their history: the conquest of a new world, of indigenous peoples, and of vast and often inhospitable terrain. Varying greatly according to the kinds of Europeans involved, the various Indian cultures encountered, and the many faces of nature in the Western Hemisphere, nevertheless in an important psychological respect, the experience has been one. As such, it has needed some quintessential expression in the literature of the Americas. Among the many tales of conquest, one seems to stand alone, lofty and detached from the details of historical context or from the general fabric of story and lore surrounding the period of discovery and colonization. The destruction of Tenochtitlán, ancient capital of the Aztecs, by the army of Cortez, is, in its charged atmosphere of triumph and pathos, the very prototype of the conquest of the New World.

In literature, the story of the Conquest of Mexico has been an important link between North and Hispanic America. North American writers, hardly less than Latin Americans, have felt its power and sensed its importance as a type of the New World experience. The Spaniard destroying in his rage for gold a savage, brilliant, and innocent people, has served North American writers as an analogue for the later continental epic of the destruction of the wilderness. Although the early Spanish writers in reporting home about the strange and marvelous city of Tenochtitlán emphasized that its high state of development was such

By permission from *With the Ears of Strangers: The Mexican in American Literature* by Cecil Robinson (Tucson: University of Arizona Press, copyright 1963).

Cecil Robinson of the English Department of the University of Arizona has published many articles and authored and edited books on cross-cultural subjects. He has served as director of programs for Spanish-speaking bilinguals and as chairman of the Bilingual-Bicultural Studies Committee at the University of Arizona. An authority on the Mexican in American literature, he has lectured throughout the United States and Latin America.

as to make the most sophisticated European gape with wonderment, the North American writers who later took up the theme often saw fit to emphasize for their own purposes the savagery and innocence which underlay this dazzling display of civilization.

However, in order to portray the Aztecs as a part of a virginal America soon to be despoiled, North American writers obsessed with this idea had to mute certain of the darker phases of Aztec life, the grisly side of its religion with its torture and human sacrifice.

Though Prescott more than any other writer influenced American authors writing about the Conquest, he gave little encouragement in *The Conquest of Mexico* to contemporary and later writers who were to present the Aztecs as a case of innocence betrayed. While not minimizing Spanish barbarities, Prescott insisted that the Conquest was in the main a deliverance from the terrors of the god Huitzilopotchli to the mildness and love of the Virgin of Guadalupe. A modern writer, Frances Gillmor, who has combined creative gifts with dogged and ingenious scholarship in recreating the lives and times of two Aztec leaders, insists that she too is not to be identified with the concept of the Aztec as noble savage betrayed. Her two books dealing with Aztec themes are written in the manner of biographical narrative. They are *Flute of the Smoking Mirror*[1], a study of the poet-statesman of Texacoco, Nazahualcoyotl (1402-1472), and *The King Danced in the Market Place*[2], a biography of Huehue Moctezuma Ilhuicamina, grandfather of the famous Moctezuma II and the leader who first made the Aztecs into a formidable power extending their domain over neighboring peoples. These books admirably convey to the reader the author's sense of the color and tone of Aztec society and the psychology of the people. A society and its leaders are dealt with as worthy in themselves of recording and interpretation, leaving untouched the question of innocence or betrayal. However, Frances Gillmor has verbally stated that Indianists inside of Mexico and without are guilty of distortion in underestimating the role that Spanish culture and Christian idealism have played in the development of Mexican society. George Vaillant, on the other hand, in his small and classic volume, *The Aztecs of Mexico*[3], while reporting fully on the horrors, placed them in their proper context in a complex and affecting religious symbolism ranging from the gayety of flower festivals to the sacrificial stone and the obsidian knife. He insists that with the destruction of Tenochtitlán a uniquely aesthetic vision of life perished.

A cherished myth, of course, is not to be overthrown by facts or by rationalistic analysis. Furthermore, the idea of the Conquest as the destruction of innocence, which has flourished in American letters for over a century, certainly expresses a truth if not the whole truth. The very

imminence of total disaster has made every knowable detail of Moctezuma's city seem especially precious to novelists and poets. Brooding
in the approved manner of early nineteenth-century romanticism over
the lost glories of the Aztecs, Robert Montgomery Bird, somewhat in
the spirit of Whitman's "Muse in the New World," heralds the Aztecs
as a source of new-world mythology for literature and theorizes that

nature, and the memory of strange deeds of renown, have flung over the valley
of Mexico a charm more romantic than is attached to many of the vales of
the older world; for though historic association and the spell of poetry have
consecrated the borders of Leman and the laurel groves of Tempe . . . [yet
does our fancy, in either, dwell upon objects which are not so much the
adjuvants of romance as of sentiment; in both, we gather food rather for feeling than imagination; we live over thoughts which are generated by memory,
and our conceptions are the reproductions of experience.] But poetry has
added no plenary charm, history has cast no over-sufficient light on the haunts
of Montezuma;[4] on the Valley of Lakes, though filled with the hum of life,
the mysteries of backward years are yet brooding; and the marvels of human
destiny are whispered to our ears, in the sigh of every breeze. . . . One chapter
only of its history (and that how full of marvels!) has been written or preserved; the rest is blank. . . . This is the proper field for romantic musings.[5]

Two modern American poets have recited, one in prose, the other
in verse, long lists of objects of commerce and art that were to be found
in the ancient capital of Mexico at the time of Moctezuma. The objects
are rendered almost tactile to the reader, and the naming is the poetry.
In his book of essays, *In the American Grain,* William Carlos Williams
assesses "The Destruction of Tenochtitlán" as a significant event in the
American experience. Of that city he writes:

Here "everything which the world affords" was offered for purchase, from
the personal services of laborers and porters to the last refinements of bijouterie;
gold, silver, lead, brass, copper, tin; wrought and unwrought stone, bricks burnt
and unburnt, timber hewn and unhewn, of different sorts; game of every
variety, fowls, quails, partridges, wild ducks, parrots, pigeons, reed-birds,
sparrows, eagles, hawks, owls, likewise the skins of some birds of prey with
their feathers, head, beak and claws; rabbits, hares, deer and little dogs, which
they raised for eating; wood and coals in abundance and brasiers of earthen-
ware for burning coals; mats of various kinds; all kinds of green vegetables,
especially onions, leeks, watercresses, nasturtium, sorrel, artichokes and golden
thistle; fruits, fish, honey, grain — either whole, in the form of flour or baked
into loaves; different kinds of cotton thread of all colors; jars, jugs, pots and
an endless variety of vessels, all made of fine clay, most of them glazed and
painted; eggs, cakes, patés of birds and fish; wine from the maguey, finally
everything that could be found throughout the whole country was sold there,
each kind of merchandise in a separate street or quarter of the market assigned
to it exclusively, and thus the best order was preserved.

To Williams the epic of Cortez and Moctezuma was the very stuff of "the American grain." He goes on to enumerate the gifts which Moctezuma sent to Cortez in an effort to placate him and forestall his march on the capital:

. . . a gold necklace of seven pieces, set with many gems like small rubies, a hundred and eighty-three emeralds and ten fine pearls, and hung with twenty-seven little bells of gold. Two wheels, one of gold like the sun and the other of silver with the image of the moon upon it, made of plates of those metals, twenty-eight hands in circumference, with figures of animals and other things in bas-relief, finished with great skill and ingenuity. — A headpiece of wood and gold, adorned with gems, from which hung twenty-five little bells of gold, and, on it, instead of plume, a green bird with eyes, beak and feet of gold. — Several shoes of the skin of deer, sewed with gold thread, the soles of which were made of blue and white stones of a brilliant appearance. — A shield of wood and leather, with little bells hanging to it and covered with plates of gold, in the middle of which was cut the image of the god of war between four heads of a lion, a tiger, an eagle and an owl, represented alive with their hair and feathers. — Twenty-four curious and beautiful shields of gold, of feathers and very small pearls, and four of feathers and silver only. — Four fishes, two ducks and some other birds of molten gold. — A large mirror adorned with gold, and many small. — Miters and crowns of feathers and gold ornamented with pearls and gems. — Several large plumes of beautiful feathers, fretted with gold and small pearls. — Several fans of gold and silver mixed together; others of feathers only, of different forms and sizes. — A variety of cotton mantles, some all white, others chequered with white and black, or red, green, yellow and blue; on the outside rough like shaggy cloth and within destitute of color and nap. — A number of underwaistcoats, handkerchiefs, counter panes, tapestries and carpets of cotton, the workmanship superior to the materials of which they were composed. — And books made of tablets with a smooth surface for writing, which being joined might be folded together or stretched out to be a considerable length. . . .

Needless to say, all these gifts rather than deterring Cortez aroused his cupidity the more and strengthened his resolve to conquer the heart of the Aztec empire.

The other poet, Archibald MacLeish, in his narrative poem *Conquistador* speaks with the voice of Bernal Díaz del Castillo, veteran campaigner who had fought under Cortez in all the battles of the Conquest. Bernal Díaz's account of the Conquest, *La Verdadera Historia de la Conquistada de Nueva España,* was the source upon which Prescott relied the most. Directly or indirectly through Prescott it has influenced most American writers dealing with the Conquest. It was written in the form of a memoir in the soldier's old age, and MacLeish catches much of the spirit of the original chronicle in its nostalgia and testiness as well as in its clarity, matter-of-factness, and eye for detail. Bernal Díaz retained a remarkable memory for the minutia of life in Tenochtitlán as it was first seen by Cortez and his men. In *Conquistador* MacLeish has him speak of the varied commerce of the city:

Merchants of sweet nuts and of chives and of honey:
Of leaves of dock for the eyes: of a calf's bone for

Gloss of the hair as the hand draws it; of dung
For salt for the tanning of leather; sellers of yarn:
Old men with the sun-bleached hair and the bunches of

Herbs: of lettuces washed cool: of garlic
Dried brown on a withy of plaited grass:
Sellers of cooked dough by the coal-fires larding the

Stained skirt with the spittle of burning fat:
Those the makers of robes: Those that shredded the
Silken down of a seed and their fingers fastened the

Stone to the twist of it turning the scarlet thread:
Sellers of good dreams: of blue clay for the
Baking of gods: of quills of the gold: of hennequin:

Sellers of beetles for red dyes: makers of
Stone masks of the dead and of stone mirrors:
Makers of fortunate knots: magistrates in the

Swept porch — and they kept the names of the year:
They took the tax on the red stones and the herons:
They judged of the levies of salt: vendors of syrups:

Of harsh drugs for the old from the coupling of hares:
Of dry seeds: of sweet straws. . . .

The contrast of elegance and barbarity arouses wonder. Pursuing his reflections in "The Destruction of Tenochtitlán," William Carlos Williams writes of Moctezuma: "Surely no other prince has lived, or will ever live, in such state as did this American cacique. The whole waking aspirations of his people, opposed to and completing their religious sense, seemed to come off in him and in him alone: the drive upward, toward the sun and the stars. He was the very person of their ornate dreams, so delicate, so prismatically colorful, so full of tinkling sounds and rhythms, so tireless of invention. Never was such a surface lifted above the isolate blackness of such profound savagery."

Another modern American writer, John Houghton Allen, in the novel *Southwest,* an original work savoring authentically of the borderlands, treats a similar theme in a strange way. He writes of the capital city of the Toltecs, predecessors of the Aztecs, and, perhaps because of his Catholic background, has a character in the novel present these people not as splendid and innocent barbarians but as victims of a fall from grace. The book, written in the first person, is mainly about the borderland between Texas and Mexico. The principal characters are Mexican rancheros and ranch hands among whom the author was raised. Loosely constructed and drawling its way from tale to tale in the manner of campfire reminiscences, the book is loaded with the lore, proverbs, and turn of speech of the borderlands and meanders back and forth through the first decades of the twentieth century as various characters remember tales of great bandits or heroes of the revolution such as Pancho Villa and his *dorados*. But there is an unexpected interpolation toward the end of the book, nightmarish, Poe-like in its weirdness and convincing otherworldliness. One remembers that Allen is quite consciously Southern, by way of Texas.

"We had a weird story told to us by a dope addict," writes Allen, casually getting his tale under way, "around the campfire at Agua Dulce one Christmas Day. Perhaps we were the sort of men who attracted weird and violent tales, but the fact remains, if you told us a story it had to be good." The Mexicans present had celebrated their Christmas the night before in traditional style "at the posada and by going to their annual Mass." Now they were back at work on the ranch and *"crudos,"* that is, suffering from hangover. "It was a pitch-dark night, and the day had been gray as a fog, with the brush twisted and tortured and bare under overcast skies. . . ." The men sitting around the fire were "passing the bottle, because of the nip in the air, and because after all, it was Christmas," when suddenly a man from out in the darkness lurched past the rim of firelight, startling all hands. It turned out that he was a harmless and pitiable creature, known to be a smoker of marijuana, "one of those grotesques that are awry and jangled from smoking this humble weed." After eating like a glutton and praising the cook "— and that alone took a *boca-de-ora* [sic] —" he launched into his story. Once as a young man he was forced to flee into the mountains west of Torreón because of a knifing. He mounted high into practically inaccessible regions of mountain wilderness, passed over a summit, and descended into an unknown valley where he discovered the "city of the Toltecs." He sneaked, full of dread, past the huge, "hawk-nosed" sentinels, who, clothed in gorgeous raiment, stood erect and looked straight ahead as though paralyzed by some enchantment. The people in the streets were frozen still, having been suddenly caught by some spell while in the attitudes of daily living. In terror the narrator fled into the principal temple where he found a throng of people kneeling and bowed frozen in an attitude of "mysterious penance" before a high priest on a throne. Horrified all the more, he escaped into a side room and found himself in a seraglio of temple maidens,

all of them remarkable in that they were blondes with golden hair that fell below their waists, and fine blue eyes like clear water, and the brave laughter that would not be heard again in the Western World. They were like Valkyries, the music of Wagner. Perhaps they had been sent as tribute to the monarchs of the Western World from the Greenland colonies a thousand years ago — for they were Vikings, and they were beautiful, the tropic sun had never touched their loveliness. There was peace about their eyes, and they were the golden thighs of Paradise. The sight of them affected me with a bitter nostalgia, and again I remembered, as we all remember, what the Spanish have lost in the Western World. They were like the blue-eyed, golden-haired Spanish descended from the Visigoths, that we all in our subconscious remember. It is not that we are people dark by nature, attracted by the light, the tall and the fair; it has been with us since we first came to the Indies, that we suffered a fall from grace — for the Captains of Cortés were massive men with red beards and light hair and blue eyes and voices like Thor — and we would remember the Visigoths. We have a bitter nostalgia for blondness, we brown little men, we yearn back to our ethnos, we would dream of the fair people with blue eyes, that even the Indians believed in — and we have remembered the Visigoths.[6]

These temple maids were imprisoned by some spell and seemed to long for the release that a Christian benediction might have given them,

but the very idea gave me a cold sweat, and I came away from the temple maidens and I found myself in the streets again, rushing through the streets of that awful city, the people crying havoc, for they seemed to cry after me to stop and heal them with a Christian benediction — this was what they had been waiting for, a thousand years! . . . I imagined the dismay on their faces, I dared not look at them from fear and shame, but they cried aloud, at last. There was a babble of voices for a moment, and then silence. They had waited for a Christian a thousand years, and I ran.[7]

The theme of the failure of the European in his relations with the original people of America is still here, but the point of view is different. The Europeans did not dare bestow real Christianity upon those who desperately needed it.

Though early American novelists dealing with the Conquest relied almost entirely on Prescott and Bernal Díaz for their source material, they did not match either of these writers in enthusiasm for the great conquistador. In the main, the Spaniard was the despoiler, and American writers have tended to find a community of spirit with that aspect of the Mexican soul which has not permitted to this day a statue of Cortez to be erected throughout the length and breadth of Mexico. The modern Mexican historian, Wigberto Jiménez Moreno, has said that the Mexican psyche still bears the scars of the trauma caused by the rape of the Indian mother by the Spanish father. A recent and rather startling revelation of how close to the surface is the intense feeling which survives in Mexico about the fate of the Aztec was the furor caused by the discovery in the south of Mexico of the alleged bones of the last of the

Aztec emperors, Cuauhtémoc (this Nahuatl name also has various spellings in English). Of a very different metal from his uncle, Moctezuma II,
Cuauhtémoc defied the Spaniards while his city was reduced to rubble,
block by block, and his people subsisted on rats. He never surrendered
but was captured and promised honorable treatment. Cortez brought him
along on one of his expeditions to the south, not daring to leave him in
the capital. In the course of the expedition, Cortez had Cuauhtémoc
hanged, claiming that the Aztec leader was plotting treason.

In an early American novel, Robert Montgomery Bird mourns the
fate of Cuauhtémoc or Cuatimozin as that writer names him: "Four
years after the fall of his empire, and at a distance of several hundred
leagues from his native valley, he expiated upon a gibbet, a crime that
existed only in the gloomy and remorseful imagination of the Conqueror.
And thus, with two royal kinsmen, kings and feudatories of Anahuac,
he was left to swing in the winds, and feed the vultures of a distant and
desert land. He merited a higher distinction, a loftier respect, and a pro-
founder compassion, than men will willingly accord to a barbarian and
infidel."[8]

In a long and idyllic novel written a decade after Bird's, Joseph Holt
Ingraham celebrates the rise and love of the first Moctezuma, whose
descendant was to lose "his power, his empire, and his life, by the hands
of an invader, whose coming was from the rising sun, and whose pathway
was deluged with blood."[9] Published the same year as Ingraham's book
was Edward Maturin's *Montezuma, the Last of the Aztecs,* which con-
jured up the vision of a pastoral, innocent, and serene Tenochtitlán on
the eve of the Conquest:

Nor had nature, in the caprice which sometimes characterizes her loveliest
creations, lavished these beauties for her own solitary enjoyment, or the isolated
honours of her own worship. Towns, studding the bosoms of the lakes, or
bordering their margins, lent the busy and populous aspect, to this sylvan
elysium, of worshippers assembled at the great altar of nature, to pour forth
their hymns of gratitude, or solemnize their simple rites in honour of her
who had made their happy valley one rich panorama of her beauties, and
endowed the temporary sojourn of earth with the fadeless joys, the unwithering
hues, and beatific visions of heaven! Clustered with flowers, or embowered in
shade, lay these cottages; their quiet inhabitants occupied in the various
employments afforded by their pastoral retreat: some of them engaged on
their *chinampas* in rearing fruit, flowers or vegetables for the market of
Tenochtitlán. Alas! little did they deem their days of happy seclusion in that
valley-retreat were so rapidly drawing to a close: its smiling orchards and
gardens so soon to be trampled by the iron-heel of the conquerer, or laid
waste by his desolating ambition; the crystal waters of its lakes darkened and
defaced by the smoke of the lombard and the quiet depths of their paradise
re-echoing the blast of the war-trumpet or the remorseless battle-cry, "God
and St. Iago!"[10]

Again in *Conquistador,* MacLeish depicts the Spanish soldiers recognizing that in Mexico they would forever be strangers:

We praised the trampling of sun as a gilt cock;
Our hearts were singing as hammered bronze and our mouths with

Sound as the corn is where the wind goes: and we mocked the
Shape of love with our thumbs: We cried aloud of the
Great sky: of the salt rock: of the land. . . .

And nevertheless it was not so: for the ground was

Silent against us: on our foreign hands
The dust was a solemn and red stain: our tongues were
Unskilled to the pulp of their fruits as a language of
Sullen stones in our mouths: we heard the sun in the
Crackle of live trees with the ears of strangers. . . .

William Carlos Williams absolves Cortez of personal blame, calling him the agent of "the spirit of malice which underlies men's lives and against which nothing offers resistance. And bitter as the thought may be that Tenochtitlán, the barbaric city, its people, its genius wherever found should have been crushed out because of the awkward names men give their emptiness, yet it was no man's fault. It was the force of the pack whom the dead drive. Cortez was neither malicious, stupid, nor blind, but a conquerer like other conquerors."

And yet, of course, all was not destruction. From practically the first day that Cortez and his men landed in Vera Cruz a racial fusion began which was to produce a remarkable new culture. In fact the very prefiguration of the new Mexican race was the relationship between Cortez and his Indian mistress, Malinche, known to the Spaniards as Doña Marina. She gave him access to the Indian world, not only in its stratagems and intrigues but in its traditions and its psychology. Indianists in Mexico have long hated Malinche as a traitor to her people. The modern painter Siqueiros presents her in a large mural being lasciviously fondled by Cortez, as she snickers at the destruction of her people, her earth-brown body making sharp contrast with the startling whiteness of the skin of the Spaniard. And yet Malinche had real grievances. The daughter of a small chieftain on the rim of Tenochtitlán, she was dispossessed of her inheritance at the connivance of her mother. Her father died while she was a child, and her mother remarried and had a son for whom she was very ambitious. If he was to inherit the chieftainship, Malinche had to be removed; so the mother sold her into slavery and staged a mock funeral to prove that she was dead. It was as a slave girl in the region of Vera Cruz that Cortez came upon her. While undoubtedly she paved the way for his successes, she also gave him an understanding and respect for the indigenous cultures of Mexico. For Cortez, unlike Pizarro, although he felt impelled on occasion to use harsh methods, had no love of cruelty per se. The histories of Mexico and Peru might be expected to have run a parallel course. In each area the Spaniards came upon highly developed and flourishing Indian civilizations, but Mexico produced a genuine fusion of races and cultures, while in Peru a Spanish oligarchy uneasily rules from Lima a dispossessed mass of Indians whose resentment is rising to a dangerous pitch. The nature of the conquest in each area and more particularly the characters of the leading conquistadores provide a key to this situation, and Malinche deserves no little credit for the road that colonial Mexico embarked upon. In the opening lines, MacLeish in *Conquistador* presents Bernal Díaz faced with the fact of *mestizaje,* a racial mixture, in the persons of his own children:

> ... my children
> Half-grown: sons with beards: the big one
> Breaking the small of his back in the brothel thrills
> And a girl to be married and all of them snarling at home
> With the Indian look in their eyes like a cat killing.

In a modern novel, *Step Down Elder Brother,* the author, Josephina Niggli, considers the social situation of the state of Nuevo León and especially its capital, Monterey, the industrial center of Mexico. Nuevo León had long prided itself on being *criollo,* that is of pure Spanish blood though born in the New World. With the industrialization of the area, *mestizos* (mixed-bloods) poured into the region from the south. They came as laborers, but within two or three generations and especially after the great revolution which began in 1910 and lasted a decade, many of the *mestizos* became petty bourgeois and began vigorously challenging the older families. The protagonist of the novel, Domingo Vasquez de Anda, though a scion of one of the great families, has come to recognize and accept the inevitable triumph of the *mestizos.* He is saturated in the history of Mexico, and as he stands over a sleeping servant girl, Serafina, who has been made pregnant by his brother, and notices for the first time the Indian cast of her features, he muses upon her lineage somewhat extravagantly: "Perhaps on Serafina's bone there was stamped the memory of Cortés' entrance to Mexico City; of Montezuma's litter with the coverlet woven from hummingbird's feathers. In her might still remain echoes of the poet-emperor, greatest of the Aztecans [Nezahualcoyotl], who, like David, came from the fields to sit on the throne and there compose psalms to God."[11] Serafina's child, though rejected by its own father, is to become, through Domingo's insistence, a recognized member of the family.

But apart from the partial survival of the Aztecs in the blood line of living Mexicans, what if anything survives of Tenochtitlán? A number of American writers have dealt with the subterranean continuance of Indian attitudes and ritual in the religious life of modern Mexico, a subject which will be treated later; but quite aside from this consideration, several American writers, some of whom are in no way regionalists, have felt impelled to re-emphasize and reinterpret the epic of Tenochtitlán as important for the self-understanding of even English-speaking America. Hart Crane ended his long poem, *The Bridge,* which had aimed at capturing all of America for the imagination, with a somewhat enigmatic reference to the eagle and the serpent, the ancient insignia of the Aztecs which is reproduced on the flag of modern Mexico. Evidently Crane felt that in the summing up of his epic this cultural symbol was not to be omitted. In another poem addressed to the stone statue of the Aztec flower god, Xochipilli, Crane challenges the reader to avail himself of that which is enduring in the life of a "dismounted people":

> . . . If you
> Could drink the sun as did and does
> Xochipilli — as they who've
> Gone have done, as they
> Who've done . . . A god of flowers in statued
> Stone . . . of love —
> If you could die, then starve, who live
> Thereafter, stronger than death smiles in flowering stone —
> You could stop time, give florescent
> Time a longer answer back (shave lightning,
> Possess in hale full the winds) of time
> A longer answer force, more enduring answer
> As they did — and have done . . . [12]

Not only in "The Destruction of Tenochtitlán," but in other essays William Carlos Williams has returned to the theme of the Aztecs and their relationship to the American consciousness. In discussing the type of the "New World Man," he rejects the notion of T.S. Eliot's enervated J. Alfred Prufrock as being representative. "Prufrock is a masterly portrait of the man just below the summit, but the type is universal; the model in his case might be Mr. J. No. The New World is Montezuma or, since he was stoned to death in a parley, Guatemozin, who had the city of Mexico leveled over him before he was taken." [13] As to the legacy of Tenochtitlán, Williams says: "One is at liberty to guess what the pure American addition to world culture might have been if it had gone forward singly. But that is merely an academicism. Perhaps Tenochtitlán which Cortez destroyed held the key. That also is beside the point, except that Tenochtitlán with its curious brilliance may still legitimately be kept alive in thought not as something which *could* have been preserved but as something which was actual and was destroyed."[14] The theme has been with us almost from the beginning of our literature; it exists in countless popular forms and has been reappraised by serious modern American writers. We have not seen the end of it, as it is enduringly a part of the matter of America.

Notes

1. Tucson: University of Arizona Press, 1949.
2. Tucson: University of Arizona Press, 1963.
3. Garden City, New York: 1941.
4. Note: The name of the Aztec emperor who met Cortés is spelled in various ways in English. Any variation is at best a rough phonetic transcription of the Nahuatl word.
5. *Calavar* (Philadelphia: Lea and Blanchard, 1847 [1st ed. 1834]), Introduction, p. iv.
6. New York: Bantam Books, 1953, p. 96.
7. Ibid., pp. 97–98.
8. *The Infidel: or the Fall of Mexico* (Philadelphia: Carey, Lea and Blanchard, 1835), vol. 2:228.
9. *Montezuma, the Serf* (Boston: H.L. Williams, 1845), vol. 1:116.
10. New York: Paine and Burgess, 1845, vol. 2:8–9.
11. New York: Rinehart, 1947, p. 238.
12. *The Collected Poems of Hart Crane* (New York: Liverwright Publishing Corp., 1933), pp. 146–47.
13. *Selected Essays of William Carlos Williams* (New York: Random House, 1954), p. 22.
14. Ibid., p. 143.

4.

From *Barrio Boy*

E RNESTO G ALARZA

To begin with, we didn't hear one but many sorts of English. Mr. Chester, my soldier friend, and Big Ernie spoke as if they were tired and always arguing. The Old Gentleman nibbled his words, like a rabbit working on a carrot, perhaps because all his teeth weren't there. Mr. Brien's words came through in a deep voice from behind the hair screen of his moustache. Big Singh spoke English in his own way, brittle and choppy, hard to understand unless you watched his lips. These people sounded nothing like the Sicilian vegetable hawker or the Greek grocer at the corner or the black lady in the alley who saved beer bottles for me. And of course none of them sounded like Miss Hopley or Miss Campbell.

It took time to realize that when the Americans said "Sackmenna" they meant Sacra-men-to, or that "Kelly-phony" was their way of saying Cali-for-nia. Worse yet, the names of many of their towns could not be managed. I tried to teach Gustavo that Woodland was not pronounced "Boor-lan," and that Walnut Grove was not "Gualen-gro." A second-hand shop on our block that called itself The Cheap Store sounded to us like the Sheep Store, and the sign did not spell it like the school books.

There was no authority at 418 L who could tell us the one proper way to pronounce a word, and it would not have done much good if there had been. Try as they did the adults in my family could see no difference between "wood" and "boor." Words spelled the same way or nearly so in Spanish and English and whose meanings we could guess accurately — words like *principal* and *tomato* — were too few to help us

Reprinted from *Barrio Boy* by Ernesto Galarza (Notre Dame, Indiana: The University of Notre Dame Press, 1971).

Ernesto Galarza of the Department of Sociology and Anthropology, University of Notre Dame, is well known for his books and articles on Mexican-Americans in the United States. In addition to *Barrio Boy,* his book *Spiders in the House and Workers in the Field,* a report on the plight of struggling agricultural workers in California, has commanded popular attention.

in daily usage. The grown-ups adapted the most necessary words and managed to make themselves understood, words like the *French loff, yelly-rol, eppel pai, tee-kett,* and *kenn meelk.* Miss Campbell and her colleagues lost no time in scrubbing out these spots in my own pronunciation. Partly to show off, partly to do my duty to the family, I tried their methods at home. It was hopeless. They listened hard but they couldn't hear me. Besides, *Boor-lan* was *Boor-lan* all over the *barrio.* Everyone knew what you meant even though you didn't say Woodland. I gave up giving English lessons at home.

The *barrio* invented its own versions of American talk. And my family, to my disgust, adopted them with no little delight. My mother could tell someone at the door asking for an absent one: "Ess gon." When some American tried to rush her into conversation she stopped him with: "Yo no pick een-glees." But at *pocho* talk my mother drew the line, although José and Gustavo fell into it easily. Such words as *yarda* for yard, *yonque* for junk, *donas* for doughnuts, *grocería* for grocery store, *raite* for ride, and *borde* for meals shocked her and I was drilled to avoid them. Woolworth's was *el fei-en-ten* to the *barrio* but it was *el baratillo* to her and by command to me also. Gustavo could say *droguería* because there wasn't anything she could do about it, but for me *botica* was required.

Prowling the alleys and gleaning along the waterfront I learned how chicano workingmen hammered the English language to their ways. On the docks I heard them bark over a slip or a spill "Oh, Chet," imitating the American crew bosses with the familiar "Gar-demme-yoo." José and I privately compared notes in the matter of "San Afabeechee," who, he said, was a saint of the Americans but which, as I well knew, was what Americans called each other in a fist fight.

When troubles made it necessary for the *barrio* people to deal with the Americans uptown, the *Autoridades,* I went with them to the police court, the industrial accident office, the county hospital, the draft board, the county clerk. We got lost together in the rigamarole of functionaries who sat, like *patrones,* behind desks and who demanded licenses, certificates, documents, affidavits, signatures, and witnesses. And we celebrated our successes, as when the worker for whom I interpreted in interviews that lasted many months was awarded a thousand dollars for a disabled arm. Don Crescencio congratulated me, saying that in Mexico for a thousand American dollars you could buy the lives of many peons.

José had chosen our new home in the basement on O Street because it was close to the Hearkness Junior High School, to which I transferred from Bret Harte. As the *jefe de familia* he explained that I could help earn our living but that I was to study for a high school diploma. That being settled, my routine was clearly divided into schooltime and worktime, the second depending on when I was free from the first.

Few Mexicans of my age from the *barrio* were enrolled at the junior high school when I went there. At least, there were no other Mexican boys or girls in Mr. Everett's class in civics, or Miss Crowley's English composition, or Mrs. Stevenson's Spanish course. Mrs. Stevenson assigned me to read to the class and to recite poems by Amado Nervo, because the poet was from Tepic and I was, too. Miss Crowley accepted my compositions about Jalcocotán and the buried treasure of Acaponeta while the others in the class were writing about Sir Patrick Spence and the Beautiful Lady without Mercy, whom they had never met. For Mr. Everett's class, the last of the day, I clipped pieces from the *Sacramento Bee* about important events in Sacramento. From him I learned to use the ring binder in which I kept clippings to prepare oral reports. Occasionally he kept me after school to talk. He sat on his desk, one leg dangling over a corner, behind him the frame of a large window and the arching elms of the school yard, telling me he thought I could easily make the debating team at the high school next year, that Stanford University might be the place to go after graduation, and making other by-the-way comments that began to shape themselves into my future.

It was during the summer vacation that school did not interfere with making a living, the time of the year when I went with other *barrio* people to the ranches to look for work. Still too young to shape up with the day-haul gangs, I loitered on skid row, picking up conversation and reading the chalk signs about work that was being offered. For a few days of picking fruit or pulling hops I bicycled to Folsom, Lodi, Woodland, Freeport, Walnut Grove, Marysville, Slough House, Florin, and places that had no name. Looking for work, I pedaled through a countryside blocked off, mile after mile, into orchards, vineyards, and vegetable farms. Along the ditchbanks, where the grass, the morning glory, and the wild oats made a soft mattress, I unrolled my bindle and slept.

In the labor camps I shared the summertime of the lives of the *barrio* people. They gathered from *barrios* of faraway places like Imperial Valley, Los Angeles, Phoenix, and San Antonio. Each family traveling on its own, they came in trucks piled with household goods or packed in their secondhand *fotingos* and *chevees*. The trucks and cars were ancient models, fresh out of a used-car lot, with license tags of many states. It was into these jalopies that much of the care and a good part of the family's earnings went. In camp they were constantly being fixed, so close to scrap that when we needed a part for repairs, we first went to the nearest junkyard.

It was a world different in so many ways from the lower part of Sacramento and the residences surrounded by trim lawns and cool canopies of elms to which I had delivered packages for Wahl's. Our main street was usually an irrigation ditch, the water supply for cooking, drinking, laundering, and bathing. In the better camps there was a faucet or a hydrant, from which water was carried in buckets, pails, and washtubs. If the camp belonged to a contractor, and it was used from year to year, there were permanent buildings — a shack for his office, the privies, weather-worn and sagging, and a few cabins made of secondhand lumber, patched and unpainted.

If the farmer provided housing himself, it was in tents pitched on the bare baked earth or on the rough ground of newly plowed land on the edge of a field. Those who arrived late for the work season camped under trees or raised lean-to's along a creek, roofing their trucks with canvas to make bedrooms. Such camps were always well away from the house of the ranchero, screened from the main road by an orchard or a grove of eucalyptus. I helped to pitch and take down such camps, on some spot that seemed lonely when we arrived, desolate when we left.

If they could help it, the workers with families avoided the more permanent camps, where the seasonal hired hands from skid row were more likely to be found. I lived a few days in such a camp and found out why families avoided them. On Saturday nights when the crews had a week's wages in their pockets, strangers appeared, men and women, carrying suitcases with liquor and other contraband. The police were called by the contractor only when the carousing threatened to break into fighting. Otherwise, the weekly bouts were a part of the regular business of the camp.

Like all the others, I often went to work without knowing how much I was going to be paid. I was never hired by a rancher, but by a contractor or a straw boss who picked up crews in town and handled the payroll. The important questions that were in my mind — the wages per hour or per lug box, whether the beds would have mattresses and blankets, the price of meals, how often we would be paid — were never discussed, much less answered, beforehand. Once we were in camp, owing the employer for the ride to the job, having no means to get back to town except by walking and no money for the next meal, arguments over working conditions were settled in favor of the boss. I learned firsthand the chiseling techniques of the contractors and their pushers — how they knocked off two or three lugs of grapes from the daily record for each member of the crew, or the way they had of turning the face of the scales away from you when you weighed your work in.

There was never any doubt about the contractor and his power over us. He could fire a man and his family on the spot and make them wait days for their wages. A man could be forced to quit by assigning him regularly to the thinnest pickings in the field. The worst thing one could do was to ask for fresh water on the job, regardless of the heat of the day;

instead of iced water, given freely, the crews were expected to buy sodas at twice the price in town, sold by the contractor himself. He usually had a pistol — to protect the payroll, so it was said. Through the ranchers for whom he worked, we were certain that he had connections with the *Autoridades,* for they never showed up in camp to settle wage disputes or listen to our complaints or to go for a doctor when one was needed. Lord of a rag-tag labor camp of Mexicans, the contractor, a Mexican himself, knew that few men would let their anger blow, even when he stung them with curses like, "Orale, San Afabeeches huevones."

As a single worker, I usually ate with some household, paying for my board. I did more work than a child but less than a man, neither the head nor the tail of a family. Unless the camp was a large one I became acquainted with most of the families. Those who could not write asked me to chalk their payroll numbers on the boxes they picked. I counted matches for a man who transferred them from the right pocket of his pants to the left as he tallied the lugs he filled throughout the day. It was his only check on the record the contractor kept of his work. As we worked the rows or the tree blocks during the day, or talked in the evenings where the men gathered in small groups to smoke and rest, I heard about *barrios* I had never seen but that must have been much like ours in Sacramento.

When my job ended I pedaled back to Sacramento, detouring over country lanes I knew well. Here and there I walked the bicycle over dirt roads rutted by wagons. The pastures were sunburned and the grain fields had been cut to stubble. Riding by a thicket of reeds where an irrigation ditch swamped I stopped and looked at the red-winged blackbirds riding gracefully on the tips of the canes. Now and then they streaked out of the green clump, spraying the pale sky with crimson dots in all directions.

Crossing the Y Street levee by Southside Park, I rode through the *barrio* to Doña Tránsito's, leaving my bike hooked on the picket fence by the handle bar.

I knocked on the screen door that always hung tired, like the sagging porch coming unnailed. No one was at home.

It was two hours before time to cook supper. From the stoop I looked up and down the cross streets. The *barrio* seemed empty.

I unhooked the bicycle, mounted it, and headed for the main high school, twenty blocks away where I would be going in a week. Pumping slowly, I wondered about the debating team and the other things Mr. Everett had mentioned.

PART TWO

Preconsideration:
SOME THEORETICAL BASES

The very imperfections and changeability of language speak against its divine origin.

— Otto Jespersen

5.

Some Traits of Language and Language Acquisition

DWIGHT BOLINGER

One estimate puts the number of languages in active use in the world today somewhere between three and four thousand. Another makes it five thousand or more. The latter is probably closer to the truth, for many languages are spoken by only a few hundred persons, and many areas of the world are still not fully surveyed. In one subdistrict of New Guinea, for example, there are sixteen languages spoken by an average of fewer than a thousand persons each.[1] Also, it is impossible to be exact, for no one knows just what constitutes "one language." Danish and Norwegian have a high degree of mutual intelligibility; this makes them almost by definition dialects of a single language. Do we count them as two? Cantonese and Mandarin, in spite of both being "Chinese," are about as dissimilar as Portuguese and Italian. Do we count mainland Chinese as one language? To be scientific we have to ignore politics and forget that Denmark and Norway have separate flags and mainland China one. But even then, since differences are quantitative, we would have to know how much to allow before graduating X from "a dialect of Y" to "a language, distinct from Y."

However that may be, the number of different languages is formidable and is quite awesome if we include the tongues once spoken but now dead. Languages are like people: for all their underlying similarities, great numbers mean great variety. Variety confronts us with this question: Do we know enough about languages to be able to describe language? Can we penetrate the differences to arrive at the samenesses underneath?

From *Aspects of Language* by Dwight Bolinger, ©1968 by Harcourt Brace Jovanovich, Inc., and reprinted with their permission.

Dwight Bolinger of the Department of Romance Languages and Literatures, Harvard University, is well known for his book *Aspects of Language,* which has been widely used in linguistics classes throughout the United States. In addition, he has co-authored *Modern Spanish* and authored *Forms of English.*

The more languages we study — and previously unexplored ones give up their secrets each year by the score — the more the answer seems to be *yes*. Learning a new language is always in some measure repeating an old experience. Variety may be enormous but similarities abound, and one can even attempt a definition, perhaps something like "Human language is a system of vocal-auditory communication using conventional signs composed of arbitrary patterned sound units and assembled according to set rules, interacting with the experiences of its users." However we word it — and obviously no one-sentence definition will ever be adequate — there is enough homogeneity to make some sort of definition possible. Languages are alike because people are alike in their capacities for communicating in a uniquely human way.

Language Is Patterned Behavior

Our five-hundred-year romance with printer's ink tempts us to forget that a language can disappear without leaving a trace when its last speaker dies and that this is still true of the majority of the world's languages in spite of the spread of presses and tape recorders. Written records and tape recordings are embodiments of language, but language itself is a way of acting. Our habit of viewing it as a *thing* is probably unavoidable, even for the linguist, but in a sense it is false.

What is somewhat thing-like, in that it persists through time and from speaker to speaker, is the system that underlies the behavior. This is what makes language so special. Breathing, grasping, and crying are also ways of acting, but we come already equipped to do them. Language is *skilled* behavior and has to be learned. Probably as the child acquires it the system is engraved somehow on the brain, and if we had the means to make it visible we could "read" it. For the present all we can see is the way people act, and linguists are useful precisely because, not being able to look into the brain, we need specialists to study the behavior and infer the system.

The Medium of Language Is Sound

All languages use the same channel for sending and receiving: the vibrations of the atmosphere. All set the vibrations going in the same way, by the activity of the speech organs. And all organize the vibrations in essentially the same way, into small units of sound that can be combined and recombined in distinctive ways. Except for the last, human communication is the same as that of most other warm-blooded creatures that move on the earth's surface: the most effective way of reaching another member of one's kind seems to be through disturbances of the air that envelops us.

Paradoxically, what sets human speech apart also sets it above dependence on any particular medium: the capacity for intricate organization. The science of phonetics, whose domain is the sounds of speech, is to linguistics what numismatics is to finance: it makes no difference to a financial transaction what alloys are used in a coin, and it makes no difference to the brain what bits of substance are used as triggers for language — they could be pebbles graded for color or size, or, if we had a dog's olfactory sense, a scheme of discriminated smells. The choice of sound is part of our pre-human heritage, probably for good reason. We do not have to look at or touch the signaler to catch the signal, and we do not depend on wind direction as with smell — nor, as with smell, are we unable to turn it off once it is emitted.[2]

Language is sound in the same sense that a given house is wood. We can conceive of other materials, but it is as if the only tools we had were woodworking ones. If we learn a language we must learn to produce sounds. We are unable to use any other medium except as an incidental help. So part of the description of language must read as if the sound that entered into the organization of language were as indispensable as the organization itself.

Sound Is Embedded In Gesture

If language is an activity, we cannot say that it stops short at the boundaries of *speech* activity, for human actions are not so easily compartmentalized. It is true that we can communicate over the telephone, which seems to prove that everything is carried by the sound wave; but we can also communicate pretty efficiently in writing, and we know that writing leaves out a great deal — intonation, for example. No communication is quite so effective as face-to-face communication, for some part of the communicative act is always contained in the expression and posture of the communicators. We call this *gesture*.

Not all gestures are equally important to language. Three kinds can be distinguished: *instinctive, semiotic,* and *paralinguistic.* The third is closest to language proper.

Instinctive gestures are automatic reactions to a stimulus. They are not learned. Dodging a blow, widening the eyes in astonishment, leaning forward to catch a sound, bowing in submission, smiling with pleasure, and others of the kind either are instincts or are based on instinct in such a way that, like the flight of a young bird, it takes no more than a slight parental or social push to set them going. Of course all such gestures give information to anyone observing them, and this is soon noted by the one performing the gesture, who then puts it on as a disguise: he smiles to please rather than to show pleasure, bows when he would rather hurl insults, and weeps when he feels no pain. In the long run all gestures acquire a social significance and take on local modifications, which is one reason why members of one culture behave awkwardly when transplanted to another.

Whereas instinctive gestures tell something — true or false — about the person making them, *semiotic* gestures are free to mean anything. They are not like distinctive sounds, because they do have their own meanings (semaphoric signs, which are just ways of signaling the alphabet, are not included here); they are more like words or even whole sentences. Thus a waving hand means 'good-bye,' both hands held palm up and outstretched with shoulders raised means 'I don't know,' the thumb and forefinger held close together means 'small' — that is, these are the meanings in our culture. Being arbitrary, semiotic gestures are not the same everywhere. In some places the gesture for 'come here' is to hold out the hand cupped palm up with the fingers beckoning; in other places it is the same except that the hand is cupped palm down, and to an outsider it may appear to be a greeting rather than a summons. Semiotic gestures are independent of language. Cooperation between the two is only incidental — a 'come-hither' gesture accompanied by the words *come here* is like a red light at a railroad crossing accompanied by a sign reading *Stop, look, and listen.*

Paralinguistic gestures are not really an independent class but a subclass of instinctive gestures, more or less systematized, much as intonation was perhaps systematized out of a set of instinctive cries and calls. They cooperate with sound as part of a larger communicative act. In the following utterance,

<pre>
        You
            don't
                m
                  e
                    a
                   n
                     it.
</pre>

everything else can remain the same, yet with one's head held slightly forward, eyes widened, and mouth left open after the last word, the result is a question ('You surely don't mean it, do you?'), while with head erect, eyes not widened, and mouth closed afterward, it is a confident assertion. Facial gestures are sometimes the only way to tell a question from a statement.

Gestures of the hands and head are used to reinforce the syllables on which the accent falls. A person too far away to hear a speaker can often tell what syllables he is emphasizing by the way he hammers with his fist or jabs downward with his jaw. How closely the two are related can be shown by a simple test: reversing the movement of the head, going up instead of down on each accent, in a sentence like *I will not do it*. It is hard to manage on the first attempt.

At the outer fringes of the system we call language is a scattering of gestural effects on speech, more curious than important. The [m] of *ho-hum* and the [p] of *yep* and *nope* come from closing the mouth as a gesture of completion: "He was the last juror and quite unconsciously smacked his lips as he finished the oath."[3] Certain gestures get tangled with sets of words and serve as a kind of semantic cohesive. The kinship of *vicious, venŏmous, vituperative, violent, vehement, vindictive, vitriolic, vile* (and indirectly *vital, vigorous, vim*) is helped by the suggestion of a snarl in the initial [v]. Similarly there is a suggestion of lip-smacking in the last syllable of *delicious, voluptuous, salacious, luscious* that results in a new slang alteration or coinage every now and then — *scrumptious* in the early 1880s, *galuptious* about 1850, *crematious* in the 1940s, the trade name *Stillicious* at about the same time, *scruptillicious* in teen-age talk in the 1960s.[4]

Language Is Largely Arbitrary

It is exceptional to find words as alike as *meow* in English and *miaou* in French. Identical meanings in different languages are almost never expressed by the same combination of sounds (the fact that the same *spellings* are often encountered is another matter). If there were a real connection between the sound of a word and its meaning, a person who did not know the language would be able to guess the word if he knew the meaning and guess the meaning if he heard the word. This almost never happens, even with words that imitate sounds: *to caw* in English is *croasser* in French; *to giggle* in English is *kichern* in German. Elsewhere it does not happen at all. *Square* and *box-shaped* mean the same but have no resemblance in sound.[5]

Arbitrariness comes from having to code a whole universe of meanings. The main problem with such vast quantities is to find not resemblances but differences, to make a given combination of sounds sufficiently unlike every other combination so that no two will be mistaken for each other. It is more important to make *wheat* and *barley* sound different than to use the names to express a family relationship as a botanist might do. Our brain can associate them if the need arises more easily than it can help us if we hear one when the other was intended.

Syntax is no less arbitrary than words. Take the order of elements. *Ground parched corn* has *first* been parched and *then* ground — the syntactic rule calls for reversing the order in which the events occur. Often the same meanings can be conveyed by quite different sequences of elements which may themselves be the same or different: *nonsensical,* which contains a prefix and a suffix, means the same as *senseless,* which has only a suffix; *more handsome* and *handsomer* are mere variants. Here and there one detects a hint of kinship between form and function — in *He came in and sat down* the phrases are in the same sequence as the actions; but other syntactic devices quickly override it: *He sat down after he came in.*

The most rigidly arbitrary level of language is that of the distinctive units of sound by which we can distinguish between *skin* and *skim* or *spare* and *scare* the moment we hear the words. It was noted earlier that the very choice of sound itself for this purpose was, while practical, not at all necessary to the system built up from it. And once it was determined that sound was to be the medium, the particular sounds did not matter so long as they could be told apart. What distinguishes *skin* from *skim* is the sound of [n] versus the sound of [m], but could just as well be [b] versus [g] — there is nothing in the nature of skin that decrees it shall be called *skin* and not *skib.* The only "natural" fact is that human beings are limited by their speech organs to certain dimensions of sound — we do not, for example, normally make the sound that would result from turning the tip of the tongue all the way back to the soft palate; it is too hard to reach. But given the sets of sounds we *can* make (not identical, of course, from one language to another, but highly similar), arbitrariness frees us to combine them at will — the combinations do not have to match anything in nature, and their number is therefore unlimited.

Arbitrariness is the rule throughout the central part of language, the part that codes sounds into words, words into phrases, and phrases into sentences. To use computer terminology, language is *digital,* not *analog:* its units function by being either present or absent, not by being present in varying degrees. If a man is asked how many feet tall a friend is and answers *six,* he gives a digital answer; for a lower height he will no longer say *six.* If words were coded analogically he might, to express 'six,' take half of the word *twelve,* say *twe.* We actually do communicate analogically in situations like this, not using words but holding up our hand to the desired height; the height of the hand is "analogous" to the height of the person.

But the digital island floats on an analog sea. If one is tired, the feebleness of the voice will show how tired one is — degrees of sound correspond to degrees of fatigue. If one is angry and not controlling oneself, the loudness of the voice will tell how angry. And wrapped around everything that is spoken is a layer of intonation which in many languages comprises an analog system that is highly formalized; for example, varying degrees of finality can be expressed by deeper and deeper lowering of the pitch at the end of an utterance.

It would not be surprising if now and then a bit of the analog sea washed over the digital island. There seems to be a connection, transcending individual languages, between the sounds of the vowels produced with the tongue high in the mouth and to the front, especially [i] (the vowel sound in *wee, teeny*), and the meaning of 'smallness,' while those with tongue low suggest 'largeness.' The size of the mouth cavity — [i] has the smallest opening of all — is matched with the meaning. We *chip* a small piece but *chop* a large one; a *slip* is smaller than a *slab* and a *nib* is smaller than a *knob*. Examples crop up spontaneously — "A *freep* is a baby *frope*," said a popular entertainer in a game of Scrabble — or in modifications of existing words, for example *least* with an exaggeratedly high [i], or the following:

"That's about the price I had in mind," said Joe Peel. "Eight to ten thousand, but of course, it would depend on the place. I might even go a *leetle* higher."[6]

But mostly the digital island stays pretty dry.

Languages Are Similarly Structured

The average learner of a foreign language is surprised and annoyed when the new language does not express things in the same way as the old. The average linguist, after years of struggling with differences between languages, is more surprised at similarities. But at bottom the naive learner is right: there are differences in detail, but in broad outline languages are put together in similar ways. A study on universals in language reached these conclusions about syntax:

1. All languages use nominal phrases and verbal phrases, corresponding to the two major classes of noun and verb, and in all of them the number of nouns far exceeds the number of verbs. One can be fairly sure that a noun in one language translates a noun in another.
2. All languages have modifiers of these two classes, corresponding to adjectives and adverbs.
3. All languages have ways of turning verbal phrases into nounal phrases (*He went* — I know *that he went*).
4. All languages have ways of making adjective-like phrases out of other kinds of phrases (*The man went* — The man *who went*).

5. All languages have ways of turning sentences into interrogatives, negatives, and commands.
6. All languages show at least two forms of interaction between verbal and nominal, typically "intransitive" (the verbal is involved with only one nominal, as in *Boys play*) and "transitive" (the verbal is involved with two nominals, as in *Boys like girls*).[7]

A more recent study views nouns as the one category of syntax that can be assumed for all languages, with the other elements being defined (differently, from language to language) by how they combine with nouns.[8]

One of the promising developments of transformational-generative grammar[9] is the hypothesis that all languages are fundamentally alike in their "deep grammar," an underlying domain of universal grammatical relationships and universal semantic features, and different only on the surface, in the more or less accidental paths along which inner forms link themselves and make their way to the top. One is reminded of what is so often said about sexual behavior — that it can be modified by social restrictions but never seriously changed. If the hypothesis is true then our bent for language is as much a part of us as our mating instincts and our hunger drives.

We Are Born To Speak

Thomas A. Edison is supposed to have parried the question of a skeptic who wanted to know what one of his fledgling inventions was good for by asking "What good is a baby?" Appearances suggest that a baby is good for very little, least of all to itself. Completely helpless, absolutely dependent on the adults around it, seemingly unable to do much more than kick and crawl for the greater part of nine or ten months, it would seem better off in the womb a little longer until ready to make a respectable debut and scratch for itself.

Yet if the premature birth of human young is an accident, it is a fortunate one. No other living form has so much to learn about the external world and so little chance of preparing for it in advance. An eaglet has the pattern of its life laid out before it hatches from the egg. Its long evolution has equipped it to contend with definite foes, search for definite foods, mate, and rear its young according to a definite ritual. The environment is predictable enough to make the response predictable too, and they are built into the genetic design. With human beings this is impossible. The main reason for its impossibility is language.

We know little about animal communication but enough to say that nowhere does it even approach the complexity of human language. By the time he is six or eight years old a child can watch a playmate carry out an intricate series of actions and give a running account of it afterward. The most that a bee can do is perform a dance that is related analogously to the direction and distance of a find of nectar, much like what we do in pointing a direction to a stranger. The content of the message is slight and highly stereotyped. With the child, the playmate's actions can be as unpredictable as you please; he will verbalize them somehow. Attaining this skill requires the mastery of a system that takes literally years to learn. An early start is essential, and it cannot be in the womb. Practice must go on in the open air where sounds are freely transmitted, for language is sound. And if language is to be socially effective, it cannot be acquired within a month or two of birth when the environment is limited to parents and crib but must continue to grow as the child becomes stronger and widens his contacts. Human evolution has insured that this will happen by providing for a brain in which the speech areas are the last to reach their full development.[10] So we might say to Edison's question that a baby is good for learning language.

First Steps

All that a child can be born with is an instinct for language, not for any particular language, just as he is born with an instinct for walking but not for walking in a given direction. This is another reason why an early beginning is necessary: languages differ and even the same language changes through time, so that an infant born with patterns already set would be at a disadvantage. One still hears the foolish claim that a child of German ancestry ought to be able to learn German more easily than some other language. Our experience discredits this. An infant of whatever race learns whatever language it hears, one about as easily as another. Complete adaptability confers the gift of survival. Children do not depend on a particular culture but fit themselves to the one into which they are born, and that culture in turn is one that is maintaining itself in a not always friendly universe. Whatever success it has is largely due to the understanding and cooperation that language makes possible.

Another reason for an early beginning and a gradual growth is *permeation*. The running account that a child is able to give of a series of actions that he performs or sees performed betokens an organized activity that is not enclosed within itself but relates at all times to something else. It would seem absurd to us to be told that every time we stood up, sat down, reached for a chocolate, turned on a light, pushed a baby carriage, or started the car we should, at the same time, be twitching in a particular way the big toe of our left foot. But just such an incessant accompaniment of everything else by our speech organs does not surprise us at all. Other activities are self-contained. That of language penetrates them and almost never stops. It must be developed not separately, like walking, but as part of whatever we do. So it must be on hand from the start.

The idea that there is an instinct for language has been recently revived by psychologists and linguists working in the field of child learning. For a long time language was thought to be a part of external culture and nothing more. Even the physiology of speech was seen as more or less accidental: our speech organs were really organs of digestion which happened to be utilized to satisfy a social need. A child in a languageless society, deprived of speech but permitted to chew and swallow, would not feel that he was missing anything. That view has been almost reversed. Now it is felt that the organs of speech in their present form were shaped as much for sound production as for nourishment. The human tongue is far more agile than it needs to be for purposes of eating. On the receiving end, the sensitivity of the human ear has been sharpened to the point that we can detect a movement of the eardrum that does not exceed one tenth of the diameter of a hydrogen molecule.

So there are three ingredients in the consummation of language:

1. an *instinct* in the shape of mental and physical capacities developed through countless centuries of natural selection;
2. a preexisting language *system,* any one of the many produced by the cultures of the world;
3. a *competence* that comes from applying the instinct to the system through the relatively long period during which the child learns both to manipulate the physical elements of the system, such as sounds and words and syntactic rules, and to permeate them with meaning.

The development of so finely graded a specialization of our organs of speech and hearing and of the nervous system to which they are attached is not surprising if we assume that society cannot survive without language and individual human beings cannot survive without society. Natural selection will take care of it.[11] And natural selection unquestionably has. Language is species-specific. It is a uniquely human trait, shared by cultures so diverse and by individuals physically and mentally so unlike one another — from Watusi tribesmen to nanocephalic dwarfs — that the notion of its being purely a socially transmitted skill is not to be credited.[12]

An instinct for language implies that a child does more than echo what he hears. The older notion of mere plasticity has been abandoned. The first months are a preparation for language in which babbling, a completely self-directed exercise, is the main activity. Imitation begins to play a part, of course, but it too is experimental and hence creative. We see how this must be if we imagine a child already motivated to imitate and being told by his mother to say *papa*. This sounds simple to us because we already know what features to heed and what ones to ignore, but the child must learn to tell them apart. Shall he imitate his mother's look, her gesture, the way she shapes her lips, the breathiness of the first consonant, the voice melody, the moving of the tongue? Even assuming that he can focus on certain things to the exclusion of others, he has no way of knowing which ones to select. He cannot then purely imitate. He must experiment and wait for approval. Imitation is an activity that is shaped creatively.

Progress

We do not know the extent to which children are taught and the extent to which they learn on their own. If learning is instinctive, then children will learn whether or not adults appoint themselves to be their teachers. But if there is an instinct to learn, for all we know there may be an instinct to teach. It is possible that parents unconsciously adopt special modes of speaking to very young children, to help them learn the important things first, impelled by the desire not so much to teach the child as to communicate with him, but with teaching a by-product.

One psychologist noted the following ways in which she simplified her own speech when talking to her child:

1. the use of a more striking variant of a speech sound when there is a choice, for example using the [t] of *table* when saying the word *butter* in place of the more usual flapped sound (almost like *budder*);
2. exaggerated intonation, with greater ups and downs of pitch;
3. slower rate;
4. simple sentence structure, as for example, avoidance of the passive voice;
5. avoidance of substitute words like *it,* as, for example, *Where's your milk? Show me your milk* instead of *Where's your milk? Show it to me.*[13]

Most parents would probably add *repetition* to this list.

Whatever the technique, the child does not seem to follow any particular sequence, learning first to pronounce all the sounds perfectly, then to manage words, then sentences, then "correct expression." A child of twelve to eighteen months with no sentences at all will be heard using sentence intonations on separate words in a perfectly normal way — *Doggie?* with rising pitch, meaning 'Is that a doggie?' or *Doggie,* with falling pitch, to comment on the dog's presence. The child's program seems to call for a developing complexity rather than doing all of one thing before taking up the next.

The first stage of communication, when parents feel that their children have really begun to speak, is reached when individual words are being pronounced intelligibly — that is, so that parents can match them with words in their own speech — and related to things and events. This is the *holophrastic* stage, when utterance and thing are related one to one. The thing named may be a single object called *mama* or a whole situation called *mapank*. The parents will interpret the latter as a sentence — *Mama spank* — but to the child it is a word. He has no basis for dividing it. A thing or situation has a proper name. There is no syntax.

The second stage is *analytic:* the child begins to divide his proper names into true sentences. Besides *mapank* the vocabulary probably includes additional words like *mama, papa,* and *baby.* The day comes when Papa spanks, and the uniqueness of *mapank* is broken up — the different elements in the situation are recognized for who they are and *ma* is properly attached to *mama.* Now *mapank* is a sentence and will probably be modified to *Mama pank.* Before long the child begins to *look* for parts within wholes and to play with them: *Baby spank.* Words become playthings. When a two-and-a-half-year-old runs to his parents and says *House eat baby* — the sort of expression that unimaginative adults brush aside as preposterous or even punish as "untrue" — he is only exulting over the discovery that he can do the same with his words as with his building blocks, put them together in fascinating ways. Much of learning a language is a pattern-flexing game. Children's monologs sometimes sound like students practicing in a language lab.[14]

To make a sentence a child must recognize certain things as the same and certain things as different, must have names for them, and must combine the names. (This achievement is simply the *collocation.*) The third stage calls for noticing more subtle kinds of sameness in the connections. It can be called the *syntactic* stage. When *mama* and *spank* are recognized as recurring sames, their presence in both *Mama spank* and *Spank mama* (the latter accompanying a playful situation in which the mother makes the baby hit her for some real or pretended misdemeanor) is recognized and the difference in the two situations is assigned to the reversal of the order. *Kiss mama, Come-to mama, See mama* then constitute a different kind of *same* — verb plus object noun — that recurs like all the others and that the child will invent or reinvent using old material to see how far he can go.

The product of the syntactic stage is a variety of sentence types, all simple but distinguished by the number and arrangement of their parts — *Get Daddy, Baby go-play, Mama eat cereal.* The component parts too are simple. There are no morphological complications like articles or verb inflections. But the syntactic stage also offers combinations like *that doggie, baby chair* ('Baby's chair'), *more cereal,* which are used as verb-less sentences but are the raw material for the fourth stage in which arrangements are added to arrangements: *Daddy sit chair* contains a simple arrangement; *Daddy sit baby chair* contains an arrangement within an arrangement. This can be called the *structural* stage. Parts are made up of other parts. When the child discovers this he is in a position to make up his own "words." If, as happened with one child, he lacks the verb *to cross,* he can say *I'm going to the other side of the whole lake,* using *go-to-the-other-side-of* as a substitute (an adult will interpret the sentence as a mistake for *I'm going all the way to the other side,* a more complex structure). As a culmination of his structural stage the child learns how to treat whole sentences as if they were elements, to insert them in larger sentences. A statement like *I go* and a question like *Will you stay?* are combined: *If I go will you stay?*

The step-by-step increase in complexity is illustrated in the responses given by one child at various ages to the command *Ask your daddy what he did at work today.* At two years and five months it was *What he did at work today,* which shows enough understanding to separate the inner question from the command as a whole (*Ask your daddy* is not repeated), but no more. At the age of three, the response was *What you did at work today?,* with the right change of intonation and with *you* for *he.* The child is now really asking a question but has "optimized" its form — that is, he has fitted a newly acquired expression into the mold of an old one that resembles it and is familiar and easy, in this case making the word order of statements serve also for questions. Finally, at three years and five months, he made the right transformation of the verb and produced *What did you do at work today?* [15]

Optimizing occurs at all stages. It may replace a difficult sound with an easy one, as when children say *woof* for *roof.* It may result in a correct sentence or an incorrect one. *What you did at work today?* is incorrect. Correct optimizing occurs when the language offers two different constructions, both correct, but one more frequent or more in harmony with familiar constructions. When four-year-olds are given a sentence like *I gave the dog the bone* they will repeat it and understand it, but if they are asked to report the same event themselves they will say *I gave the bone to the dog.* [16] The construction without *to* is less general (for instance, it seldom occurs in the question *Who(m) did you give the money?* — the more normal form is *Who(m) did you give the money to?*) and is not like the related constructions in which prepositions are required: *I got the money from Dad, I got the present for Dad and then I gave it to him,* etc.

The final stage is *stylistic.* The child now has a repertory of constructions among which he can choose. Choice makes for flexibility. He is no longer restricted to conveying just the primary information but is able to show a certain way in which the message is to be taken. *Give the bone to Dingo* and *Give Dingo the bone* "mean the same," but if there is also a cat named Tillie who gets raw liver and both pets are about to be fed, *Give Dingo the bone* is the choice to make when Dingo was about to be given Tillie's ration; it puts the emphasis in the right place.

Attainment

A favorite generalization of one school of linguists used to be that every child has complete control of his language by the age of five or six. Without disparaging the truly phenomenal control of an enormously complex system that six-year-olds do achieve, we must realize that no limit can be set and that learning by the same old processes continues through life, though at a rate that diminishes so rapidly that well before adolescence it seems almost to have come to a stop. It might be described as a curve that starts by virtually touching infinity and ends by approaching zero, as shown on Chart 5.1.

Chart 5.1

**Rate of Learning Expressed as a Proportion of
New to Old Over Equal Intervals of Time**

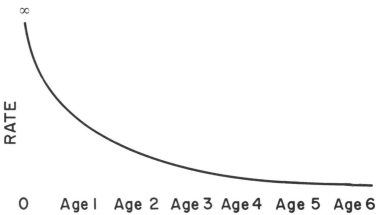

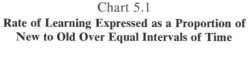

O   Age 1   Age 2   Age 3 Age 4   Age 5   Age 6

If learning never ceases, it follows that a language is never completely learned. There is always someone who knows a bit of it that we do not know.[17] In part this is because with the experimental and inventive way in which learning is done, no two people ever carry exactly the same network of shapes and patterns in their heads. A perfect command eludes us because as we catch up it moves off — "the" language exists only as imperfect copies, with original touches, in individual minds; it never stays exactly the same. All we can say is that interplay is so fast, frequent, and vital that great differences are not tolerated, networks are forced to acquire a similar weave, and all within cooperating distance are said to "speak the same language."

Notes

1. Richard Loving and Jack Bass, "Languages of the Amanab Sub-district," report published by the Department of Information and Extension Services, Territory of Papua and New Guinea, Port Moresby, April 1964.
2. Thomas A. Sebeok, "Coding in the Evolution of Signaling Behavior," *Behavioral Science* 7 (1962): 435.
3. Raymond Postgate, *Verdict of Twelve* (New York: Simon and Schuster, Pocket Books, 1946), p. 70.
4. *Boulder Camera* (Boulder, Colorado), June 10, 1963.
5. What happens when two words come to sound the same is treated in chapter 7 of *Aspects of Language* by Dwight Bolinger (New York: Harcourt, Brace, Jovanovich, 1968).
6. Frank Gruber, *The Silver Jackass* (New York: Penguin Books, 1947), p. 45.
7. Paraphrased from Samuel E. Martin's review of *Universals of Language,* ed. J.H. Greenburg, *Harvard Educational Review* 34 (1964): 353–55.
8. John Lyons, "Towards a 'Notional' Theory of the 'Parts of Speech'," *Journal of Linguistics* 2 (1966): 209–36.
9. Bolinger, *Aspects of Language,* pp. 201–4.
10. Leonard Carmichael, "The Early Growth of Language Capacity in the Individual," in *New Directions in the Study of Language,* ed. Eric H. Lenneberg (Cambridge, Mass.: M.I.T. Press, 1966), pp. 1–22, especially pp. 17–19.
11. See Charles F. Hockett and Robert Ascher, "The Human Revolution," *American Scientist* 52 (1964): 71–92.
12. Eric H. Lenneberg, "A Biological Perspective of Language," in Lenneberg, *New Directions,* p. 65–88.
13. Lila R. Gleitman and Elizabeth F. Shipley, "A Proposal for the Study of the Acquisition of English Syntax," grant proposal submitted March 1, 1963, to National Institutes of Health, p. 24.
14. See Lenneberg, *New Directions,* p. 181 for a child's substitution drill: *what color blanket, what color mop, what color glass.*
15. Gleitman and Shipley, "A Proposal," p. 14.
16. Colin Fraser, Ursula Bellugi, and Roger Brown, "Control of Grammar in Imitation, Comprehension, and Production," *Journal of Verbal Learning and Verbal Behavior* 2 (1963): 133.
17. Some linguists tend to retort, "This may be true of vocabulary — we obviously keep on learning new words all our lives — but it is not true of grammar." Yet one investigation, which studied the sentences written by ninth and tenth graders, after noting that by rigorous standards of sentence formation "almost half of the sentences written by the ninth graders were mal-formed," concluded that it is probably true that "the grammar of English is never fully mastered." (Abstract of dissertation by Donald Ray Bateman, "The Effects of a Study of a Generative Grammar upon the Structure of Written Sentences of Ninth and Tenth Graders," Ohio State University, 1965, in *Linguistics* 26 (1966): 21–22.

6.

Some Theoretical Aspects of
Language Learning and Language Teaching

DAVID L. WOLFE

1. Preliminary Statements

1.1 *Differences and similarities between (a) the child's acquisition of his first language, (b) the child's acquisition of a second language, and (c) the adult's acquisition of a second language.* The infant-child acquires his first language in the most natural or least artificial manner possible. There is normally nothing in his mind to prevent him from ultimately learning a native language; on the contrary, if Chomsky is correct in his twentieth century version of the sixteenth century notion of innate ideas,[1] the infant brain is predisposed toward the acquisition of the grammar of natural language. On the basis of his contacts with *parole* — the outer, surface manifestations of the speech of his home and community — and regardless of how fragmentary, uninventive, or degenerate this corpus may be, the child internalizes a highly complex, abstract set of interrelated systems, minimally a phonological system, a syntactic system, and a semantic system. Vygotsky[2] has shown how the speech function and the thought function have two separate origins in the developing infant, speech having its roots in babbling and emoting through sound, and thought deriving from problem-solving and the use of tools. Vygotsky concludes that apes are capable of both types of behavior, but that only human beings learn to fuse the two separate functions into a single use, i.e., that combination of vocalizing and thinking which leads to the creation of symbolic language and eventually to the formation of concepts. Vygotsky shows experimentally how the child's thinking develops from (a) an initial primitive mental organization of the environment into "heaps" or

Reprinted from *Language Learning* 17, nos. 3 & 4 (1968): 173–88.

David L. Wolfe of the Department of Romance Languages and Literatures, University of Michigan, has taught Spanish linguistics in Spain and Mexico. In addition, he has co-authored *A Structural Course in Spanish* and *El español a través de sus escritores* and authored the texts *Curso básico de español* and *Curso intermedio de español*.

unorganized congeries through (b) several different types of thinking in complexes (still a primitive type of thinking) until it reaches in about the twelfth year of the child's life the final stage (c), where abstract concepts are understood and used.

Once the child reaches this age of linguistic puberty and is capable of handling true concepts, he has completed the language-learning cycle. This does not imply that he has stopped learning his native language; even if the lexicon of every language were not open-ended, as indeed it is, the child simply could not in a lifetime of learning exhaust the lexical wealth of any language, nor could he put into actual practice the infinite possibilities available to him from the recursive devices of the syntax.

The notion of linguistic puberty is useful because it provides a natural linguistic dividing line between the child and the adult. The adult is aware (unconsciously, to be sure) of the nature and use of language in the sense that he has completed the language-learning cycle, whereas the child, at any point in his linguistic development is still not linguistically mature. Furthermore, the adult has developed, in the course of his maturation, a general overall psychological consciousness equipped to deal in generalizations and abstractions as well as with linguistic concepts. This may explain in part why a child will quickly and accurately acquire a second language "unconsciously" from playmates in the street or from a nanny, whereas the same child may acquire only a very imperfect knowledge of a second language in many years of "conscious" classroom study. The adult, on the contrary, may through "conscious" drill acquire an excellent command of a second language, although the same adult, in a natural situation, such as that of an immigrant in an alien speech community, may acquire only a "broken," imperfect fluency after many years of natural exposure. It would appear that few adults can learn a language in the street and that few children can learn a language artificially. Although there may be elements acquired unconsciously by the adult in his learning of a (second) language and although there may be elements consciously learned by the child in his acquisition of a (second) language, broadly speaking, a child acquires a language (his first or a second) unconsciously, and an adult learns a language consciously. Until the elementary classroom abandons adult "conscious" learning procedures and is converted into a more natural streetlike situation, it will continue to be the case that adults in school learn languages much faster than children in school; and, since few adults retain the flexibility of mind required to acquire linguistic knowledge "unconsciously," the converse of this statement is also true: the child will learn a language much faster than the adult in a natural situation. Language acquisition by the adult is, then, an artificial process.

1.2 *Language-learning devices which run counter to the nature of language.* The fact that language learning in the adult is an artificial process does not excuse the many practices common in language teaching today which run counter to the nature of true language behavior. The necessity for artificial language-learning situations and techniques does not imply a corresponding necessity for distorting or changing the nature of what is being learned. Perhaps the most widespread textbook technique for needlessly increasing the artificiality of language learning in the adult is the use of drills and exercises which force the student to lie. In many classrooms up to one hundred percent of the student's time is spent in the repetition of drill sentences such as these:

(a) Teacher:		Student:
Yesterday I went to the movies.		Yesterday I went to the movies.
	play	Yesterday I went to the play.
	game	Yesterday I went to the game.
Last night		Last night I went to the game.
Last week		Last week I went to the game.
	Charles	Last week Charles went to the game.
	etc.	
(b) Teacher:		Student:
Mary studies every day.		Mary studies every day.
I		I study every day.
We		We study every day.
	work	We work every day.
John		John works every day.
	etc.	

These seemingly harmless sentences are, from the point of view of the real life situation of the teacher and the student, probably all untrue. From the point of view of true linguistic communication they border on the nonsensical; after all, who is referred to by "John" or "Charles" or "Mary"? Certainly no one in the environment of the teacher and the student. The evil in this type of repeated lying is that it produces a deadening effect in the mind of the student and reduces him to a parrotlike existence where repetition of form occurs in the vocal tract, but repetition of meaning does not occur in the mind. This runs exactly counter to the insight into the nature of language provided by the great linguists of the last one hundred years or so. Pike calls language a "form-meaning composite,"[3] a unity which cannot be split up in theory and certainly not in practice. In this respect Pike follows Bloomfield, who states that "in language, forms cannot be separated from their meanings."[4] Chomsky has characterized language as being "rule-governed creativity."[5] We are not engaged in language behavior unless we are expressing ourselves syntactically as well as semantically by saying what we want or need to say (the creative aspect) and, at the same time, saying it correctly (the rule-governed aspect). Humboldt has said that language "makes infinite use of finite means,"[6] which is to say that there is no limitation on creativity (in Chomsky's sense) or meaning (in Bloomfield's sense), although the means, the grammar (Chomsky's rule-governed aspect and Bloomfield's form aspect) are finite, limited — in short, teachable and learnable. ("Teaching" in the present context refers to the contribution of the teacher and "learning" refers to that of the student; there is no single term in English for this process, thus forcing us to talk about language learning and/or language teaching. It is a single process, however, in which the teacher perhaps goes fifty percent of the way and the student the other fifty percent of the way. The teacher cannot put something into the student's mind without some degree of receptivity or cooperation on the part of the student, nor can the student learn a language completely on his own without any external stimulus or force.) One important way, then, in which adult language learning can be considerably improved is to eliminate from the classroom the necessity for continual lying. Only by talking factually about things and events inside and outside of the classroom will teachers and students really be engaged in true, undistorted language behavior, that is, in rule-governed creativity or in making infinite use of finite means. Part of the purpose of this discussion is to show how this may be done.

Another common way in which the subject matter of elementary language courses is unnecessarily distorted is through the technique of memorized dialogues. If language behavior is rule-governed creativity, students reciting a memorized dialogue are not engaged in language behavior, since there is no originality or creativity involved in this type of recitation; the student obviously does not in such a case express himself naturally. It might appear at first glance that the rule-governed aspect of language behavior does occur accurately in the recitation of a memorized dialogue, but one must not be deceived into believing that because the student is producing, say, Spanish sentences without syntactic errors he has thereby internalized the syntax and the vocabulary he is displaying. The student will not be able to use the syntactic and lexical elements of a memorized dialogue as part of his active linguistic corpus[7] unless these elements are thoroughly drilled as separate linguistic units. The fixed dialogue does not necessarily provide a better or more natural context in which to learn lexical items. In this respect the single context of the fixed dialogue is inferior to the multiple contexts of a drill or series of drills. Very little experience in the classroom is required to demonstrate this fact. One may indeed memorize the libretti of all of the operas of Verdi and still not be able to manage the rudiments of Italian grammar or be able to summon to one's aid a given lexical item buried in the context of a memorized dialogue. It is true, of course, that there are certain formulas used in a speech community — greetings and farewells come under this category — which may be memorized as lexical units and drilled strictly as formulas. In general, however, the phonological, syntactic, and lexical units of a language will not be mastered outside of drill materials specifically designed to achieve such mastery. The use in the classroom of natural, unlimited, spontaneous dialogues that correspond to Chomsky's notion of rule-governed creativity will be discussed in part two of this discussion.

A third common practice in the classroom which serves to undermine many of the goals of the language teacher is the failure on the part of the textbook writer and the teacher to distinguish between concrete sentences and abstract sentences in both drills and tests. Sentences such as

(c) Now I am standing up.
     Now I am walking to the table.
     Now I am picking up the red book.
     I am not picking up the green book.
     Now I am returning to my chair.
     Finally, I am sitting down again.

are concrete, that is, of a very low level of abstraction in that they may be easily demonstrated or acted out in an immediate, visual, dramatic way. They can also be easily visualized in the student's mind on further repetition of the sentences with variations. These sentences refer to the immediate reality of the student-teacher-classroom situation and make use of realia or props that may be seen and handled and passed around. This is the most immediate and vivid use of language: reacting verbally and physically at the same time to objects and events in the surrounding environment.

On the other hand, sentences such as

(d) Where are you from?
     I am from Toledo.
     How old are you?
     She is 23 years old.
     Where do you live?
     Ask me where I live.
     Tell me what your name is.

are not concrete in the same sense as the sentences in (c). None of the sentences in (d) refers to objects in the immediate environment of the student. They all refer to more abstract information or facts that cannot be seen or handled in the same way in which a book or pencil can be visualized and held. Nor can any of these statements be acted out dramatically so that the meaning becomes obvious to the beholder.

It is important for the language teacher to know that the use of sentences of type (c) makes possible the elimination from the classroom of the confusing and tedious technique of translation between the target and the native languages, whereas the use of sentences of type (d) makes translation inevitable. Since sentences of type (c) can be demonstrated visually by acting on the part of the teacher and/or students, there is no necessity for their being translated into the native language of the student. In the first few weeks of a language course (the most crucial weeks, since at this time the student will establish a technique of learning), the teacher must avoid sentences of an abstract nature such as those quoted in (d). Only sentences of the lowest level of concreteness should be practiced if the teacher wishes to make the learning of the language less artificial. Translation as a learning technique means (1) operating in terms of the native language as a base from which one departs and to which one invariably returns and (2) considering the target language as a distant object of curiosity which acquires meaning only in terms of a recasting into the lexical and syntactic categories of the native language. If such a learning technique is employed, the target language acquires meaningful values, if ever, only after many years of language study and then usually by means of a year or two of practice abroad. This external approach to a language is not as natural as the internalizing approach, which avoids translation and in so doing avoids the so-called interference of the native language. (The learning and teaching of translation as a skill is, of course, distinct from the unnecessary use of translation as a device for teaching the target language. The art of translation is probably best drilled after the native and target languages have both been independently mastered.)

In the later stages of language learning, when the student may be safely permitted to handle abstract sentences or sentences with a remote referent without the danger of resorting to the native language as a crutch, he must still be required to use his imaginative powers to the fullest in order to see or "feel" with maximum impact each sentence he utters. The normal, sophisticated, adult reaction to the sentence *The dog bit the lady,* for example, is to consider this information in the most abstract way possible, i.e., to focus one's intellectual attention on the abstract outline of the facts. The small child — or the poet for that matter, when he is functioning as a poet — would react to this sentence by seeing in his mind's eye the many details of color, size, and texture of the dog, of the woman, of her clothing, and so forth. This vivid exercising of the powers of the imagination must be explained and drilled in the classroom if the adult student is to realize the full potential of his language learning experience, that is, if he is to master the target language on its own terms and not in terms of so-called equivalents in the native language.

1.3 *Contrastive analysis.* A contrastive analysis is intended to reveal the degree to which two linguistic systems differ from each other as well as the extent to which they might overlap in structure. On the basis of such an analysis it is thought possible to predict a hierarchy of learning difficulties to be encountered by a native speaker of language X learning target language Y. At all points in this systematic contrast where difficulties are likely to be encountered by the learner of Y — whether they are phonological, syntactic or lexical — special and extensive drills must be constructed in order that the student may combat and overcome the interference caused by the powerful structural habits formed in learning the native language. According to this theory, the teacher need not necessarily contrast the two languages in the classroom as part of his teaching technique, but he will use materials based on the results of a contrastive analysis, and he will at all times be aware of the precise nature of the interference that continues to plague his students. In this way students will not spend too much time drilling what is assumed to be easy for them, but will devote most of their time to overcoming "real" problems.

It should be noted, however, that the target language itself may present interference. If, for example, students learning English have succeeded in mastering the difficult question patterns illustrated by the sentences

(e)   Where does he live?
      Where did he go?
      What time is it?
      When are they arriving?
      What should I say?

then they will have difficulty producing included questions, as in the sentences

(f)   Can you tell me where he lives?
      Do you know where he went?
      Will you tell me what time it is?
      I don't know when they are arriving.
      Please tell me what I should say.

since the pressure resulting from a possible overlearning of the first set of structures will cause them to say

(g)   *Can you tell me where does he live?
      *Do you know where did he go?
      *Will you tell me what time is it?
      *I don't know when they are arriving.
      *Please tell me what should I say.

which are all serious mistakes. Here is another example: If students have learned the structure underlying the sentences

(h) I want to study.
     We need to work.
     They have to go.
     You wish to stay.

this structure will interfere when they learn the structure underlying the sentences

(i) I must study.
     We should work.
     I can go.
     They will stay.

causing them to say

(j) *I must to study.
     *We should to work.
     *I can to go.
     *They will to stay.

which are wrong. It should be noted that such interference as is illustrated by the preceding examples is extremely common in language learning and does not have its origin in the native language, since the same mistakes occur regardless of the learner's language background. This indicates a serious weakness in any course materials based solely on contrastive analysis between the target and the native languages. Drilling contrasts *within* the target language may turn out to be more significant to language teaching than drilling structures that contrast with certain structures of the native language. Thus, it is a serious technical error on the part of the teacher to explain the difference between the Spanish preterit form *tomé* and the Spanish present perfect form *he tomado* in terms of their English equivalents, *I took* and *I have taken*. The average student is not conscious of the linguistic analysis of his native language and in all probability cannot explain the difference in usage between the two English forms. The proper approach in the classroom in this case would probably be to ignore English and to explain the actual difference in point of view that is implied by the use of *he tomado* (which refers to an event occurring prior to the present moment in time, just as *habré tomado — I will have taken —* refers to an event occurring prior to a future moment in time and *había tomado* refers to an event occurring prior to a past moment in time, regardless of whether or not the moment in time is actually expressed in any of these cases) versus the use of *tomé* (which includes the time period covered by *he tomado* and *había tomado,* but without reference to any time-point-of-view). Once the various uses of each of these two tenses have been drilled and contrasted, and once the uses of both of these tenses have been contrasted in drills with each other, the learning job is completed and English equivalents are not only irrelevant, but, if needlessly introduced, possibly harmful.

Courses constructed according to the principle of contrastive analysis assume that the student will automatically, or with very little practice, transfer from his native language to the target language all that he can; this is not necessarily true. Once the student grasps the idea that the new language differs from his native language in many matters of structure, he will then not know when it is safe to operate in terms of his native language (it seldom is), and he may try to create his own structures on the basis of previous contact with the new language. Teachers of written and oral composition will be familiar with this type of interference. Some students, not knowing a correct form, will make up a form which does not parallel either the native or the target language. Or, a student will persistently fail to make a grammatical distinction in the target language which he actually does make consistently in his native language. These facts lend further weight to the proposition that teaching a foreign language primarily in terms of drills based on a contrastive analysis of the native and target languages with a strong emphasis on the differences between the two systems is not enough.

There are many other factors which commonly interfere in the language-learning process. Students who have studied a language other than the target or native languages will probably experience interference from the other foreign language, especially if the course they are currently taking is poorly designed. Certain students may suffer from psychological interference; many students are afraid to abandon their native language, even temporarily, in the fear that they could never operate in life solely on the basis of another language. These students must learn to relax and to enjoy the game of using actively a new language system. Other students must contend with the interference of bad speech habits which they drilled under the influence of a textbook full of errors or under the influence of a non-native speaker of the target language who could not supply a native model, even on tape. Poor study habits play a large role in preventing smooth progress in language learning; many students believe they can learn a foreign language in large doses at infrequent intervals, whereas language learning is only achieved in small doses at frequent intervals.

The important contrasts the learner of a new language should be required to master, then, are those inherent in the system of the target language. If the native speaker of English, for example, can suspend his interest in English long enough to practice — at different times and in different contexts — the several uses of, say, Spanish *tocar, tomar,* and *jugar* until he can easily apply the proper word to the proper situation, he as well as his teacher need never actually become aware of the fact that these words represent a so-called problem in translation, i.e., that *tocar* and *jugar* are both translated as *play,* whereas *tomar* may be translated as *drink* or *take.* The problem of how to say *play* in Spanish has been eliminated by ignoring English completely and operating entirely in terms of natural Spanish contrasts within the system. Likewise, the problem of translating *tomar* into English need not arise as long as *tomar* is used in Spanish in the appropriate situations. The two Spanish verbs *ser* and *estar,* both often translated by English *be,* are supposed to constitute a problem for the English-speaking student of Spanish. This problem disappears when each use of *ser* and each use of *estar* is properly drilled; the two verbs need never actually be drilled in contrast except for the necessary contrast between such usages as *está flaco (he is skinny right now)* and *es flaco (he is a skinny person).* The reason students of Spanish never or rarely make the mistake of saying **soy hablando* instead of *estoy hablando (I am speaking)* is simply because they have been adequately drilled on this one particular use of *estar* with the gerund. Contrastive analysis between two languages, then, should be taught in a course in translation. In an elementary language course the important contrastive analysis that must be taught is the contrastive analysis of the linguistic units *within* the target language.[8]

2. The Minimal Stages Required in the Teaching of Language Elements to Adults

2.1 *Selection and ordering of linguistic units.* Once the linguist has provided the language teacher with an adequate presentation of the elements and processes of a given natural language — including the recursive devices that underlie and explain the infinite surface forms of speech — the language teacher (or the textbook writer) must then break down the linguist's synthesis into a series of discrete elements, selecting out the elements to be included in a specific course of study, and ordering these elements into a pedagogically effective sequence. The selection of elements will be based on such criteria as frequency of occurrence of the linguistic element in speech or in literature (depending on the goals of the course), and the utility of the element in the classroom situation (a low-frequency item may be particularly useful in the classroom).

For teaching purposes linguistic elements must be broken down *maximally:* if a single form has two or more meanings or uses, then it must be considered, from the standpoint of course design, as constituting two or more distinct units, each one of which will be drilled separately and perhaps at distant points in the course sequence. Similarly, if a single meaning or use is manifested in speech in two or more forms (as the imperfect tense is in Spanish, for example), then the linguistic element must be considered, in the course design, as two or more distinct elements to be drilled separately and perhaps at distant points in the course sequence.

Linguistic units may be phonological (a single allophone, for example, or a single meaningful intonation curve, or a letter of the alphabet), they may be lexical (any verb, noun, or adjective stem, for example), or they may be syntactic (a single ending or affix, for example, or a discontinuous form such as *have -en,* or a sentence type that constitutes a single unit of meaning, such as IF SUBJECT VERB-ED, SUBJECT WOULD VERB; this latter structure is a single linguistic unit used to refer to a hypothetical situation in the present or future time, as in these sentences: *If I worked, I would earn money, If I studied I would learn, If I went to New York I would take a plane*).

In practice it appears that the most effective classroom procedure is to introduce to the adult student a single linguistic unit at a time, drilling it as a distinct unit before drilling it in contrast with other similar units. It may turn out to be more appropriate to introduce two units in contrast with each other, and this can be done effectively in the classroom, but the presentation of more than two units at a time, such as a complete verb paradigm or a complete noun or pronoun declension, results in too much complexity for smooth, adequate learning on the part of the adult student.

2.2 *Focus of attention on the linguistic unit.* Since the adult learns a language consciously, at some point in the presentation of a linguistic element the student's attention must be focused on the element itself in isolation from the rest of the sentence being repeated. This is usually done by repeating the element in isolation, by writing the abstract element — a sentence skeleton, for example — on the board, or by underlining in a sample sentence written on the board those parts which constitute the linguistic unit, as in the following example: *Si Pepe tuviera dinero, pagaría la cuenta (If Pepe had money he would pay the bill).* Here, the underlined elements constitute a linguistic unit which must be drilled. Such a focusing of attention on the linguistic unit to be explained and drilled is not necessary in teaching children, since they may acquire the unit without being conscious of it. The adult, however, requires the intellectual focus. Quite often the teacher himself needs to learn intellectually exactly what it is that he is teaching. Focus of attenion does not imply that a new linguistic unit cannot be introduced for the first time in a subtle, natural manner in the context of situations arising in the classroom; on the contrary, the ideal approach is to create a situation or make use of a naturally existing situation in order to introduce a new linguistic element. The teacher may then proceed naturally to the drill of this item. What is claimed here is that at some point, perhaps not until a post-drill review, the linguistic element should be, for the adult learner, focused on in a conscious way. This may be done by inductive generalization on the part of the student himself.

2.3 *Articulatory fluency in the item to be drilled.* In an oral approach to the learning of a language, a given linguistic unit may be repeated hundreds of times in the course of a series of drills. It is only logical to insist on a pronunciation check of the item to be drilled in advance of the drills. If a student is pronouncing an English [h] at the beginning of the Spanish word *ha* as in *ha tomado (he has taken),* giving this silent *h* a foreign spelling pronunciation, and he continues to do this during hundreds of repetitions of this linguistic unit, then he will have acquired a habit difficult to break. Thus, a pronunciation check of the unit to be drilled must occur before (and during) the drills. This is not so important in connection with the substitution items in a drill, since these may be pronounced once and not repeated.

2.4 *Vitalization.* The crucial concept of vitalization refers to the manner in which the meaning, the use, the practical utility, the application to reality of a linguistic unit is demonstrated, dramatized, explained or made vital and clear to the student. Vitalization is particularly important during the moment in which a new linguistic unit is introduced to the student, and it constitutes an essential element − the creative or meaningful element − in every learning stage that is to follow. No drill that is not vitalized will contribute much to the language learning process. Phonological elements are vitalized when a student perceives the humor in the phonemic difference between, say, *He came by ship* versus *He came by sheep* or when a wrong intonational pattern is used, as, say, in *What are we having for dinner tonight − Mother?* versus *What are we having for dinner tonight, Mother?* (with a rising intonation on *Mother* in the first, but not the second sentence). Vitalization is particularly important on the level of syntax; the precise use and time application of tense endings, for instance, must be demonstrated by the teacher and "felt" by the student. Lexical meanings are usually easier to vitalize than syntactic uses and phonological contrasts, but there still remains, regarding lexical items, the difficult problem of demonstrating exactly the range of meaning of a particular linguistic unit.[9]

2.5 *Repetition by the student (not by the teacher) of the linguistic unit being learned together with variation of all other elements in the sentences being repeated.* The only way a linguistic unit may be learned in a single repetition is under conditions of extreme emotional stress. If a student were taught the meaning and pronunciation of a profane expletive, for example, and then the teacher proceeded to slap the student's face until, enraged, the student used the swear word against the teacher, the student in this case would probably remember the item without the need for further repetition of it. The amount of repetition required to learn a linguistic unit is reduced proportionately according to the intensity of the emotion involved in the repetition. In most cases a considerable amount of repetition is required before a linguistic unit is mastered by the student. It is important that *only* the linguistic unit being drilled be repeated and that all other elements be varied; otherwise the student will wrongly associate a needlessly repeated element with the structure being learned. In some cases this is necessary to a certain extent; that is, the teacher may want the student to associate a word such as *yesterday* with a past tense structure. But at some point in the drills the word *yesterday* should be changed to *last night, last week,* etc., so that the student will not assume that *yesterday* is part of the linguistic structure itself. It is of equal importance that the teacher not "give away" the linguistic unit in the cue sentences supplied to the student during the course of the drills; the student must always generate the structure on his own, and no part of the structure should occur in the teacher's statements and questions that cue the student's response.

2.6 *Forced transfer of attention from structural form to general meaning.* In a drill the student will begin his uttering of sentences with attention focused on the structure to be learned, but, if the drill is carefully constructed, in the course of the drill the student's attention will be shifted from the form of the structure itself to the total meaning of the sentence, especially the meaning of the lexical substitution items. This transfer of attention is achieved by a progressively more stimulating vitalization of the drill on the part of the teacher. The substitution items that appear in the teacher's questions and which will form part of the student's response must become increasingly more striking and attention-provoking so that the interest of the student will be drawn away from the mechanical form of the structure being practiced and placed entirely on the total meaning of the sentence. The actual moment in which the student begins to transfer his attention from the linguistic unit to the general meaning of the sentence being uttered is usually obvious to the teacher, since the student quite often will "break down" and fail to produce accurately the form of the linguistic unit being drilled. Thus, if the teacher says to a male student, in reference to the girl sitting next to him, "Are you going to invite Miss Wilson to the movies tonight?" expecting the response "No, but if I invited her, she would accept my invitation" (which practices the structure IF SUBJECT VERB-ED, SUBJECT WOULD VERB) and the student responds, "No, but if I would invite her, she accepted my invitation," the teacher may conclude – provided that the student has not made any mistakes previously in the drill – that the student has just shifted attention completely to the content of the utterance and is no longer thinking consciously about the syntax underlying the statement. The teacher must then continue drilling until the student succeeds in transferring his attention *and at the same time* produces the new structure correctly and unconsciously. In this type of exercise, learning actually occurs and the teacher may be certain that he has not wasted his or the student's time.

This approach to drill is implied by Fries when he writes:

The adult need not repeat the slow processes of the child, when he attempts to learn a foreign language. Instead of the haphazard mixture of structural patterns that confront the child in the speech of those around him, in which the occurrence or the repetition of a particular pattern is a matter of chance, it is possible to have a series of practice exercises which begin with the fundamental structural patterns of the language, which provide sufficient repetition of each pattern to develop a habit, and which are arranged in such a sequence as to lead the student systematically through the whole range of devices which form the complicated structural machinery of a language. These structural exercises should in their content, as far as possible, have practical relevance to the circumstances or the situations in which the student is actually living in order that they may avoid artificiality and gain their meaning from immediate experience.[10]

Lado specifies these ideas of Fries in greater detail when he states:

Pattern practice – completely oral – is presented here as one such technique. It consists paradoxically in the conscious substitution of some element *other than the chief element* being taught so that primary attention is drawn away from it while the entire pattern is repeated![11] [Lado's italics]

By stressing the importance of varying all elements except the element to be learned (i.e., to be made unconscious, automatic), and by insisting that the teacher not reveal in his cue the form of the structure to be generated, I have attempted to refine the theoretical contributions of Fries and Lado in this respect.

2.7 *Creative uses of the linguistic unit in original dialogues.* It will be noted that, thus far, the creativity of the student has been limited to responding to the teacher's linguistic stimulus; he has done this usually by answering questions affirmatively or negatively depending on the truth of the situation, or he has responded by supplying a missing word or two. It is now necessary for the student to become genuinely creative and to say, within the framework of the linguistic unit being drilled and the limitations of his vocabulary, what he wants to say. This is most conveniently accomplished by having students talk to each other in pairs, inventing questions and answers that practice the linguistic unit being learned. This frees the teacher to circulate, eavesdrop, occasionally participate, and to spend some time with the slower learner, giving him what amounts to private tutoring.

2.8 *Contrast drills.* The linguistic unit being learned must now be drilled in contrast with other similar linguistic units. It is not possible to contrast each new linguistic item with all other elements in the language, but it is necessary, in order to show the relationship of the unit to other units, to drill it in contrast with other units of the same linguistic class. Thus, if the Spanish third person singular preterit ending for first conjugation verbs (-ó) has already been learned and the student is at present learning the corresponding first person ending (-é), then, after this new ending has been learned, it must be contrasted with the third person ending, since both endings form part of a small linguistic subset of elements. The newly learned ending will also be drilled in contrast with any other tense endings that have been taught, such as, for example, the present indicative endings.

2.9 *Creative contrastive use of the linguistic unit in original dialogues.* This stage parallels 2.7 above, except that now the student must incorporate the new structure into the whole of his active corpus. The student must converse freely, drawing upon all that he has learned in the language, but his talk must refer to a situation also requiring the use of the newly learned element. This amounts to free conversation that relates to the new linguistic unit.

2.10 *Testing.* The student may now be tested on the linguistic unit under consideration (in contrast, of course, with all previously learned linguistic units). It is beyond the scope of this chapter to discuss methods of testing; the reader is referred to R. Lado, *Language Testing: The Construction and Use of Foreign Language Tests* (London, 1961) and R. Valette, *Modern Language Testing* (New York, 1967).

Notes

1. Cf. Noam Chomsky, *Aspects of the Theory of Syntax* (Cambridge, Mass.: M.I.T. Press, 1965), pp. 47–59 and Noam Chomsky, *Cartesian Linguistics* (New York: Harper and Row, 1966).
2. Lew S. Vygotsky, *Thought and Language*, trans. by E. Hanfman and G. Vakar (Cambridge, Mass.: M.I.T. Press, 1962).
3. Kenneth L. Pike, *Language in Relation to a Unified Theory of the Structure of Human Behavior,* part 1, preliminary edition (Glendale, Calif.: Summer Institute of Linguistics, 1954), p. 24.
4. Leonard Bloomfield, "Meaning," *Monatshefte für Deutschen Unterricht* 35 (1943): 102.
5. Noam Chomsky, "The Logical Basis of Linguistic Theory," in *Preprints of Papers for the Ninth International Congress of Linguists* (Cambridge, Mass.: M.I.T. Press, 1962), p. 512.
6. Quoted in Chomsky, *Aspects*, p. 8.
7. I use the word *corpus* in the sense expounded by Charles and Agnes Fries in *Foundations for English Teaching* (Tokyo: English Language Exploratory Committee, 1961).
8. Many of the ideas set forth here were originally discussed by David Wolfe in "Some Uses and Limitations of Contrastive Analysis in Teaching Foreign Languages," *The Education Quarterly* 11, no. 3 (1963): 19–22.
9. The term *vitalization,* as applied to language learning is, to my knowledge, the invention of Manoutchehr Varasteh of the University of Teheran; it was he who first illustrated to me the importance of this concept in language teaching.
10. Charles C. Fries, *Teaching and Learning English as a Foreign Language* (Ann Arbor: University of Michigan Press, 1945), p. 35.
11. Robert Lado, "Pattern Practice — Completely Oral," in *Selected Articles from Language Learning,* no. 1 (Ann Arbor: University of Michigan Press, 1963), pp. 42–45.

7.

Communication in Multilingual Societies

JOHN J. GUMPERZ

No one would claim that there is a one-to-one relationship between languages and social systems, yet we continue to think of speech communities as discrete, culturally homogeneous groups whose members speak closely related varieties of a single language. To be sure, no human group of any permanence can exist without regular and frequent communication. But such communication does not necessarily imply monolingualism. Recent ethnographic literature deals increasingly with stable multilingual societies, where populations of widely different cultural and linguistic backgrounds live in close geographic proximity. They are subject to the same political authority, attend the same schools, exchange services, and cooperate in many other respects. But they carry out their joint activities by means of not one, but a variety of languages. A major contemporary linguistics problem is the description of the verbal skills involved in speakers' concurrent use of the languages used in such communities.

Whenever all members of such a community do not have equal facility in all the languages in use there, language choice is, of course, determined by requirements of intelligibility. But we also have evidence to show that a majority, or at least a significant minority of residents, can frequently communicate effectively in more than one language, and that they alternate among languages for much the same reasons that monolinguals select among styles of a single language. That is to say, the same social pressures which would lead a monolingual to change from colloquial to formal or technical styles may induce a bilingual to shift from one lan-

From *Cognitive Anthropology* edited by Stephen A. Tyler. Copyright© 1969 by Holt, Rinehart and Winston, Inc. Reprinted by permission of Holt, Rinehart and Winston, Inc.

John J. Gumperz of the Language Behavior Research Laboratory at the University of California, Berkeley, is a recognized authority on linguistic diversity and bilingual communication. Among his publications are *Language in Social Groups* and *Directions in Sociolinguistics* (with Dell Hymes).

guage to another. Where this is the case, the difference between mono-lingual and bilingual behavior thus lies in the linguistic coding of socially equivalent processes. In one instance speakers select among lexical or phonetic variants of what they regard as the same language; in the other case, speakers choose between what they view as two linguistic entities. We shall now inquire into the special verbal skills required by interlanguage shift and what differentiates them from the skills needed to shift among styles of the same language.

Since the classification of speech varieties as belonging to the same or different languages is in fact determined largely on sociopolitical grounds, it can easily be shown that the purely qualitative distinction between monolingualism and bilingualism is by no means adequate to answer our question. Language pairs like Serbian and Croatian in Yugoslavia; Hindi and Urdu in India; Bokmal and Nynorsk in Norway, all of which have figured prominently in recent accounts of language conflict, are, for example, grammatically less distinct than some forms of upper- and lower-*call* English in New York. An individual who shifts from one member of such a pair to the other is bilingual in a social sense only. On the other hand, colloquial and literary varieties of Arabic would be regarded as separate languages were it not for the fact that modern Arabs insist on minimizing the differences between them. Thus speakers' views of language distinctions may depart considerably from linguistic reality.

Even when two speech varieties are obviously grammatically distinct, convergence resulting from language contact over time materially affects their distinctness. Scholars working in the Balkans, where multilingualism has long been widespread, have frequently noted considerable overlaps in lexicon, phonology, morphology, and syntax among local varieties of Slavic and adjoining dialects of Greek, Rumanian, and Albanian. They also point out that these relationships are independent of historical relatedness.

The effect of convergence on the structure of languages is often questioned.[1] Structural linguists have tended to criticize writings on convergence on methodological grounds. Edward Sapir's view that the grammatical core of a language is relatively immune to diffusion is still widely accepted. Nevertheless, more recent, structurally oriented studies by such linguists as Weinreich[2] reveal a number of clear instances of grammatical borrowings. Such borrowings are particularly frequent in those cases where we have evidence of widespread multilingualism.

Ethnographically oriented work on bilingual behavior further shows that not all varieties of a language are equally affected. Casual styles of either language tend to be less distant than more formal varieties. Diebold, for example, finds that phonological interference is greatest in code-switching situations.[3] The colloquial Canadian French expression, *Pourquoi tu l'a fait pour?* cited by Mackey[4] is a close translation equivalent of the English, *What have you done that for?* John Macnamara cites a similar example from rural dialects of Irish English, where sentences such as *I have it lost* for *I lost it* can be explained as direct translation equivalents of Gaelic.[5] Both formal Canadian French and educated Irish English avoid such translation equivalents. Charles Ferguson[6] in his discussion of diglossia — the use of grammatically separate varieties among educated residents of several societies — states that the varieties concerned in each case constitute a single phonological structure, in spite of their grammatical differences.

There is ample reason to suppose, therefore, that whenever two or more languages are regularly employed within the same social system, they differ significantly from the same languages as spoken in separate social systems. They are grammatically more similar and at the same time show greater intralanguage differentiation. Language distance is not a constant but varies with the intensity and quality of internal communication. Any answer to our question about the skills required in language switching therefore requires empirical investigation by methods which do not depend on any prior assumption about linguistic or social reality on the part of the analyst.

Measure of Language Distance

Much of the linguistic research on bilingualism relies on measures of interference, "the use of elements from one language while speaking or writing another."[7] The usual procedure is to search the bilingual performance for features of pronunciation, grammar, and lexicon not present in the monolingual standard, which can be attributed to second language influence. Interference analysis has provided important insights into the more general processes of borrowing[8] and their effects on linguistic change. It also serves as an important tool in language pedagogy, where the object is to study what is involved in the monolingual's learning of a new language and acculturating to a different monolingual community. Interference measurements of all kinds, however, assume that the structure of the standard is known and that speakers have direct access to the standard and seriously attempt to imitate it. These assumptions are justified for the ordinary second language learner or for isolated speakers of minority languages, whose significant contacts are largely with the surrounding monolingual community and who can thus be expected to conform to its norms. They do not, however, apply in our case. Members of stable bilingual communities interact largely with other bilinguals, and it can be shown that such interaction generates its own norms of correctness.[9] Although learning through prestige imitation takes place in all societies, the particular linguistic object of this imitation in bilingual societies must be established through empirical research; it cannot be assumed.

A second technique of interlanguage comparison is that of contrastive analysis, which finds extensive application in the preparation of pedagogical language texts. This method consists of a direct point-by-point comparison of the two systems at each component of structure. Differences are evaluated according to their places within the respective system (whether they are phonetic, phonemic, syntactic, and so forth). They are then counted, under the assumption that "what the student has to learn equals the sum of the differences established by this comparison."[10] Prediction of the hierarchy of difficulties is thus based on the linguist's analysis of their structural importance. For example, the fact that in Spanish the segments [d] and [ð] are in complementary distribution, with the former occurring initially in words like *dar* and the latter medially in words like *lado,* whereas they contrast in English words like *dare* and *there,* may lead to the diagnosis that the Spanish-speaking student has the problem of assigning phonemic status to two phonetic entities which are allophones and not phonemes in his own language.[11] But the assignment of phonemic status to a linguistic feature is generally based on the performance of "ideal speakers living in a homogeneous community."[12] Since bilingual speakers are excluded from consideration here, ordinary structural categories can hardly be used to predict bilingual performance.

The fact that bilingual communities show more than the usual amount of intralanguage diversity also raises some doubt about the carry-over of traditional elicitation techniques into fieldwork in bilingual situations. If the linguist, as is commonly done, simply seeks out individuals who speak both languages well and asks them to repeat utterances in the two languages, he is likely to elicit largely formal (maximally distinct) styles. Colloquial expressions like the French and Irish expressions cited earlier are quite likely to be suppressed as unsuitable as long as the speakers themselves perceive of the interview situation as a formal encounter. Since the rules of language choice are largely beyond conscious control, even repeated requests to speak and behave informally are not likely to produce the desired results.

If instead of starting with the a priori assumption that two languages are distinct, we take the opposite view and treat them as part of a single whole, many such difficulties can be avoided. This means that in his fieldwork the linguist would disregard the speaker's view of the languages as distinct entities and treat them as part of the same *linguistic repertoire.*

The distinction between grammars and languages current in recent linguistic theory provides some justification for this approach. A grammar is a theoretical construct, a set of rules which underlies verbal performance. A language consists of the set of utterances generated by the grammar. Implicit in the notion of grammar is the assumption that some rules are universal, that is, characteristic of human behavior as a whole, and that others are language specific. If we say that grammars may show varying degrees of relatedness we are only carrying this notion a little bit further. We then assume that bilingual behavior reflects both an underlying set of general rules which applies to the entire linguistic repertoire and lower-order, nonshared, language-specific rules. It is the task of linguistic analysis to discover the dividing line between these two sets of rules.

Work in machine translation provides a technique for accomplishing this, enabling the investigator to focus directly on the relationship between two sets of texts without requiring any a priori linguistic or social assumptions. In some earlier work in machine translation, it had in fact been assumed that grammatical information could be disregarded. But this assumption was soon proved wrong when it was shown that grammatical analysis is the most efficient way of organizing the information required for translation so as to fit into a computer's storage capacity.[13] If we then ask what is the minimum coding necessary to translate the speaker's performance in Language A to the same speaker's performance in Language B, we must in fact do a linguistic analysis. But note that a grammar in these terms is merely an information storage device; it is not an independently patterned organic entity. Its categories are justified only to the extent that they facilitate the translation process. The best solution is simply that which provides the simplest translation rules. Since the greater the grammatical overlap the easier the translation process, it is simplest to assume that there is a single underlying system from which the differences of the two languages can be derived. Language distance can then be measured as a function of the number of nonshared rules.

If translatability measures are based only on a single set of texts, the number of grammatical rules needed will be an arbitrarily restricted selection. But the greater the number of speakers measured, and the greater the variety of contexts in which the texts are collected, the more complete will be the body of rules. Translatability measures thus are akin to sociological forms of measurement in that they depend for their validity on sample size and on interaction processes and are therefore ideally suited for sociolinguistic analysis, where interspeaker variation is the central problem.

The speech of the Spanish-English bilingual in New York approaches our usual image of bilingual behavior. In spite of some overlap, the systems concerned are distinct in every component. Nevertheless, even in this case, the translatability approach raises some new questions about the nature of bilingual skills. To give a phonological example, much of the difference between the two languages results from the presence in one language of articulations not occurring in the other. Thus Spanish lacks the [š] of English *shoe* and English lacks the [ñ] of Spanish *baño*. Further distinctions, however, emerge when we compare the articulation of phonetically equivalent words. Thus the word *photo* will be [fowtow] in English and [foto] in Spanish in the same speaker's pronunciation. Spanish-English bilinguals, then, maintain two parallel sets of phonetically similar articulation ranges corresponding to functionally equivalent phones.

It would seem that the necessity of keeping the above ranges separate is an important problem in Spanish-English code-switching. Comparison of the formal speech of educated bilinguals with that of uneducated bilinguals or with the same speakers in informal speech shows in fact that these distinctions are frequently collapsed.

Conclusion

The view that language distance is a function of social interaction and social context raises some interesting general problems. The common view that multilingualism, wherever it occurs, also reflects deep social cleavages is clearly in need of revision. If we wish to understand the social significance of language behavior, we must go beyond popular language names and simple language-usage statistics. Furthermore, if in spite of surface appearances, language is not necessarily a serious barrier to communication, why do such differences maintain themselves over long periods of time? What is it within the system of roles and statuses or in the norms of social interaction that favors the retention of such overt symbols of distinctness? Under what conditions do such symbols disappear?

Of more direct practical value is the question of the relative importance of social and language barriers to communication. Intralanguage variation clearly plays an important part in bilingual behavior, and measures of bilingual competence must account for it if they are to be socially realistic. Furthermore, the common assumption that uneducated speakers of minority languages learn better when instructed through the medium of their own vernacular is not necessarily always justified. Instructional materials in these vernaculars may rely on monolingual norms which are culturally quite alien to the student and linguistically different from his home speech. Considerably more research is needed on these and similar questions, and ethnographically oriented linguistic measurement is an important factor in this task.

Notes

1. George Carpenter Barker, *Pachuco: An American-Spanish Argot and Its Social Functions in Tucson, Arizona* (Tucson: University of Arizona Press, 1950).
2. Uriel Weinreich, *Languages in Contact* (New York: Linguistic Circle, 1953).
3. Richard A. Diebold, "Incipient Bilingualism" in *Language in Culture and Society,* ed. Dell Hymes (New York: Harper and Row, 1964), pp. 495–508.
4. William F. Mackey, "Bilingual Interference: Its Analysis and Measurement," *Journal of Communication* 15: 239–49.
5. John T. Macnamara, *Bilingualism in Primary Education: A Study of Irish Experience* (Edinburgh: Edinburgh University Press, 1966).
6. Charles A. Ferguson, "Diglossia" in *Language in Culture and Society,* ed. Dell Hymes (New York: Harper, 1964), pp. 429–39.
7. Mackey, "Bilingual Interference."
8. Weinreich, *Languages in Contact.*
9. Susan Ervin-Tripp, "An Analysis of the Interaction of Language Topic and Listener" in *The Ethnography of Communication,* ed. John Gumperz and Dell Hymes, *American Anthropologist* 66, part 2: 103.
10. Bela Banathy, Edith Trager, and Carl D. Waddle, "The Use of Contrastive Data in Foreign Language Course Development," in *Trends in Language Teaching,* ed. A. Valdman (New York: McGraw-Hill, 1966).
11. Ibid.
12. Noam Chomsky, *Aspects of the Theory of Syntax* (Cambridge, Mass.: M.I.T. Press, 1965).
13. Sydney Lamb, "The Nature of the Machine Translation Problem," *Journal of Verbal Learning and Verbal Behavior* 4 (1965): 196–210.

8.

The Psychological Bases of Second Language Learning

LEON A. JAKOBOVITS

The topic of this discussion is the psychological bases of second language learning, but the subject that really concerns me is that human being we refer to as "the learner," and I consider a mere coincidence the fact that I happen to focus at this time on the activity involved in second language learning. I consider this kind of topical subdivision quite arbitrary, convenient and helpful for certain purposes, but at the same time potentially harmful when its arbitrariness and artificiality are forgotten and the division is taken as real.

Many factors, conditions, and situations in the educational system at all levels conspire to concretize and reify divisions in learning topics which originate from considerations that are separate from and irrelevant to the learning process itself. It is my feeling that the reasons that maintain curricular compartmentalization are either unrelated or actually detrimental to the student and the process of education. Disciplinary specialization has distinct advantages for certain purposes: for conducting research of a certain kind, for becoming a so-called expert in the field and the social, intellectual, and economic advantages that go along with having the status of an expert in our society, for professional and sociopolitical reasons having to do with influence and power, and so on. But it seems to me that too often considerations of this kind are allowed to interfere with the best interests of the student and his education.

Consider the trappings that surround the academic subject of second language learning, professional, educational, academic, and political: the foreign language profession with its organizations, conventions, journals, licensing procedures, and career opportunities; the FL literature and research, themselves subdivided into areas of specialization and methodological applications; the sociopolitical activities that revolve around the

Reprinted from *Language Sciences* 14 (Feb. 1971): pp. 22–28.

See biographical note on Leon A. Jakobovits in Chapter 2 of this book.

maintenance of ethnic identity, the specialized laws enacted with these interests in mind, and so on. These various divergent lines of interaction are somehow expected to converge into a meaningful topical unit of a classroom subject. But do they?

"Second language learning" as a classroom subject is one thing, and being a bilingual person is another thing, and these two things have often very little to do with one another. I believe that both of these can have valid educational objectives, but to confuse them is to neutralize the advantages that either may have to offer. When I went to high school I took Latin and Ancient Greek as school subjects, and it was clear to me, and it seemed so to the teacher as well, that the objective was not that of producing a bilingual individual. But when I took Flemish and Spanish and German and French and Hebrew, a confusion existed: the objective was ostensibly to produce a multilingual individual, but the educational activities surrounding these subjects did not differ much from those involving Latin and Greek.

This was over twenty years ago, and it is now a matter of historical interest in foreign language education how this kind of confusion was supposedly eliminated. We speak of the advent of the audiolingual age in FL teaching, and we even have dates associated with the inauguration of this new era. The last three or four generations of high school and college students are products of the language laboratory and of pattern practice, and the activities that these imply are supposed to attest to the changing educational objectives of second language learning. The objective of the current "modern" era in FL education is to produce a living, viable bilingualism that is involved in talking, reading, and writing in two or more languages.

I shall deal in a moment with the reasons that make me believe that such an objective is quite inadequate, ill defined, and unrealistic, but for the present, let us examine the degree of success of our current educational objectives in FL teaching. On the one hand, the number of students taking a FL has steadily increased over the years so that currently it is estimated that as many as eighty percent of all high school students in this country are exposed to such a course at one time or another in their educational career, and at the college level this proportion is even higher. This state of affairs attests to the vigor and influence of a profession dedicated to the universalization of FL learning. Let us consider that as a success.

But now, let us consider some other criteria. How do the students involved in this massive effort feel about it; do they think they are getting anything worthwhile out of it? What proportion of them achieve a state of living bilingualism whereby they can talk, read, and write bilingually? Here, we are entering an area of great controversy, and on past occasions when I have had the opportunity of discussing this issue in my writings and talks I found myself doing it in an atmosphere of polemics and defensiveness. For the very act of raising the issue becomes a potential threat to that vast constituency of established and vested interests that is the FL profession. The question is threatening only because we have allowed a confusion to arise between the interests of a profession and the interests of the student population, while they should have been kept separate in the best interests of both.

I shall not go into the details of an empirical and experimental nature to support the following two claims: (1) that a majority of high school and college students remain unimpressed by the value of FL study and a good number of them have very distinctly negative attitudes toward these courses, and (2) that the proportion of students who develop sufficient competence in their second language to make it possible for them to use it outside the classroom is extremely small. I have attempted in some previous writings to document the students' negative attitudes and their total lack of binguality, but these two facts are so widespread and well known to all concerned that they in themselves are not the points of controversy. (See L.A. Jakobovits, *Foreign Language Learning: A Psycholinguistic Analysis of the Issues* [Rowley, Mass: Newbury House Publishers, 1970].)

The controversy revolves around the explanation that accounts for these facts. There are those who claim that the fault lies in the audio-lingual method. This is countered by the proponents of that method by laying the blame on its misapplication in the form of the uninspiring use of language laboratories and rigid boring pattern practice exercises in the classroom. There are those who view the students' negative attitudes toward FL study as a symptom of a wider educational malaise that affects all courses and subjects that a "rebellious" younger generation no longer finds "relevant." There are those who consider the notion of "FLs for everyone" a totally unrealistic and misplaced objective. There are those who advocate FLES programs as the only viable ones, given the alleged relationship between early age and language learning. And, so goes on the gamut of claims and counterclaims, fault-finding, and whitewashing.

I believe we should attempt to extricate ourselves from this level of discourse and take another look from a different vantage point. In the remainder of this discussion, I would like to outline what it would take to achieve this new perspective on FL learning.

To begin with, let me state a number of premises that need prior discussion and some subsequent agreement:

1. Bilingualism entails biculturalism.

2. Bilingualism cannot as a rule be achieved in the FL classroom.

3. There are valid educational objectives in learning a second language that are other than the attainment of bilingualism.

4. Learning a second language has associated with it factors and considerations that are unique to it and are different from learning other school subjects.

5. When a large proportion of students fail to learn a second language in school, their "failure" is not a reflection of the teacher's competence or the method he uses.

6. The conditions that hold under a mass educational system are unfavorable to the development of an effective FL curriculum.

I'd like to take up each of these points in turn.

Bilingualism and Biculturalism

I suppose it would be possible to define bilingualism in a way that would invalidate the proposition that bilingualism entails biculturalism. In fact, people's use of the term, both academic and other, varies considerably from one extreme that defines bilingualism as a state of linguistic interference involving two or more languages, to the other extreme that reserves the term to describe the state of an individual who is equally at home in two or more languages under all conditions of usage and in addition sounds indistinguishable from native speakers of either language. Actually, one can argue with some merit that the proposition that bilingualism entails biculturalism holds true for both of these extreme definitions, as well as all those in between. In that case, we need to discuss what it is to be bicultural.

We are faced here with exactly the same problem as that of bilingualism. I find it useful to think of biculturalism in terms of the sharing of two cultures that have some identifiable identity of their own. This is ultimately a matter of classificatory convenience. Thus, in the case of political or national reasons, cultural boundary lines are set up that may or may not overlap with the boundaries set up on the basis of economic, religious, ideological, or historical reasons. Thus, I along with many of my fellow Canadians, consider Canada a bilingual and bicultural country, meaning English and French, and this is a matter of historical classification. In fact, the Canadian population is made up of a number of other ethnic-linguistic groups as well, and this has become on the part of the latter groups a point of contention to the work and official designation of the Royal Commission on *Bi*-lingualism and *Bi*-culturalism.

It is clear, then, that biculturalism can be defined on the basis of a number of different and equally relevant criteria. Therefore, it is important to always be clear as to the particular criteria used in any discussion.

I would like for my present purposes to define biculturalism in terms of a communications criterion. Communication between two individuals is made possible as a result of their sharing certain types of knowledge and certain types of inferential reasoning behavior. The shared knowledge includes a linguistic code, semantic structures, certain attitudes, rules of conversation, and rules of the social and physical order of things. The shared inferential reasoning behavior includes expectations of what leads to what under particular conditions. When people interact on repeated occasions and do so for mutual benefit, they will learn each other's communicative premises. Thus, subgroups of habitual interactants form cultural or subcultural identities. When a member of one subgroup interacts with a member of another subgroup he has to readjust his communication premises. It is at this point that he begins the process of becoming bicultural.

Now, if we look at the nature of this readjustment process, we note that it involves acquiring new knowledge, new expectations, and new ways of making inferences. A new linguistic code or changes in the linguistic code may or may not be involved. Thus bilingualism is not a prerequisite for speakers of that language, a notion that has led to the development of such serious disciplines as ethnolinguistics and cognitive anthropology. Learning a second language requires the acquisition of a new semantic structure that reflects a new order of things in the world. The learner makes the momentous discovery that lo and behold the world isn't as it is, and the cognitive dissonance that this realization creates may very well transform him into a more understanding, more humble, more compassionate, more flexible thinking human being.

These, then, are some of the values of FL study other than functional bilingualism, and I submit that they are not unimportant. Let no FL teacher, contemplating the so-called failure of the FL curriculum, feel defensive or sheepish about his contribution to the educational development of our youth. The attainment of bilingualism is by no means the only justifiable objective of a FL program.

Learning a Second Language is Unlike Learning Other School Subjects

I have already referred to some of the particular attitudes that revolve around the study of FLs, and these attach to it a cultural significance that is distinctly different from that of other school subjects. But now I have in mind another sort of difference which is related to the developmental learning steps involved in studying a second language and their attitudinal consequences. That "mathematics is difficult" is a common piece of folklore that most students and parents hold with unshakable conviction. Not to run into trouble there is no mean achievement, let alone be good in it. That "Spanish is a cinch" while "German is for the brainy people" are also interesting little bits of knowledge that you can discover when you spend your time administering opinion surveys to high school students, as I and some of my academic colleagues are fond of doing. But very few students enrolling in a second language course have any inkling of the pain they have let themselves in for by that action. Imagine how difficult it is to learn how to talk! This can't be! There must be something wrong somewhere! Either the teacher is no good or I have no aptitude for languages. And there goes another lost cause.

There are three kinds of problems that face second language learners that I feel are unique: the self-evaluations concerning rate of progress and degree of achievement, the peculiar cumulative nature of their developing competence, and the psychological resistance to free expression. Let me discuss these in reverse order.

There appears to be a qualitative difference for many learners in the significance they attach to making errors while speaking in a FL versus getting an answer wrong in another school subject. Getting the wrong answer for a problem in algebra or the wrong date for an historical battle is a pity because of the grade missed, but there is something either sacrilegious or idiotic in unintentionally murdering a sentence. There is an interesting psychological phenomenon here that would surely be worth further investigation, but for the moment, let us simply note that this attitude serves to inhibit and retard the expressive leap in a second language. Teachers, too, I might add share this attitude with their students, and although their rationalization for it might be different (for instance, "it is more difficult to unlearn errors later on") their low tolerance for phonological distortions and syntactic irregularities no doubt serves to maintain the students' resistance to communicative speech. (I cannot go into this now, but I have no doubt that error analysis would show up developmental patterns that necessitate intermediary forms of speech for which correction is futile and attitudinally harmful.)

Next, another second language learning problem is that so much of it is initially in the form of latent knowledge, and progress seems so uneven to the learner. For instance, the so-called "active" skills — speaking and writing — are far behind the "passive" skills of listening and reading, and while the latter proceed in noticeable steps, the former seem never to get off the ground. Actually, "active" and "passive" are misnomers here because the deep structure analysis of a sentence is similar whether you generate it or someone else does it for you. The only passive thing about listening is that your peripheral vocal apparatus creates less disturbance in the air than when you talk, but syntactically you are equally active in both situations. This is not to say that the processes are identical — otherwise they would develop at comparable rates — but the nature of the difference might not be what we suppose it to be.

There are, furthermore, problems associated with diagnosing areas of difficulty. A mistake in an algebra problem can be traced to a forgotten formula (that can then be relearned) or an error in subtraction (that can be shrugged off). Not so when an expression in the FL is misunderstood or when a sentence fails to materialize in the quivering throat of the student. When second language learners are asked to list their major problems, one that is high on almost everyone's list is vocabulary. This is a doubtful assessment, and experienced teachers know this. Another common candidate is gender and verb tense. But here too there are reasons to believe that the problem is more complex than that. There is room here for a great deal of more systematic observations than we now have available, and I am simply throwing the problem up for discussion.

Finally, the third kind of problem that seems to be peculiar to second language learning, one that is not unconnected to the other two, is the student's self-evaluation of the rate of his progress and the extent of his achievement. He seems to share with many a teacher and parent the delusion that he ought to know more than he does at any one point and that unless he ultimately achieves functional, easygoing, native-like fluency in his expressions his efforts have been in vain. As I have pointed out earlier, not only is bilingualism not the sole valid objective of FL study, but that objective is quite unrealistic for many learners within the school system, and perhaps teachers could play a more active and constructive role in the formation of more realistic self-evaluations on the part of their students.

The Relation Between Student "Failure" and Teacher "Failure"

There is a very pernicious sort of biculturalism. Or to put it another way, while bilingualism always entails biculturalism, biculturalism entails bilingualism only in the special instance where a new linguistic code is to be acquired when interacting with a member of the second culture. It is this special case that we are faced with in learning a second language, but the properties of the general class of which it is an instance should always be kept in mind. Unless this is done it would be difficult to distinguish the learning of a second language from the learning of an alternate code for communication within a subculture, such as the language of the deaf or the Morse Code. For instance, if two friends decided one day to learn finger spelling and started interacting that way, this would not be an instance of biculturalism. I suppose you might call this an instance of unicultural bi-codalism. Bilingualism, on the other hand, is more than bi-codalism, since the second language is not intentionally patterned on the first. It includes a reorganization of knowledge as embodied in the phonological, syntactic, lexical, and semantic structures of that language as well as certain sociolinguistic rules. This reorganization of knowledge contains different communication premises and constitutes biculturalism. It is for this reason that I stated that any degree of bilingualism entails some degree of biculturalism.

This way of looking at second language learning allows a different perspective on FL teaching. The latter thus becomes a question of training in biculturalism. Once this premise is accepted, the problems involved in FL teaching methodology take on different dimensions. I believe that the issues involved in bicultural training are more productive than those involved in bilingual training. I do not have time here to explore this issue in detail. Let me simply sketch some of the parameters that I think might be involved in such an investigation.

To begin with, a focus on bicultural training would give a more appropriate status to the role of language training per se. There is a widespread attitude among teachers and educators involved in FL training, which is shared also by students and their parents, that mastering the elementary mechanics of language is a necessary prerequisite for getting to the subsequent stage of some degree of bilingualism, this latter stage being the really worthwhile aspect of the experience because it then allows the incipient bilingual to some into contact with the culture of the people either directly through oral communication or indirectly through reading and exposure to the mass media. The assumption that lies behind this attitude seems to me to give an unwarranted amount of weight and importance to a particular form of bicultural communication, that which is directly mediated by the second code.

It seems to me that other forms of bicultural communication are equally worthwhile for various purposes and under many conditions. For instance, the amount of bilingualism gained through a few weeks travel in Japan is fairly negligible when unsupported by prior or concurrent language training, yet the degree of biculturalism one might absorb during the same time may have very lasting consequences for the individual. Similarly a serious interest in Oriental art, or Eastern philosophy, or even the regular practice of karate, may transform an ethnocentric unicultural individual into a culturally more sophisticated person, who, even though he may know nothing of a second language, is well on his way to bicultural and multicultural competency. On what bases can it really be claimed that mastering the mechanics of a second language is a superior educational objective to these other forms of biculturalism, especially when that kind of demand actually stands in the way of bicultural experiences, as I believe it does for the majority of students in our FL programs?

I think educators must face this issue head on and reexamine their attitude toward the universalization of the FL curriculum in its current manifestation. I have grave doubts about the value of cramming knowledge down the throat of anyone, whether it be a FL or Oriental art or trigonometry. I believe that expending massive educational efforts in teaching FLs in the absence of a genuine interest in that type of knowledge is not only futile but harmful. It seems to me that for the educational process to be effective it ought to be dispensed in a miserly fashion: give only as much as is demanded. To feel comfortable with this kind of educational philosophy, the teacher must have two prior beliefs: one is that merely acquiring facts in the absence of an intrinsic interest is not ultimately very useful, hence to attempt it is futile; the other is a belief in the intrinsic worth of the individual, that what matters is the process of satisfying his creative and intellectual needs that in fact exist, rather than needs defined for him by others. Are FL teachers prepared to take off the colored glasses of their provincial perspective and view the problem in its wider educational implications? I shall have a few more things to say on this issue in the last section of this discussion.

Can Bilingualism Be Achieved in the Classroom?

Earlier, I stated the answer to this question in the negative. Let me now elaborate. When FL teachers and administrators are faced with the fact that the vast majority of their students do not attain a state of functional bilingualism at the end of their training, their most common reaction is to look around for more effective methods of teaching. This is not an irrational or surprising reaction. But if repeated searches for the best method fail to graduate a greater proportion of bilinguals, another conclusion should be seriously considered, namely that bilingualism cannot as a rule be achieved in the classroom. There are a number of considerations that can serve to rationalize this conclusion. Let me mention a few.

1. Developing communicative competence in a language requires conditions in which communicative needs exist. One can put this in a slightly different way which might be more useful: the degree of communicative competence acquired by an individual is proportional to the extent of his communicative needs. Now, what are the communicative needs of an American student in the classroom taking French, say? I can't think of very many that cannot be satisfied in English, short of the case of the pupil who falls in love with his pretty unilingual French teacher. While being present in FL classes where the use of English was forbidden, I have repeatedly noted that whenever a genuine communicative need arose, the students automatically and insistently lapsed into the use of English. Carrying on a classroom discussion on some topic did in a few instances create genuine communicative needs when the students got involved in the subject, but the requirement of using the second language

was purely artificial, and by the time the painful process of constructing a reasonably correct sentence was achieved, the need has come and gone and the discussion turned into an artificial language exercise. I am not knocking the usefulness of discussions in the FL classroom; in fact, I believe they are distinctly more advantageous than pattern practice exercises. But I am drawing attention to the difficulty of creating genuine communicative needs in the classroom setting, and hence, according to the proposition I stated above, to the difficulty of developing functional bilingualism.

2. Achieving functional bilingualism in the classroom requires a fairly high degree of FL aptitude. I take aptitude to be an inverse function of time required to achieve a set criterion. Thus, even though it may be the case that almost all adults are capable of becoming bilingual, only a small proportion of them could achieve that status given the time limitations that hold in the school setting.

3. Achieving functional bilingualism in the absence of extensive contact with unilingual native speakers requires an integrative orientation on the part of the learner. By "integrative orientation" I mean an attitude whereby the learner identifies with native models and perceives an intrinsic value in acquiring cultural characteristics that the native models possess, including their language. It is simply the fact that the vast majority of American students do not have such an integrative orientation toward foreign models.

In the absence of any of the three conditions that I stated, namely genuine communicative needs, high aptitude, and integrative orientation, let alone their combination, it is then unrealistic to expect that the classroom can produce very many functional bilinguals.

Are There Valid Objectives in Learning a Second Language Other Than Bilingualism?

Earlier I stated the answer in the affirmative. (And here I can almost hear the sigh of relief on the part of FL teachers whom I have not as yet totally alienated and who are still reading this chapter.) What are some of these objectives?

Let me start with the extrinsic ones. American culture attaches value to FL learning. While this attitude is neither simple nor universal, it has been strong and pervasive over the years and has made possible the recent drive toward universalization of the FL curriculum in our schools. Language loyalty and maintenance activities on the part of ethnic groups in this country have remained very strong and active. I would guess that no less than half of the Americans living today can count in their parental or grandparental generation an individual whose first language is other than English. In addition, there still lingers today the traditional European value whereby one is not fully educated unless one "knows" a second language. Furthermore, many Americans have come to believe that international peace requires greater understanding and contact between the peoples of the world, and thus by taking a FL course in school they feel that they are somehow contributing to world peace. Finally, many more Americans today travel abroad, or at least consider traveling abroad, and this fact is consistent with the study of FLs.

It should be noted that some of these extrinsic motivations to FL study may not in fact be valid from the point of view of an impartial observer. That is, one may be considered to be an educated person even though one is unilingual in English; one may not actually contribute to world peace by enrolling in a FL course; one may not make use of Spanish while traveling in France and Italy; and so on. But this is not the point. Given a prevalent cultural value for FL study, it can be considered a valid educational objective to have a strong and active FL curriculum.

Now, to mention some other objectives that might be more intrinsic in nature. Exposure to a FL constitutes bicultural training. The teacher may be a foreigner. The content of the day's lesson may offer a new perspective on a different social order. Or it may be a foreign magazine, or a movie, or a book, or a meal. A new insight may be gained on the neighbors next door or on the foreign dignitaries that the president is seen meeting on the White House steps. History, geography, and anthropology may take on a slightly different perspective, one that might be closer and more relevant to personal experience.

Language, as a device for communication, becomes more concretized as the individual leaves the automatic, unthinking facility of his native language, and moves into the painful, halting hesitancies of a foreign tongue as he deliberately tries to place the adjectives and verbs in their proper order. For the first time, the artificial structuredness of human language enters his awareness and becomes a living reality. There are undoubtedly rare but recurrent moments when he feels the architect's elation when viewing the finished product of his imagination as he beholds that rare phenomenon of a novel, well-formed sentence in the second language for which he himself is responsible. Then, for the very few, there is that supreme satisfaction that comes from viewing a French movie without having to bother to read the English subtitles, or settling down with a novel without pencil and dictionary. The mere contemplation of these two delights is sufficient to drive many a student to one more hour of a boring language laboratory session.

Finally, let me mention along with these intrinsic values, a more esoteric argument that comes out of the psycholinguist's bag. In this view, unilingual speakers are compared to the egocentrism of young children who innocently believe that the word is the thing, and the concept is the word. The semantic structure of a language reflects the conceptual framework of argumentation whereby some unjustified goal is set for a program, then, when it is not attained, the program is dubbed a failure. I believe this is the type of argument that is responsible for the crisis atmosphere in FL education today and the ensuing frantic search for better methods, better bilingual programs, better manipulative techniques for motivating students to learn, and so on. Naturally, my remark is not intended to license another kind of extreme attitude whereby all is well under the sun and we need not worry about continuing excellence in education. The point is that the setting of goals for a program ought not to be done very lightly and in the absence of careful justification.

The other day a graduate student in linguistics dropped in to see me in my office and, being from Thailand, he wanted me to tell him why their ESL program over there was a failure. "Was it true," as he had heard, "that I was against the audiolingual method, and if so, which method would be better?" I asked him what the purpose of their ESL program was and he told me, "Why, of course, so that the Thais could learn the two active and the two passive skills in English." Undaunted, I asked, "What for? Why do the Thais want to know the four skills in English?", upon which he said, "In order to be able to read English textbooks." Several minutes of silence ensued, whereupon he said "I see what you mean; you mean, what's the use of learning the four skills in English when what they want is to learn how to decode English textbooks."

I relate this episode — and I hope I am not doing the student an injustice — because it so clearly points up the excesses of goal setting for many existing programs, excesses that I believe are quite habitual in the second language teaching field. Perhaps one explanation for the acuteness of this problem is that few people in this field actually believe that it is either possible or useful to develop specialized skills in the use of a second language. It is as if they treated language learning as a monolithic block to be digested in toto or not at all. This appears to be indeed a matter of belief, for I have been unable to find any serious attempt to investigate the problem. And yet, it seems to me that there are cogent arguments against the monolithic theory. We know that reading in one's native language is a specialized skill, and particularly when it comes to reading textbook English, the variance to be found there in individual differences in competence does not seem to match the much smaller variance in competence we can note in the daily use of native English speakers. Similarly, the skill with which the French Canadian bus driver in Montreal handles me in English, when the need arises, totally belies his English competence as soon as I engage him in a political discussion. The same non-communicative situation arises with the English saleslady to whom I make conversation in French after she has very competently sold me the piece of merchandise in French.

Thus observation supports the separateness of various communicative skills in a language. There remain then two problems in this connection. First, is there not a minimum common core of linguistic knowledge that transcends specialized communicative settings and that should be taught to all language learners? And second, is the teaching of specialized goals justifiable and feasible given a great deal of heterogeneity in need and unpredictability in later use?

Neither of these questions, it seems to me, is open to a pat answer, but I believe that it is possible to set guidelines that apply differentially to particular situations.

In the first instance it ought to be recognized that the resources available to any particular language training program, be it in a high school setting or a special language school, are limited. Certain decisions have then to be made about the priority of needs to be met. Then one must examine whether the learning conditions in that school and the larger community are favorable for meeting the priority needs. For instance, offering a conversational course in Russian in a high school and community where there is one living speaker of Russian is asking for trouble, unless it is made quite clear to all concerned that bilingualism is not the goal of the course. Or, offering an audiolingual course in German to chemistry majors in college whose sole interest is to decipher journal articles, can only be done at the chagrin of the students and the peril of the teacher. And to teach the "two active skills and the two passive skills" to Thai college students who only wish to get through their engineering texts is not only futile, as experience shows, but positively heartless. Obviously, we have to proceed with deliberate planning in the specialization of second language courses, but equally obviously a process of unfreezing the current monolithic programs is long overdue.

Toward Compensatory or Individuated FL Instruction

The last of my six premises stated that an effective FL curriculum is not possible under present conditions of mass education. There is nothing so peculiar to FL instruction that this should be true only of it and not of other school subjects, and so my premise here is but an expression of the more general thesis that effective education and mass teaching do not go together. By "mass teaching" I wish to refer to the teaching that is guided by the principle that pupils are in school to be fed *x* amount of knowledge divided up in *y* units and chunks and administered in *t* amount of time. Thus it is not merely a question of teacher-student ratio but the conception itself of the educational process.

I am in agreement with Carl Rogers' student-centered conception of the educational process, wherein the responsibility for learning is placed where it truly belongs, on the student and not on the teacher. I don't know who it was that said that that which can be taught is not worth learning, and that which is worth learning cannot be taught. A teacher's role is that of a catalyst that under the right conditions can facilitate the student's learning. This of course is an ideal model, a conception, a guiding principle. It is neat and oversimplified. What are the right conditions? What happens in the meantime, while the right conditions decide to appear on the scene? Can the teacher create these conditions? I don't think anyone has the answers to these questions, but this state of ignorance need not render us helpless. There are little things that can be tried by the teacher. He need not wait for official policy and the expert's overall program. It's a question of attitude on the part of the individual human being that is in the person of the teacher and the quality of relationships he can tolerate when interacting with those other individual human beings that are in the person of the student.

For instance, in one type of a FL class the students and the teacher must be willing to play a particular kind of a game whereby they pretend that they know no English and the only possible mode of interaction is either nonverbal or through the medium of the target language. Now, the students, if they become truly involved in this game, would attempt to use the knowledge of the teacher for facilitating the interaction within the rules of the game. They would ask for instance, "How do you say thus-and-thus in French?" and then would repeat it. At any time, the information the students are asking is determined by, not what is in lesson sixteen in a textbook, but the communicative needs of the moment that the person-to-person interaction creates. I have tried to create such a classroom for the French class in an English school in the Montreal area with the cooperation of a teacher, and although what I have just described did take place in some measure, another interesting, and to me unexpected, thing happened as well. These were ninth graders who already had had two or three years of French classes in the usual classroom setting and knew that they would be returning to that setting following this experimental year. After about three weeks of instruction along the student-centered, teacher-as-facilitator pattern, they introduced certain demands into the situation. They wanted the teacher to lecture on the use of the subjunctive and to assign reading and writing homework. They furthermore insisted on being corrected by the teacher. What a marvelous development. Can you imagine students demanding a grammar lecture and homework! When I interviewed them after about two months of instruction they were critical of the course because they felt they weren't learning enough — and this despite a visible and tangible increase in communicative facility on their part, which could be noted on a set of tests I devised for them. Needless to say, the teacher gladly acceded to the demands for grammatical explanations and homework assignments for those students who wanted them, for, although this was the sentiment of a majority of them, it was by no means unanimous.

It seems to me that arrangements of this sort can be set up in most classrooms, whatever the specialized goals of subgroups of students in the class. While it would be nice if a separate teacher were available for each subgroup, we cannot at the moment afford this kind of luxury of resources. But neither is it necessary, for as I indicated earlier, it is not merely a question of teacher-student ratio, but an attitude on the part of teacher and student toward the kind of relationship they have.

This completes my discussion of the six premises I stated at the beginning. I should like to summarize briefly. There are valid educational objectives in learning a second language that are other than the attainment of bilingualism. Bilingualism is a process of enculturation, and although the acquisition of some forms of biculturalism represents a realistic and worthwhile goal, the achievement of a state of bilingualism is not to be expected for the majority of students. Learning a FL in school has associated with it certain unique aspects, and the student's successes or failures in learning are not a reflection of the teacher's competence or the language teaching method he uses. Instead, they are a joint function of the student's attitudes, needs, and aptitude; the quality of the existing relationship between the teacher and the student; and the specific objective of the course in terms of the specialized language skills the teacher and the student agree upon to pursue.

These, to me, are the major premises that define the psychological bases of second language learning.

9.

How Bilingualism Has Been Described and Measured

W. F. MACKEY

The concept of bilingualism poses basic problems of identification and delimitation, such as those between language and dialect, between dialect and idiolect, between idiolect and discourse, between code and message – problems made more complex by the bilingual situations in which each language functions.

The Description of Bilingualism

How can we therefore describe bilingualism? Let us rather ask how bilingualism has been described. It has been described by category, dichotomy, and scale.

By category, bilingualism has been described according to proficiency and according to function. From the point of view of proficiency, such categories as "complete bilingualism," "perfect bilingualism," "partial bilingualism," "incipient bilingualism," and "passive bilingualism" have become current. From the point of view of function, we have heard of "home bilingualism," "school bilingualism," "street bilingualism," and similar terms, denoting the use to which bilingualism is put.

The disadvantage of such categories in the description of bilingualism is that they are either impossible to delimit (When does a person become a perfect bilingual?), or they overlap (Bilingualism of the street can also penetrate the home).

Bilingualism also has been described by the use of dichotomies. For

Adapted from *Description and Measurement of Bilingualism,* edited by L. G. Kelly, by permission of the University of Toronto Press. Copyright, Canada, 1969, by the University of Toronto Press.

William F. Mackey of the International Center for Research on Bilingualism at Laval University in Quebec, has taught at universities in Canada, England, and the United States. A well-known editor and author in the fields of bilingualism and second language teaching, his books include *Language Teaching Analysis, The Canadian Reader's Dictionary* (with M. West), *Principes de didactique analytique* (with L. Laforge), *Theory and Method in the Study of Bilingualism,* and *Bilingual Education in a Binational School: A Case Study of the Equal Maintenance of Languages by Free Alternation.*

example, there is coordinated versus compound bilingualism, individual versus national bilingualism, stable versus unstable bilingualism, balanced versus unbalanced bilingualism, pure versus mixed bilingualism, simultaneous versus sequential bilingualism, comprehensive versus limited bilingualism, organized versus incidental bilingualism, general versus specific bilingualism, regressive versus progressive bilingualism, personal versus institutional bilingualism, and so forth.

The difficulty in describing bilingualism through dichotomies has been that the categories are rarely mutually exclusive, and individual cases are rarely an either/or proposition. If they are made up of variables, we shall have to ask ourselves whether some of these could not be converted into scales and whether a number of such scales could not interlock to provide profiles.

This leads us to the third type of descriptive mode: bilingualism has sometimes been described in scales. For example, there are dominance configurations, profiles of bilingual background, and bilingual semantic differentials. The difficulty here is that many such scales presuppose standard units of measure which do not exist, and valid procedures for their delimitation. Such units also presuppose an understanding of the nature of what is measured as it does in other fields; before time could be measured, there had to be a concept of time; before energy could be gauged, there had to be an idea of what heat was. The concepts of time and energy led to the creation of units — hours, minutes, seconds — watts, volts, and horsepower.

Although the creation and standardization of units create a practical difficulty, the basic research required constitutes a theoretical advantage, since it forces us to establish valid measures for each of the many dimensions of bilingualism. It is also this type of description which is a prerequisite and most conducive to the establishment of measures.

The Measurement of Bilingualism

How can bilingualism be measured? Bilingualism has been measured according to the function, stability, and distribution of the languages involved, in relation to their location, origin, and dominance. These dimensions can apply both to the individual and the group.

Most measures presuppose the creation of units. In the measurement of bilingualism, this is rendered difficult by the fact that these units are not self-evident. They are, therefore, often simply measures of indices which are assumed to reflect certain variables of bilingualism, such as dominance, skill, and regression. Are these true indications of such variables? What does the presence of a certain feature really indicate?

Before being used as basis for units of measurement, such indices require validation. The problem has been threefold. First, there is the validation of suitable indices. To what extent, for example, is word-association skill an index of individual language dominance? What sort of data can be used as indices for the proportion of bilinguals of a certain degree in a given area?

Secondly, the obtaining of valid samples has often been difficult. For example, questionnaires have been used to measure language proficiency. Recorded samples have been obtained for the measurement of language function.

Thirdly, the elaboration of units of measurement poses a number of problems. Type-token ratios have been used as measures of interference. Percentages of loan-words have been used as measures of language dominance. Some measures have been based on various branches of statistics and information theory.

Dimensions of Enquiry

Systematic examination of all these indices, sampling techniques, and units of measure presents a number of problems. We must determine the extent to which they are valid, discard or modify some, and propose others. The necessary steps include delimitation of variables, the validation of appropriate indices, the choice of effective and acceptable units, and the elaboration of measurement techniques (developmental, psycholinguistic, linguistic, sociolinguistic, sociocultural, and demographic).

The first step is examination of the developmental aspects: the indices, sampling, and measures used in case studies. In this field of inquiry, researchers have used written questionnaires, oral recording, and descriptive introspection. Most studies, however, have taken into account only the bilingual's output. Few of them, if any, have also recorded input; that is, what the developing bilingual hears and reads.

Secondly, we must study the indices, sampling, and measures of bilingual proficiency, capacity, and performance. Most measures of this psycholinguistic dimension of bilingualism have been based on tests ranging from conventional, skill-based language tests through time-reaction tests on rapid word translation; oral reading of homographs and mixed word lists; word detection and word completion tests; reading of color names written in colors other than the name indicates; and a number of local tests invented for specific experiments.

What needs to be studied is the extent to which such tests are indices of bilingual proficiency or capacity. Does a standard word-translation test, for example, measure only language proficiency, only translation skill, only switching facility, or all three skills — and to what extent?

Our attention should also be directed to the linguistic aspects, including the measurement of interference and language distance. One of the main problems here is that of distinguishing between code and message, that of identifying each item in the bilingual's chain of speech and allocating it to one language or the other in the idiolect of the individual. The fact that the bilingual uses an item from the other language is not necessarily an indication of interference if this item has already become part of that individual's language norm. Among measures used, there have been word counts and type-token ratios in running texts.

After studying the measurement of how well the bilingual knows his languages, it is necessary to study what he does with them. This sociolinguistic dimension has to do with language function. Various models and configurations of dominance, bilingual background profiles, and other measures have been used, most of the data coming from questionnaires. One of the main problems here is to make sure that the measures give an accurate picture of the distribution of both languages throughout the entire behavior of the individual.

From the individual, we can pass to the sociocultural aspects, and consider the bilingual group as a group. How can we describe and measure the behavior of bilingual groups? The first problem here is the isolation of behavioral features of the bilingual group which are distinct from those of each unilingual group with which there is contact. This behavior may be both linguistic and nonlinguistic. It may reflect group attitudes and prejudices, group values and customs. The description of these may range from the anecdotal to the statistical. Measurements have included direct tests of group attitudes and indirect tests based on questionnaires and pre-recorded voice guises.

Finally, there are the demographic aspects: the measurement of bilingual populations. In many countries, this is a practical problem of great importance. Several countries keep language statistics, but these either say very little or are largely meaningless. The problem is first that of collecting large masses of data with simple questionnaires, and second, that of finding out how to classify people as bilinguals from the evidence of their answers to a question which, for practical reasons, has to be simple. What sort of question should it be? This will depend of course on the arbitrary significance which we can give to the word bilingual. And here, we come full circle and are again faced with the problem of definition. We could next look into the possibility of devising a series of questions which would design a profile of language contact, thus obviating the problem of definition and that of deciding on a dividing line.

In the study of these six dimensions of bilingualism, we will find that we are faced with different types of data normally dealt with by such diverse disciplines as psychology, linguistics, sociology, anthropology, and perhaps politics, law, and government. Each discipline has been in the habit of categorizing and representing these data according to its own conventions and dealing with the results in its own way to arrive at its own theory of bilingualism.

If we are to succeed in our objectives of effectively describing and measuring bilingualism, we must attempt to elaborate common categories and common or related types of representation of the same phenomena to describe such inherent differences as may exist between the bilingual and the unilingual, the differences among bilinguals themselves, the interpersonal and intergroup relations among and between bilinguals and unilinguals. A great help here would be a general and unified theory of bilingualism.

In our search for measures, however, it might be salutary to remember that, in the final analysis, all measures are arbitrary. Even the hours and minutes, which are so much part of our daily lives, are simply arbitrary measures of time. The important thing is that they have been so efficient for the sort of time measures which we required.

We can hardly expect measures of bilingualism to be less arbitrary. But we can insist that they effectively measure what we shall agree to call the constituent elements of any given dimension of bilingualism.

We cannot reasonably expect immediate and unanimous adoption of any proposals, when we consider that as recently as the late 1700s twenty competing thermometer scales were still in use, and England, after 170 years of hesitation, had finally got around to adopting the Gregorian calendar. So there is still hope for the decimal monetary unit, the centigrade thermometer, and the metric system. And also, we hope, for universal measures of bilingualism.

10.

English as a Second Language for Navajos

ROBERT W. YOUNG

Cultural Borrowing

In everyday parlance we use the term *culture* in a wide variety of contexts and meanings ranging from "proper" social deportment to the acquisition of "refined" tastes in music, literature, and the arts. In addition, the term forms part of the specialized vocabulary of several disciplines, including agriculture, bacteriology, and anthropology. In the latter, and in this chapter, *culture* refers to the varied systems developed by human societies as media for adaptation to the environment in which their members live; in its totality, a cultural system constitutes the means through which the group to which it pertains achieves survival as an organized society. Such systems range from simple to the complex and sophisticated, and among themselves they exhibit a wide variety of differences in form and content.

When we speak of the culture of a society or community, we have reference to the entire gamut of tools, institutions, social values, customs, traditions, techniques, concepts, and other traits that characterize the way of life of the group. The specific items that make up a cultural system, or *elements* as they are called, fall into two broad categories: material and nonmaterial. In the first are included such features as tools (axes, hammers, jacks), vehicles (wagons, cars, airplanes), clothing (shirts, dresses, shoes) and shelter (houses, tents, hogans); and among the nonmaterial elements of culture are such institutions as social organization, kinship systems, marriage, government, religion, and language.

Adapted from *English as a Second Language for Navajos: An Overview of Certain Cultural and Linguistic Factors,* revised edition, by Robert W. Young (Albuquerque: Bureau of Indian Affairs Area Office, 1968).

Robert W. Young of the Department of Linguistics, University of New Mexico, served as Albuquerque area tribal operations officer with the Bureau of Indian Affairs for more than thirty years. A leading authority on the Athapaskan languages, he is well known as one of the developers of the Navajo language alphabet.

The content of a given cultural system is determined by a wide range of factors, including the physical environment, inventiveness of the people, influence of surrounding communities, trade, opportunities for borrowing, and many others. For obvious reasons the material content of traditional Eskimo culture contained elements of a type not found in the cultures of the peoples living in the tropical rain forests or of those living in the hot deserts. The physical environment, in each instance, imposed different requirements for survival, and a different framework for cultural development.

Borrowing and trade have had a tremendous influence on cultural content, in modern as well as in ancient times, and a cursory glance at the present day Eskimo, the Navajo or, for that matter, virtually any community of people anywhere on earth, is sufficient to reflect the importance of these avenues for cultural change and growth. Guns, steel axes, knives, metal fishhooks, motorboats, rubber boots, stoves, tobacco, liquor, and a host of items have been borrowed and incorporated into Eskimo culture in the course of contact with outside cultural communities; horses, sheep, goats, iron tools, wagons, automobiles, radio, television, and many other elements have been borrowed by, and have become part of the cultural systems of such people as the Navajo since their first contact with Europeans. And in Japan, Western European and American influences have changed the way of life in less than a century.

In Alaska, in the American Southwest, and elsewhere, the pace of cultural change has quickened with each generation, as aboriginal peoples respond to changing conditions of life. To no small degree, the dominant Anglo-American system, with its emphasis on molding the environment itself to human need, has established new conditions for life and survival; new conditions so complex in nature that the institution of the school has come to occupy a position of primary importance providing, as it does, the training necessary for successful living.

Formal education, in modern American society, is designed to facilitate the successful adaptation and survival of its members within an environment and under conditions that the society itself, to a large extent has created. The educational system is not only one that cultural minorities have *borrowed,* but one which the Anglo-American cultural community has imposed upon them. With reference to such culturally divergent minorities, formal education is the instrument used by the dominant society to generate and accelerate cultural change through the medium of induced "acculturation" — that is, the process through which such communities as the Navajo are induced and trained to participate in the dominant national cultural system. It is, in a broad sense, a form of cultural borrowing, differing however from the more usual process of voluntarily picking and choosing, on the part of the borrower, in that some of the stimuli for change are imposed and the initiative is taken by the "lending" system itself. Unfortunately, the process of induced or — as it often turns out, *compelled* — acculturation is not without its problems for the "lender" as well as for the "borrower." The need for change is not always as apparent to the latter as it is to the former, and in the absence of recognition of compelling necessity, the borrower is sometimes reluctant to accept what is held out to him. It may not appear, from his viewpoint, to fit his requirements, or its acceptance may threaten existing institutions and practices upon which he places value.

Consequently, compulsory education, when first imposed upon Indian communities by the federal government just before the turn of the century, met with strenuous resistance. From the hopeful point of view of the would-be "lender," schooling offered improved tools for survival in a changing environment; but from that of the "borrower" the educational process threatened cultural extinction. It removed the child from the home where he received his traditional training in the language, values, religion, and other institutions of his own culture and promised to leave him ill-prepared for life in the only world his parents knew. They resisted and the "lenders" applied force. A long tug-of-war followed.

A comparable situation developed when, in the 1930s, the compelling need to conserve natural resources in the Navajo country led to livestock reduction and the introduction of a wage economy as a new economic base for the Navajo people. From the point of view of the lending society, this was a new and superior device for survival; but from the Navajo viewpoint it threatened cultural extinction. Coupled with the process of formal education, the new economic system constituted a threat to the traditional social organization of the tribe, as well as to the religious life of the people, not to mention the economic pursuits, residence patterns, and associated values that were basic to the traditional Navajo way of life. Like compulsory education in the days of Black Horse[1], the new economic urgings so necessary from the viewpoint of the "lender" met with violent resistance by the prospective "borrowers."

Time, among other factors, is usually an important ingredient in cultural change, whether the change takes place through a process of voluntary borrowing or through one of induced acculturation. *In the latter case, the degree of success and the quantity of time required hinge, to no small degree, on the depth of understanding attained by the "lender," and on the effectiveness of applied techniques.*

The fact is that a culture is more than a system of material and nonmaterial elements that can be listed, catalogued, and classified. A culture constitutes a complex set of habits of doing, thinking, and reacting to stimuli — habits that one acquires in early childhood and which, for the most part, he continues to share, throughout his life, with fellow members of his cultural community. In its totality, a cultural system is a frame of reference that shapes and governs one's picture of the world around him. Within this framework and, as Whorf[2] pointed out in 1956, within the frame of reference imposed by the structure of the language he speaks, one is conditioned to look upon the world about him in a manner that may differ substantially from that characterizing another and distinct cultural system.

As a consequence, from the point of view of his own system, one man, looking at a vast expanse of trees through his cultural window, may choose the expansiveness of the forest as the salient feature of the landscape, without reference to the species that compose it, and so describe the scene by applying appropriate terms in his language; another man, viewing the same scene from the vantage point of another cultural window might see and describe it quite differently as large numbers of specific types of trees — oaks, elms, maples. From the point of view of his own system one man, looking at the passage of time within the limits imposed by his cultural perspective, may conceive of it, measure, and describe it *only* in terms of the rising and setting of the sun, the recurring phases of the moon, or the sequence of seasons; another man may add mechanical and mathematical or astronomical measurements, including hours, minutes, seconds, days, months, years, decades, centuries, millennia, and light years — one system may place maximum importance on the element of time and its exact measurement, while another may attach little or no importance to the same phenomenon. Similarly, one may look at an object and describe its color as *green* in contradistinction to *blue;* but another may apply a term meaning both green and blue (Navajo *dootł'izh,* for example), and if the distinction is of paramount importance may make it by comparison with something possessing the proper shade (Navajo *tátł'id naxalingo dootł'izh* — blue like water-scum — green).

The manner in which the members of one cultural community conceive of the world around them, and their relationship with it, may differ substantially from the manner in which the members of another such community look upon and react to it — this is true even where the cultural groups concerned occupy similar physical environments, and in situations where the concepts are not conditioned by geographical factors.

Likewise, what is "logical" and "reasonable" to one system may be quite the contrary to another. There are few, if any, cultural absolutes but many "relatives," in this regard. To a Navajo or Pueblo Indian, whose culture has developed an elaborate system through which man strives for the maintenance of harmony with nature, the Anglo-American concept of actively controlling natural forces in the interest of man's survival, and the media through which to accomplish this may not always appear reasonable. In the late fifties the Navajo Tribal Council, after long debate and against the better judgment of most of the Navajo community, authorized the use of a small amount (ten thousand dollars) of tribal funds to employ a technician to seed the clouds with silver iodide in an effort to break a period of severe drought. The experiment met with very limited success, especially in view of the paucity of appropriate clouds — and there were those who complained that the propellers of the airplane blew away such rainclouds as appeared over the horizon. In subsequent council action, which met with the enthusiastic support of most tribal leaders and members, the unused residue of the appropriation was diverted to defray the cost of reconstructing and carrying on a ceremony that had fallen into disuse, and which had formerly been relied upon to produce rain. The ceremonial procedure was "logical" to traditionally oriented members of the tribe because it was consonant with the position that man must maintain himself in harmony with nature; at the same time, the cloud-seeding process was "logical" to non-Navajos who were culturally conditioned to a scientific approach in attaining control over nature for man's benefit. The two processes reflect fundamentally different points of view regarding natural phenomena and man's relationship to them; they pertain to different cultural frames of reference — and, to the delight of the proponents of the ceremonial approach, it did, in fact, rain!

Borrowed elements of material culture generally find ready acceptance if they represent an obvious improvement or otherwise meet an immediate need in the estimation of the borrower. Replacement of a stone ax by one made of steel does not require radical complimentary cultural changes; both instruments have the same function. Such patently practical improvements are capable of smooth incorporation into a system, with few if any repercussions. Even the horse, whose introduction revolutionized the way of life of peoples such as the Navajo and the Indians of the Great Plains, was readily accommodated within the Indian cultures, apparently without seriously shaking the foundations on which those systems rested. Wagons, automobiles, trucks, radios, television, Pendleton blankets, and a host of other objects have since entered the Navajo scene, and have become part of the system without creating insuperable problems or generating a high level of resistance. The cultural system merely flowed around such innovations, after the fashion of an ameba around its prey, and made them part of itself without seriously modifying its own basic structure. History seems to reflect the fact that people literally threw away their stone axes and knives when steel tools became available; and the production of pottery for utilitarian purposes has all but disappeared since the advent of more durable utensils for the Indian housewife.

Not so, however, with the nonmaterial elements of culture — the institutions pertaining to religion, social organization, kinship, language, marriage, or social values. The Navajo or the Pueblo did not junk his own religion for Christianity; discard his own language for Spanish or English; or drop his clan, kinship, or other social system in favor of a borrowed replacement. Such nonmaterial elements as these are among the mainstays in the cultural framework and, as such, they undergo change at a much slower rate than do those relating to the tangible material culture. The successful incorporation of such Anglo-American institutions as formal education, representative democratic government, the father-centered family, a system of justice based on coercive laws, and modern medicine into Navajo culture has been slow and painful because they are or were elements that did not fit the accustomed cultural framework; their incorporation necessitates a host of radical adjustments in the complex of fundamental cultural habits of the people before they can be accommodated — in fact, incorporation of the entire range of such alien institutions has profound implications for the very survival of the borrowing system itself.

The immediate value of these institutions as improved tools for survival, intangible and complex as they are, has not been as readily apparent to the potential borrower as it was in the case of the steel ax, the horse, or the gun. Material elements from non-Indian culture have continued to be accepted, and incorporated wholesale into that of the Navajo and other Indian tribes, but incorporation of the values, customs, concepts, language, associated habits, and institutions of the outside community enter slowly and painfully, often only as the result of heavy pressure.

The concept of coercion, in the sense of imposing one's will on another person or animate being without physical contact or force, is part of the Anglo-American cultural heritage, and the English language is replete with terms expressing various aspects of the concept — *cause, force, oblige, make, compel, order, command, constrain, must, have to, ought to, shall* — come quickly to mind. They are part of the heritage of a culture with a long history of kings, emperors, dictators, deities, governments, and family patriarchs, whose authority to impose their will on others has been long accepted as part of the world view of the communities participating in the system. So deeply ingrained is this area of habitual acceptance of the compelling, coercive need to do certain things that Anglos are astonished and annoyed by the lack of concern in the same area on the part of people like the Navajo, as reflected by the paucity of terms in the language of the latter corresponding to those listed above. How does one say *ought to, must, duty,* or *responsibility* in Navajo? Such circumlocutions, from the English point of view, as *ákǫ́ǫ́ deesháałgo t'éiyá yá' át'ééh — It is only good that I shall go there,* seems to lack the force of compelling necessity implicit in *I* **must** *go there, I* **have to** *go there.* Likewise, when *I* **make** *the horse run,* the action of the horse is implicitly the result of the imposition of my will over his. *Łį́į́' shá yilghoł — The horse is running* **for** *me,* implies an action, on the part of the horse, that is essentially voluntary. Again, to the English-speaking person the Navajo expression appears to be weak and lacking the important overtone of coercive authority — of forcing the beast to yield to the will of a master. And when Anglos find that not even the deities of the Navajo pantheon or the political leaders of the tribe are wont to issue mandates to be obeyed by men, they are likely to be as perplexed as the Navajo who finds the reverse to be true in Anglo-American society.

Navajo culture does not have a heritage of coercive religions or of political or patriarchal family figures, and in the Navajo scheme of things one does not usually impose his will on another animate being to the same extent, and in the same ways as one does from the English point of view. *I* **made** *my wife sing* becomes, in Navajo, simply *even though my wife did not want to do so, she sang when I told her to sing (she' esdzáán doo íinízin da ndi xótaał bidishníigo xóótááł.)* From the Navajo point of view, one can compel his children to go to school in the sense that he *drives* him *(bíníshchéén)* or them *(bíníshkad)* there; or he can *place* them in school *(nínínil),* but none of these terms reflect the imposition of one's will independently of physical force — the children do not comply with a mandate. They are animate "objects" with wills of their own.

On the other hand, with reference to inanimate objects, lacking a will of their own, appropriate causative verb forms exist. *Yibąs,* in Navajo, means *it* [a wheel-like object] *is rolling along,* while a causative form, *yoołbąs,* conveys the meaning *he is* **making** *it roll along; he is rolling it along* [by physical contact]. *Naaghá* means *he is walking around,* and a causative form, *nabiishłá,* can be translated *I am making him walk around* — but only in the sense of *I am walking him around* (as a baby or a drunk person, for example, by holding him up and physically moving him about). The causative action expressed by *yoołbąs* and *nabiishłá* has, in both instances the same connotation; both actions are produced as a result of physical contact, and not by the imposition of the agent's will with acquiescence by the actor. To express the concept of obliging a person to walk against his will, by mandate, one is likely to take the same approach as that described with reference to "making" one's wife sing, even though she does not wish to do so. One can, of course, *order* or *command* another person *(yił'aad)* but the term carries the connotation of *sending* him to perform an action; it does not follow that he complies. In the Navajo cultural-linguistic framework, animate objects are more frequently and commonly viewed as acting voluntarily than as acting as the result of imposition of another animate object's will.

The Navajo parent is likely to ask a child if it *wants* to go to school, rather than issuing a mandate to the effect that it *must* go. By the same token, coercive laws are distasteful from the Navajo point of view, and the tribal leadership has long preferred persuasion to force, even in applying "compulsory" education laws on the reservation. As a result, acceptance of the Anglo-American police and court system, based as it is on the principle of compulsive behavior — the enforcement of coercive laws — has still not been comfortably accommodated within the Navajo cultural framework, despite the fact that the tribal government supports a system of tribal courts and a well-equipped police force. Nor is the concept of impersonal punishment through the imposition of a fine or jail sentence, in lieu of payment to the victim of a crime or act of violence, "reasonable" from the traditional Navajo viewpoint. Many types of disputes, both civil and criminal, were customarily resolved in local community meetings in the very recent past, and the procedure probably continues to the present day. In some instances, such solutions involve payment of money or goods by one party to another.

The contrasting Anglo and Navajo viewpoints regarding coercion merely serve to exemplify the many other conflicting cultural values that serve to complicate interaction between these two societies.[3] In addition, we might elaborate a bit upon the cultural differences that exist regarding the nature of knowledge and the purposes and methods of education. Traditionally in Navajo society, the acquisiton of knowledge involved rote learning of practical experience. The process of rote learning was predicated on the premise that the answers to all philosophical questions were already contained in the body of Navajo religious literature (mythology, as it is often termed), and one had only to seek it out; while adequate methods relating to such practices as animal husbandry and agriculture had already been developed in Navajo culture, and therefore one had only to learn them by experience. The learner was not expected to question the body of facts or the traditional methodology. To no small degree rote learning is a factor in the Anglo-American education system, but generally Anglos have accepted the fact that they do not possess all knowledge in an absolute sense, and they encourage their children to question and test theories and hypotheses and to strive to make their own contribution to the fund of human knowledge. This approach to the acquisition of knowledge reflects Anglo-American acceptance of change in the interest of "progress," and the requirement that opinions and practices be supported by a strong rationale. Rote learning is defensible on the premise that it provides the tools required to support initiative thinking, but it is not universally accepted in Anglo-American society as an ideal end in itself.

Such cultural conflicts cannot be readily resolved. They constitute divergent habits, habitual attitudes and systems, which are part of the main fabric of the societies to which they belong, and change in one area carries the need for change in others. Such situations sometimes resemble cards: the removal of one card in a key location threatens to tumble the entire structure.

Culture is a complex system of interrelated habits.

Linguistic Borrowing

The nature and function of language assume different perspectives as they are examined by different disciplines. The psychologist, the philosopher, the linguist, the physiologist, and the anthropologist are each concerned with different facets of the phenomenon of speech — but from the standpoint of the social scientist a language becomes an integral part of the culture of the people who speak it or, for that matter, who use it in any of its several secondary forms (writing, gestures, signals, signs, mathematical formulas, artistic and other representations). Whatever its form, language comprises a set of signals that serve the need, in human society, for the intercommunication of ideas and concepts. In addition, the structure and content of a given system of speech, as Whorf[4], Sapir[5], Hoijer[6], and others have pointed out — in combination with associated cultural features — establishes a frame of reference within which the process of reasoning itself takes place; it is a framework that molds the worldview of the speakers of a given language and one that tends to confine that view to the boundaries and perspective of the cultural system in which such speakers are participants. Like the rest of culture, a system of language, with its characteristic patterns of expression, elements of phonology, and structural features, comprises a complex set of distinctive habits. In short, the sum total of the values, attitudes, concepts, and modes of expression of a community constitute the frame of reference within which its members conceive of, look upon, describe, react to, and explain the world in which they live and their relationships with it — it is their window on the universe.

The lexicon, or elements of vocabulary, of a speech system can be compared to the material elements (tools, weapons, etc.) of culture — such elements of speech, like tools, may be borrowed from another language system, or existing terms, like existing tools, may be modified to meet new requirements. Words, as these units are commonly called, again like tools, may come and go. But unlike elements of vocabulary, the structural-grammatical features of a language and the characteristic pattern in which they are used to reflect the world of its speakers constitute a framework that changes much more slowly; structural, grammatical features (and the patterns governing the expression of ideas) are analogous, in this context, to the fundamental elements of a culture — its institutions of religion, social and political organization, and values.

As cultures change — and none are static — those changes reflect in language, because, as we have pointed out, language itself is a reflection of the total culture of its speakers — a catalog and transmitter of the elements and features of the entire social system. There are few, if any, "primitive" cultures in the sense that they are rudimentary in form and content; and by the same token there are few, if any, truly "rudimentary" speech forms. Cultural and linguistic systems may be, of course, relatively more or less complex, in a comparative sense; but their viability hinges on the extent to which they meet group requirements, and the demands of successful social living are rarely, if ever, simple. In fact, the languages of relatively simple cultural systems may be structurally highly complex, while those of comparatively complex societies may be quite simple, as exemplified by a comparison of Navajo and English.

Neither culture generally, nor language in particular, are static; both are in a constant state of change for a large variety of reasons, including cultural and linguistic borrowing. English *tobacco* is, in its origin, a Carib Indian word; and Navajo *béeso (money)* has its origin in Spanish *peso.* Sometimes vocabulary grows to meet new needs through a process of extending the meaning of a pre-existing label: English *car* now describes any vehicle on wheels, but it was once a term applied to a Celtic war chariot; Navajo *K'aa'* is the name for *arrow* and, by extension, *bullet (bee'eldǫǫh bik' a', gun's arrow = bullet),* and *łeetsoii — yellow ochre* is, by extension, applied to uranium ore. In other situations, new words are coined as labels for the identification of new objects: English *kodak, radar;* Navajo *chidí naa' na'í* (caterpillar tractor — literally *crawling automobile).* Verb labels, as well as names (nouns) are extended in meaning to meet new needs. Thus English *start* came to be applied to the process of causing a combustion engine to begin operation, and *run* came to be applied to the operation itself. Navajo *diits'a'* means *it is making a noise,* and the term was transferred to describe the operation of a gasoline motor, to meaning *it is running.* By analogy with other verbal constructions the term *disétts' ą́ą́' — I caused it to make noise,* came into use to describe the act of starting a motor — that is, *causing* it to make noise.

These borrowings, with other developmental changes, are part of the process through which language grows to compliment other types of cultural change. However, like the replacement of a stone ax with a steel implement, changes of this type do not seriously disturb the structural and conceptual framework underlying a given speech system: rather, they enrich it and maintain it abreast of changing communicational needs.

Sweeping cultural change sometimes results in the discarding of an entire language, with adoption of the speech system of the new culture — or such change may result in the relegation of a language to a position of secondary importance. The introduction of English and other European speech forms as the languages of science and education in so-called "underdeveloped countries" (that is, countries inhabited by cultural minority peoples) seriously affects the status of the local language and may result in its sharp decline or extinction. Many American Indian languages, as well as many tribal languages of Africa and Asia have followed, or may well follow, such a course to more or less quickly join the ranks of the myriads of dead languages (and associated cultures) of the world. At the same time, in other situations, the languages of minority cultures have survived (Welsh, for example), or have themselves become the vehicle of communication with reference to a radically changed cultural system (Japanese, for example). A system of language that does not keep pace with cultural change is not likely to survive.

Notes

1. Black Horse was a Navajo leader of the 1890s who was violently opposed to education. *See* The Bureau of Indian Affairs, "The Trouble at Round Rock," Navajo Historical Series No. 2 (Washington, D.C.: U.S. Government Printing Office, 1952).
2. Benjamin Lee Whorf, *Language, Thought and Reality* (Cambridge, Mass.: M.I.T. Press, 1956).
3. An excellent analysis of conflicting cultural values relating to Southwestern Indian and Mexican-American communities is provided in Miles V. Zintz, "Final Report, Indian Research Study" (Albuquerque: University of New Mexico College of Education, 1960).
4. Whorf, *Language, Thought and Reality.*
5. Edward Sapir, "Language and Environment," in *Selected Writings in Language, Culture, and Personality,* ed. David J. Mandelbaum (Berkeley: University of California Press, 1949).
6. Harry Hoijer, "Culture Implications of Some Navaho Linguistic Categories," *Language* 27 (1951): 111–20.

11.

Navajo Language Maintenance:
Six-Year-Olds in 1969

BERNARD A. SPOLSKY

While the general question of the status of American Indian languages is often discussed, there are few statistics available to support claims of loss or retention. Fishman[1] does not treat the topic except to refer to Chafe[2] as the source of the estimate that only 40% of the 300 languages or dialects extant have more than 100 speakers, and that more than half of these have speakers of very advanced ages. Kinkade[3] gives data on the language spoken at Haskell Institute in 1969. These figures might be compared with those published by Stuart[4] on the same school a number of years earlier. But, as Kinkade points out, the data are not strictly comparable, nor do they form a basis for reasonable hypotheses about language retention or currency. The key difficulty is the nature of the sample: Indian children who have spoken their own language at home are much less likely to reach Haskell than those who speak English at home. A language census based only on older people is contaminated by the fact that school is always a factor in the acquisition of English and the loss of the native language. Even an exceptional school like Rough Rock Demonstration School, with its acceptance of the principle of teaching in Navajo, still uses English as the medium of instruction after the first year or two.

One way around this problem is to look at the language used by six-year-old children at the time when they first come to school. Whatever other measures of language maintenance may be established, the most important is surely the parents' choice of language to speak to their chil-

Reprinted from *Language Sciences* 13 (Dec. 1970): pp. 19–24.

Bernard A. Spolsky of the departments of Linguistics and Elementary Education at the University of New Mexico has been educational consultant for the Bureau of Indian Affairs since 1967. A specialist in descriptive linguistics, he has edited (with Paul Garvin) *Computation in Linguistics: A Case Book* and *The Language Education of Minority Children: Selected Readings.*

dren. Thus, while parents with strong ethnic or national or religious ties may choose to have their children learn an ethnic language in school or church, the fact that they themselves speak English to them at home is clearly the best guide to their basic attitude. When one finds, for instance, a pueblo expressing interest in having its language taught in Head Start programs or elementary school, one is tempted to see this as evidence of a strong desire to maintain the language; but in fact it reflects the situation that English is now a first language for their children. Official tribal policy is language maintenance, but the actual home policy is to switch to English.

The survey detailed in this chapter was carried out in order to provide a picture of the present status of the Navajo language, to serve as a baseline for later studies of any change, and to permit some degree of prediction of the direction and speed of language loss. The size of the Navajo nation and the fact that it is settled in a reasonably self-contained area means that maintenance is much more practical for Navajo than for the hundreds of smaller tribal groups that have lost or are losing their language; nevertheless, there is a steady increase in the amount of English spoken on and off the reservation, and a related percentage decrease in knowledge of Navajo. (But, of all Indian languages, there has been an absolute increase in speakers.)

The general method adopted in our study was to prepare a simple questionnaire to be completed by teachers in schools on or near the reservation. The data gathered on the language of six-year-old children were then correlated with two measures of acculturation: the type of school, and the distance from the nearest off-reservation town. The results permit the following generalizations:

1. Over-all, 73% of Navajo six-year-olds in the study come to school not speaking enough English to do first grade work.
2. The farther a school is from an off-reservation town, the more likely its pupils are to speak Navajo.
3. The farther children live away from a school, the more likely they are to speak Navajo at home.
4. Language is maintained for some time even when other traditional features of life are given up.

The questionnaire sent out to teachers asked them to describe the language capabilities of each of their six-year-old Navajo pupils at the time of starting school. Teachers were advised to ask help from other staff members if they needed it; this was to encourage them to ask Navajo aides about the students' knowledge of Navajo. They were asked to place each child on a five-point scale:

N: When the child first came to school, he or she appeared to know only Navajo, and no English.

N-e: When the child first came to school, he or she appeared to know mainly Navajo; he or she knew a little English, but not enough to do first grade work.

N-E: When the child came to school, he or she was equally proficient in English and Navajo.

n-E: When the child came to school, he or she knew mainly English and also knew a bit of Navajo.

E: When the child came to school, he or she knew only English.

In case they were uncertain, teachers were asked to use a question mark rather than a check mark in the appropriate column; only 12 out of 171 used the question mark.

The questionnaire was distributed by the Bureau of Indian Affairs area office in Window Rock to all BIA schools on the reservation; completed forms were received from all but 5 of the 69 schools. It was also distributed to all schools in the Gallup-McKinley County school district, and to a number of other public school districts. (The Gallup-McKinley school board also sent a modified form of the questionnaire to the public schools at Zuni. Returns from these placed 101 out of 110 children in a Z-e column: Children who speak mainly Zuni, know a few words of English, but not enough for first grade work.)

Complete raw scores and percentage scores for each school were collected. (See Table 11.1 following in this chapter.) We also calculated an index for each school of the degree of Navajo use by its six-year-olds. This index was calculated by assigning a value to each column (N = 5, N-e = 4, N-E = 3, n-E = 2, E = 1), and finding the average for the pupils in the school. A second index, the total of the percentages in the first two columns, was also calculated; this gave some estimate of the percentage of children considered by their teachers not to know enough English to to first grade work. The next measure determined was a figure to represent the relative accessibility of the school itself to the nearest comparatively large off-reservation town; towns used were Gallup, Farmington, Flagstaff, Winslow, Holbrook, and Cortez. The accessibliity index was calculated as follows. Using a good up-to-date road map (Map No. 2345, "Indian Country," published by the Automobile Club of Southern California), we took distances on improved paved roads at face value; multiplied by two distances on gravel roads; multiplied by three distances on graded dirt roads; and multiplied by four distances on ungraded dirt roads. Thus, an accessibility index of 80 could mean 80 miles on paved road; or 20 miles on graded dirt road and another 20 miles on paved road; and so on. Anyone who has tried to travel on reservation roads in wet weather will appreciate the reasoning here. The two indices of amount of Navajo and the index of accessibility were correlated (Table 11.2).'

Results

Table 11.1 lists all the schools from which returns were received, and shows the number and percentage of children assigned to each category. It will be noted that we have data on a total of 2,893 six-year-olds. Of these, 943 or 33% were reported to know Navajo only, and 1,188 or 41% were reported to know Navajo mainly, with some English but not enough to do first grade work. It would be valuable to know more about the background of these two categories. One reasonable assumption is that many of the children placed in the column N-e get there because they have been to a preschool program of some kind: a Head Start or a kindergarten program of the sort that is starting to be established on the reservation. These preschool programs are often taught by Navajo-speaking teachers, and have Navajo aides, but a start is always made on teaching English. Thus, N-e could reflect either a community where there is some contact with English, and some English spoken around the children, or, more generally, a school with a preschool program.

The middle category, N-E, is of course the most unsatisfactory. There are at present no simple instruments to determine language dominance in a six-year-old Navajo child; it is also too much to expect a non-Navajo-speaking teacher to be able to make a reliable judgment on the Navajo proficiency of her pupils. Basically, though, we may assume that a teacher checking this column is saying: "I've heard this child speak Navajo with his peers or the aide, but I know that he can understand me when I talk to him, and he seems to manage first grade work in English all right." One feels somewhat doubtful that there are in fact 473 (or 16%) such paragons of bilingualism; future studies will be needed to assess the reliability and validity of this category in particular.

The questionnaire we used did not permit us to decide how many of the 298, or 10% graded n-E or E, native speakers of English, are in fact children of Anglos rather than Navajos. There are a number of Anglo employees on the reservation, and in some cases, employees' children are permitted to go to BIA schools. In the more crucial case of the Gallup-McKinley schools, however, we may be confident that only Navajo children have been included in the sample.

Some evidence of the regional variation may be arrived at by looking at the figures (raw totals and percentages) for the five agencies of the BIA (Table 11.3). As might be expected, the Fort Defiance Agency and the Shiprock Agency turn out to have the highest percentage of

English speakers; this reflects the two main settlement areas at Window Rock and Shiprock. The other three agencies have low English use. This tendency is explained in part by the distance factor considered below; the average distance of schools from off-reservation centers for each agency is given in Table 11.4.

A calculation of the correlation of the indices of degree of Navajo and accessibility (Table 11.2) shows that the two indices of Navajo correlated with each other very highly: .913 (Pearson); the first index correlated .517 and the second .413 with the index of accessibility. The first index is, as mentioned above, probably a better general measure for the data; it takes into account the general distribution, while the second ignores distribution within the columns. We can see clear evidence then in support of the notion that the loss of Navajo correlates with accessibility of off-reservation towns. Behind this is the notion that the closer one lives to the edge of the reservation, the more likely one is to have given up on traditional reservation values. (By "edge" we mean not the edge of the reservation as it appears on a map, of course, but the edge as provided by the presence of an off-reservation shopping center.) The correlation of about .5 is probably a reasonable picture of the significance of the factor, for there are of course other factors that account for language maintenance.

A second fact, on which we do not have direct evidence, but for which evidence can be derived from our data, is the factor of distance of a child's home from the school. This we may assume to account for some of the inter-child variation, but we have no evidence for that. It should also account for some of the interschool variation. That this is so can be seen when we compare the results we get for BIA and public schools. One of the factors that decides whether a child goes to a public school or a BIA boarding school is his distance from the school, or rather from a school bus route: the general principle is that a child must live more than 1½ miles from a public school bus route before he is permitted to be enrolled in a BIA boarding school. There are probably exceptions, but this gives a measure of general tendency. Now, the comparison between BIA schools as a whole and public schools is clear. For the BIA schools we have an index of Navajo of 4.30, and for the public schools in the sample, omitting Gallup urban schools, an index of 3.58. Again, if we compare individual schools in the same area, we find that Kayenta BIA boarding school for example has an index of 4.72 and Kayenta public elementary school an index of 3.67. (See Table 11.5 for other pairs.) It would be of value to support these data by collecting actual figures of the distance that individual pupils live from school so that one could determine the contribution of this factor to the general picture.

To use these results to predict future trends is difficult. Let us for the moment accept our figure that about 25% of the children on the reservation are being spoken to by their parents in English. One suggestive comparison is possible if we consider some data collected by Witherspoon (personal communication); he estimates that one-third of the over-forty generation had any schooling in English, two-thirds of the 20-40 year olds, and most of 6-20 year olds. Now, assuming that the middle group are the present child-raising group, we find that with two-thirds of the parents exposed to English at school, four-fifths of them continue to speak Navajo to their children. Of course a great number of the 20-40 year olds who completed school will be living off the reservation, so that we do not have data on the language spoken to their children. It is nonetheless a reasonable assumption that going to school is not enough to lead to a loss of language. But the figure of those completing elementary school and going on to high school is nearer to one-third of the 20-40 generation. Allowing that these are also the ones who are likely to stay off the reservation, we see a much closer fit between a person's completing elementary school and the likelihood that as a parent he will speak English to his children. If this is so, we might expect to see a great decrease in the amount of Navajo spoken as soon as the educational system on the reservation starts to be effective and as soon as more and better roads are built.

One of the central questions in the study of bilingualism is the degree to which it is possible for a group to maintain their language even when accepting other cultural values. There are of course numbers of cases of peoples who have managed to develop a modern industrial society without giving up their national language. It is not easy, but it can be done. A necessary concomitant of such a result is a highly developed sense of national identity, and a movement supporting the national language as symbol of that identity. Whether this will develop with the Navajos remains to be seen. An earlier attempt at language standardization and modernization, with a widespread Navajo literacy campaign and an associated newspaper, petered out. A new impetus has started, closely tied with education, and focused in a couple of schools. If it succeeds, it will of course have a considerable effect on future language maintenance.

We see our survey then as a first step. In future studies, we plan to find methods of testing the reliability and validity of the teachers' judgments on which we depend, and to attempt to gather other data that might be relevant (such as whether a child has older brothers or sisters at school and whether he attended a Head Start program). But at the moment we can safely say that one Indian language, at least, is not about to die between the completion of the linguist's description and its publication.

Table 11.1
Summary of Questionnaire Results

SCHOOLS	N		N-e		N-E		n-E		E	
BUREAU OF INDIAN AFFAIRS:										
Chinle Agency:										
Chinle	22	(79%)	6	(21%)	0		0		0	
Low Mountain	12	(32%)	18	(49%)	5	(14%)	1	(3%)	1	(3%)
Lukachukai	26	(44%)	23	(39%)	10	(17%)	0		0	
Many Farms	16	(67%)	0		8	(33%)	0		0	
Nazlini	18	(82%)	3	(14%)	1	(5%)	0		0	
Piñon	52	(75%)	16	(23%)	0		0		1	(1%)
Rock Point	19	(43%)	24	(55%)	1	(2%)	0		0	
Cottonwood Day	9	(22%)	30	(73%)	2	(5%)	0		0	
Eastern Navajo Agency:										
Baca	2	(33%)	4	(67%)	0		0		0	
Cheechilgeetho	7	(24%)	18	(62%)	1	(3%)	3	(10%)	0	
Crownpoint	7	(27%)	17	(65%)	2	(8%)	0		0	
Lake Valley	14	(100%)	0		0		0		0	
Mariano Lake										
Pueblo Pintado	14	(38%)	15	(41%)	5	(14%)	3	(8%)	0	
Standing Rock	5	(33%)	10	(67%)	0		0		0	
Thoreau	7	(37%)	11	(58%)	1	(5%)	0		0	
Torreón	15	(75%)	5	(25%)	0		0		0	
Whitehorse	1	(7%)	14	(93%)	0		0		0	
Ft. Wingate	18	(75%)	6	(25%)	0		0		0	
Borrego Pass	9	(82%)	2	(18%)	0		0		0	
Bread Springs										
Jones Ranch	5	(46%)	5	(46%)	1	(9%)	1		0	
Ojo Encino	5	(33%)	8	(53%)	1	(7%)	0	(7%)	0	
Ft. Defiance Agency:										
Chuska	10	(21%)	18	(38%)	18	(38%)	1	(2%)	0	
Crystal	3	(16%)	13	(68%)	2	(11%)	0		1	(5%)
Dilcon	26	(43%)	22	(36%)	10	(16%)	0		3	(5%)
Greasewood	0		5	(63%)	3	(38%)	0		0	
Hunter's Point	28	(58%)	17	(35%)	3	(6%)	0		0	
Kinlichee	15	(52%)	13	(45%)	0		1	(3%)	0	
Pine Springs	2	(12%)	6	(35%)	9	(53%)	0		0	
Seba Dalkai	0		24	(83%)	3	(11%)	2	(7%)	0	
Tohatchi	0		4	(67%)	2	(33%)	0		0	
Toyei	28	(51%)	26	(47%)	1	(2%)	0		0	
Wide Ruins	15	(52%)	4	(14%)	9	(31%)	0		1	(3%)
Shiprock Agency:										
Aneth	13	(34%)	25	(66%)	0		0		0	
Nenahnezad	17	(30%)	12	(35%)	5	(15%)	0		0	
Red Rock	11	(44%)	14	(56%)	0		0		0	
Sanostee	13	(27%)	25	(52%)	10	(21%)	0		0	
Shiprock	10	(38%)	15	(58%)	0		1	(4%)	0	
Teecnospos	26	(33%)	42	(54%)	4	(5%)	4	(5%)	2	(3%)
Toadlena	4	(9%)	18	(40%)	11	(24%)	10	(22%)	2	(4%)
Beclabito Day	0		1	(50%)	1	(50%)	0		0	
Cove Day	14	(82%)	3	(18%)	0		0		0	

Table 11.1 (continued)

SCHOOLS	N		N-e		N-E		n-E		E	
Tuba City Agency:										
Dennehotso	13	(35%)	22	(59%)	2	(5%)	0		0	
Kaibeto (Upper)										
Kaibeto (Lower)										
Kayenta	54	(73%)	20	(27%)	0		0		0	
Leupp										
Navajo Mountain	24	(77%)	3	(10%)	1	(3%)	2	(6%)	1	(3%)
Rocky Ridge	30	(79%)	8	(21%)	0		0		0	
Shonto										
Tuba City	55	(53%)	46	(45%)	2	(2%)	0		0	
Red Lake Day										
PUBLIC SCHOOLS:										
Gallup-McKinley — Urban:										
A. Roat	2	(5%)	20	(49%)	5	(12%)	7	(17%)	7	(17%)
Indian Hills	1	(8%)	5	(42%)	4	(33%)	0		2	(17%)
Jefferson	4	(36%)	1	(9%)	2	(18%)	1	(9%)	3	(27%)
Lincoln	0		2	(15%)	2	(15%)	5	(39%)	4	(31%)
Red Rock	3	(12%)	15	(63%)	4	(17%)	1	(4%)	1	(4%)
Roosevelt	0		1	(13%)	2	(25%)	1	(13%)	4	(50%)
Sky City	0		1	(100%)	0		0		0	
Sunnyside	0		1	(11%)	3	(33%)	3	(33%)	2	(22%)
Washington	5	(11%)	6	(13%)	9	(20%)	6	(13%)	19	(42%)
Gallup-McKinley — Rural:										
Church Rock	19	(25%)	29	(39%)	16	(21%)	6	(8%)	5	(7%)
Crownpoint	15	(11%)	40	(30%)	63	(48%)	5	(4%)	9	(7%)
Navajo	10	(15%)	26	(39%)	21	(32%)	9	(14%)	0	
Ramah	6	(19%)	19	(58%)	6	(19%)	1	(3%)	0	
Thoreau	24	(35%)	40	(58%)	5	(7%)	0		0	
Tohatchi	30	(35%)	26	(31%)	19	(22%)	5	(6%)	5	(6%)
Tse Bonito	0		10	(100%)	0		0		0	
Kayenta:										
Kayenta	21	(25%)	32	(39%)	17	(21%)	8	(10%)	5	(6%)
Ganado:										
Ganado	21	(28%)	46	(62%)	6	(8%)	1	(1%)	0	
Central:										
Naschitti	3	(7%)	11	(24%)	29	(64%)	1	(2%)	1	(2%)
Mesa	16	(14%)	44	(39%)	39	(35%)	7	(6%)	7	(6%)
Wilson	15	(23%)	19	(30%)	20	(31%)	8	(13%)	2	(3%)
Valley	1	(2%)	31	(46%)	16	(24%)	10	(15%)	9	(13%)
Newcomb										
Chinle:										
Many Farms	13	(30%)	17	(40%)	3	(7%)	2	(5%)	8	(8%)
Chinle	18	(15%)	59	(50%)	21	(18%)	11	(9%)	10	(8%)
Round Rock	3	(19%)	8	(50%)	2	(13%)	3	(19%)		
Window Rock:										
Ft. Defiance	15	(20%)	18	(23%)	17	(22%)	20	(26%)	7	(9%)
Window Rock	4	(8%)	11	(22%)	8	(16%)	14	(29%)	12	(25%)

Table 11.2
Degree of Navajo vs. Degree of Accessibility

SCHOOLS	No. of six-year-olds	% of N + N-e	Mean	Accessibility Index
BUREAU OF INDIAN AFFAIRS:				
Chinle Agency:				
Chinle	28	100%	4.78	91
Low Mountain	37	81%	4.05	115
Lukachukai	59	83%	4.27	102
Many Farms	24	67%	4.33	103
Nazlini	22	95%	4.77	101
Piñon	69	99%	4.71	122
Rock Point	44	98%	4.40	88
Cottonwood Day	41	95%	4.17	104
Eastern Navajo Agency:				
Baca	6	100%	4.33	19
Cheechilgeetho	29	86%	4.00	56
Crownpoint	26	92%	4.19	58
Lake Valley	14	100%	5.00	141
Mariano				63
Pueblo Pintado	37	78%	4.08	124
Standing Rock	15	100%	4.33	39
Thoreau	19	95%	4.31	32
Torreón	20	100%	4.75	126
Whitehorse	15	100%	4.06	139
Ft. Wingate	24	100%	4.75	13
Borrego Pass	11	100%	4.81	75
Bread Springs				
Jones Ranch	11	91%	4.36	54
Ojo Encino	15	87%	4.13	157
Ft. Defiance Agency:				
Chuska	47	60%	3.78	24
Crystal	19	84%	3.89	52
Dilcon	61	79%	4.11	53
Greasewood	8	63%	3.62	86
Hunter's Point	48	94%	4.52	33
Kinlichee	29	97%	4.44	53
Pine Springs	17	47%	3.58	68
Seba Dalkai	29	83%	3.75	46
Tohatchi	6	67%	3.66	26
Toyei	55	98%	4.49	80
Wide Ruins	29	66%	4.10	85
Shiprock Agency:				
Aneth	38	100%	4.34	49
Nenahnezad	34	65%	4.35	14
Red Rock	25	100%	4.44	80
Sanostee	48	79%	4.06	67
Shiprock	26	96%	4.30	27
Teecnospos	78	87%	4.10	47
Toadlena	45	49%	3.26	86
Beclabito Day	2	50%	3.50	50
Cove Day	17	100%	4.82	102

Table 11.2 (continued)

SCHOOLS	No. of six-year-olds	% of N + N-e	Mean	Accessibility Index
Tuba City Agency:				
Dennehotso	37	95%	4.29	91
Kaibeto (upper)				
Kaibeto (lower)				
Kayenta	74	73%	4.72	117
Leupp				
Navajo Mountain	31	87%	4.51	251
Rocky Ridge	38	100%	4.78	102
Shonto				
Tuba City	103	98%	4.51	79
Red Lake Day				
GALLUP-McKINLEY SCHOOLS:				
Urban:				
A. Roat	41	54%	3.07	1
Indian Hills	12	50%	3.24	1
Jefferson	11	46%	3.18	1
Lincoln	13	15%	2.15	1
Red Rock	24	75%	3.75	1
Roosevelt	8	13%	2.28	1
Sky City	1	100%	4.00	1
Sunnyside	9	11%	2.33	1
Washington	45	24%	2.37	1
Rural:				
Church Rock	75	64%	3.67	14
Crownpoint	132	42%	3.35	58
Navajo	66	55%	3.56	42
Ramah	32	77%	3.93	43
Thoreau	69	93%	4.27	32
Tohatchi	85	66%	3.85	26
Tse Bonito	10	100%	4.00	24
PUBLIC SCHOOLS:				
Kayenta:				
Kayenta	83	64%	3.67	117
Ganado:				
Ganado	74	91%	4.17	52
Central:				
Naschitti	45	31%	3.31	42
Mesa	113	53%	3.49	27
Wilson	64	53%	3.58	8
Valley	67	48%	3.07	27
Newcomb				
Chinle:				
Many Farms	43	70%	3.58	103
Chinle	119	65%	3.54	91
Round Rock	16	69%	3.69	101

Table 11.3
Summary of Questionnaire Results
by BIA Agency

AGENCY	N	N-e	N-E	n-E	E
Chinle	174 (54%)	120 (37%)	27 (8%)	1 (1%)	2 (1%)
Eastern					
Navajo	109 (45%)	115 (48%)	11 (5%)	7 (3%)	0
Ft. Defiance	127 (36%)	152 (44%)	60 (17%)	4 (1%)	5 (1%)
Shiprock	108 (35%)	155 (50%)	31 (10%)	15 (5%)	4 (1%)
Tuba City	176 (62%)	99 (35%)	5 (2%)	2 (1%)	1 (1%)

Table 11.4
Degree of Navajo vs. Degree of Accessibility
by BIA Agency

AGENCY	Mean Navajo Index	Accessibility Index
Tuba City	4.56	131
Chinle	4.44	103
Eastern Navajo	4.39	79
Shiprock	4.13	58
Ft. Defiance	3.99	55

Table 11.5
Navajo Indices of BIA Schools and Public Schools

BIA SCHOOLS			PUBLIC SCHOOLS		
Name of School	% of N + N-e	Mean Navajo Index	Name of School	% of N + N-e	Mean Navajo Index
Chinle	100%	4.78	Chinle	65%	3.54
Crownpoint	92%	4.19	Crownpoint	42%	3.35
Kayenta	73%	4.72	Kayenta	64%	3.67
Shiprock	96%	4.30	*Mesa	53%	3.45
			Valley	48%	3.07
Thoreau	95%	4.31	Thoreau	93%	4.27
**Tohatchi	67%	3.66			
Chuska	60%	3.78	Tohatchi	66%	3.85
Red Rock	100%	4.44	Red Rock	75%	3.75
Many Farms	67%	4.33	Many Farms	70%	3.58

*Two public schools compared to one BIA school.
**Two BIA schools compared to one public school.

Notes

1. Joshua A. Fishman, "The Historical and Social Contexts of an Inquiry into Language Maintenance Efforts," in *Language Loyalty in the United States: The Maintenance and Perpetuation of Non-English Mother Tongues by American Ethnic and Religious Groups,* ed. Joshua A. Fishman (The Hague: Mouton, 1966).
2. Wallace L. Chafe, "Estimates Regarding the Present Speakers of North American Indian Languages," *International Journal of American Linguistics* 28, no. 3: 162–71.
3. M. Dale Kinkade, "Indian Languages at Haskell Institute," *International Journal of American Linguistics* 36, no. 1: 46–52.
4. C.I.J.M. Stuart, "American Indian Languages at Haskell Institute," *International Journal of American Linguistics* 28, no. 2: 151.

12.

Children's Comprehension of Standard and Negro Nonstandard English Sentences

Thomas S. Frentz

Contemporary linguistic research comparing standard English (SE) and Negro nonstandard English (NNE) has identified numerous differences between the two dialects.[1] For example, one common syntactic contrast is that whenever a present tense form of *to be* is expected in SE, NNE may have no form at all.[2] Consequently, SE sentences like *She is a nurse* and *John is at the store* find their NNE correlates in the sentences *She a nurse* and *John at the store,* respectively. With regard to phonological contrasts, when a stop is present as the final member of a consonant cluster in SE, the stop is often absent from the cluster in NNE.[3] Thus, SE words like *told* and *desk* find their NNE counterparts in *tol'* and *des',* respectively.

The question arises whether such observed differences between SE and NNE reflect merely alternative ways of expressing grammatical distinctions (i.e., surface structure differences), or whether they represent more fundamental differences regarding the capabilities of the dialects to express such distinctions (i.e., deep structure differences).[4] One approach to this question would be to identify the nature of the grammatical rules which explain the observed differences. In most generative grammars, phrase structure rules generate deep structures which in turn specify what a sentence means, while transformational rules generate surface structures which specify approximately how a sentence is produced. If the differences between SE and NNE are deep structure differences, then such contrasts should be explainable only in terms of phrase

Reprinted from *Speech Monographs* 38 (March 1971): 10–16. Research was supported by funds granted to the Institute for Research on Poverty at the University of Wisconsin by the Office of Economic Opportunity pursuant to the provisions of the Economic Opportunity Act of 1964.

Thomas S. Frentz of the Department of Speech Communication, University of Southern California, has concentrated on several aspects of human communication from a language perspective. The study which follows was developed from his doctoral dissertation.

structure rules, whereas if the differences reflect surface structure differences, they should be explainable by transformational rules.

To date, the most explicit answer to this question comes from Labov.[5] Labov has argued that most of the syntactic differences between NNE and SE are explainable in terms of transformational rules which define surface structure, and that the deep structure components of the dialects are virtually identical. For example, the difference between the NNE surface form *They mine* and the SE surface form *They're mine* is readily explained by different transformational contraction rules. In SE, the rule converts the underlying deep structure *They are mine*[6] to the surface structure *They're mine*. In NNE, however, the rule may convert *They are mine* to *They're mine* as in SE, or, more commonly, it may convert *They are mine* to *They mine*. If syntactic differences between NNE and SE are accommodated by transformational rules, then such differences should be restricted to the surface structures of the dialects, and the deep structures should be the same.

The present study was designed primarily to test a performance corollary of the above reasoning. If SE and NNE have the same deep structures underlying specified surface variations, then NNE user comprehension of NNE sentence meaning as determined by deep structure should be the same as SE user comprehension of SE sentence meaning.

Research by Baratz[7] adds two dimensions to this reasoning. In a sentence repetition task which focused upon surface structure detail, Baratz found that NNE users performed better than SE users with NNE sentènces, but that SE users performed better than NNE users with SE sentences. These findings suggest that users perform best with their preferred dialect. If the Baratz results reflect a general behavioral pattern when SE and NNE users use both SE and NNE sentences, then such findings should recur in an experimental task which focuses primarily upon deep structure processing — for example, a comprehension task.

Accordingly, in a test situation involving comprehension of singular and plural NNE and SE sentences, it is hypothesized that:

1. NNE user comprehension of NNE sentences will not differ from SE user comprehension of SE sentences.
2. NNE users will comprehend NNE sentences better than SE users.
3. SE users will comprehend SE sentences better than NNE users.

Method

Subjects

The primary criterion for subject selection was that subjects be bona fide users of either SE or NNE — that is, that they speak and hear primarily either SE or NNE in everyday communication. Based upon extensive pre-testing and the advice of an expert with both dialects, sixty subjects were chosen — thirty white third-grade children from a Wisconsin elementary school and thirty black children from an inner-city elementary school in Chicago. White children represented SE users, while black children represented NNE users. Fifteen white subjects were male and fifteen female with a mean age of 8.85 years. Twelve black subjects were male, eighteen female with a mean age of 8.50 years.

Materials

The third person, present tense, singular vs. plural was the distinction considered in the study. This distinction is realized by the SE sentences *The boy writes* and *The boys write,* and by the NNE sentences *Duh boy wri"* and *Duh boys wri',* respectively.[8]

Test items were 24 three-word sentences: 12 in NNE, 12 in SE. Half of the sentences in each dialect were singular, and half were plural. All were recorded by a female, black adult, fluent in both dialects. Eight sentences and their corresponding pictures were used as examples in the instructions, and 16 sentences were used in the experiment. Table 12.1 presents these sentences.

Table 12.1

Orthographic Representations of All Sentence Replicates

Standard English	Nonstandard Negro English
1. The boy writes	1a. Duh boy wri"
2. The boys write	2a. Duh boys wri'
3. The girl plays	3a. Duh girl play'
4. The girls play	4a. Duh girls play
5. The boy drinks	5a. Duh boy drin"
6. The boys drink	6a. Duh boys drin'
7. The girl eats	7a. Duh girl ea"
8. The girls eat	8a. Duh girls ea'
9. The boy sits*	9a. Duh boy si"*
10. The boys sit*	10a. Duh boys si'*
11. The girl sweeps*	11a. Duh girl swee"*
12. The girls sweep*	12a. Duh girls swee'*

*Used in instructions only.

Two pictures were constructed for each sentence: one singular, the other plural. "Singular pictures" showed one of two children performing the activity specified in the sentences (e.g., writing, playing, drinking, etc.), while "plural pictures" depicted both children engaging in the activity. Singular and plural pictures were identical except for the grammatical marking. Two sets of pictures were constructed which differed only in the skin color and other ethnic features of the children depicted. In the testing, black children saw only pictures showing black children, while white children saw only pictures depicting white children. All pictures were created by a commercial artist and reproduced on 35mm slides.

Procedure

In presentation, sentences and pictures were combined as follows: (1) singular sentence/singular picture, (2) plural sentence/plural picture, (3) singular sentence/plural picture, and (4) plural sentence/singular picture. This procedure yielded two major conditions. The "means same" condition was any sentence/picture combination with corresponding grammatical markings (i.e., singular sentences/singular pictures or plural sentences/plural pictures). The "means different" condition was defined as any sentence/picture combination with opposing grammatical markings (i.e., singular sentences/plural pictures or plural sentences/singular pictures). All sentences and pictures appeared at least once in both "means same" and "means different" conditions.

Combining sentences and pictures in this fashion resulted in 48 different sentence/picture combinations. Only 32 combinations appeared in the experiment. The remaining 16 appeared in the instructions only. Each subject was exposed to the same sentence twice, once in a "means same" condition, and once in a "means different" condition, and to the same picture four times, once in a "means same," once in a "means different" condition with NNE sentences, and once in a "means same," once in a "means different" condition with SE sentences. Three random orders of the stimuli were constructed. Each subject experienced only one of the orders.

All subjects were tested individually at school during the school day. For each subject, the testing procedures were as follows: (1) He was seated in front of a screen and fitted with earphones. (2) He heard the instructions presented twice, once in SE, the second time in NNE. Both versions of the instructions were recorded by the same black adult who recorded the test sentences. (3) After hearing the instructions, he was exposed to the 32 sentence/picture combinations. The subject was exposed to a picture for three seconds, then he heard the sentence, and finally he had five seconds to press either a "means same" or "means different" button depending upon the perceived relationship between sentence and picture.

Design

The active, independent variables were (1) dialect of user (NNE, SE), (2) dialect of sentences (NNE, SE), (3) sentence form (singular, plural), (4) picture form (singular, plural). In addition, four assigned variables were considered — namely, (5) "word pool" replicates defining the four specific noun-verb pairings: *(boys writing, girls playing, boys drinking, and girls eating).* (6) sex of user (male, female), (7) random orders (A, B, and C), and (8) position of the "means different" button (left, right).[9]

Two dependent variables were used — namely, a subject's meaning response score, and the subject's latency of response. For the meaning score, a subject was given "1" for a correct response and "0" for either an incorrect response or for no response in the allotted five-second interval between stimulus presentations. Latency scores varied between 0.00 and 5.00 seconds. Data for analysis consisted of the percentage of correct responses and the mean latency scores for each subject in each sentence/picture condition.

Results

Data were analyzed by two univariate analyses of variance. Table 12.2 presents the cell means directly relevant to the hypothesized relationship between dialect of users and dialect of sentences. Contrary to expectations, the dialect user by dialect of sentences interaction was not significant for either dependent measure. Since a detailed consideration of the specific hypotheses defining the pattern of that interaction was contingent upon the interaction being significant, no further analyses were performed.

Table 12.2

Mean Percentage of Correct Meaning Responses and Mean Latency Scores for the Dialect of User by Dialect of Sentences Interaction

Dialect of Users	NNE		SE	
Dialect of Sentences	NNE	SE	NNE	SE
Meaning Response	$.75_b$	$.75_b$	$.88_a$	$.91_a$
Latency	$.89_c$	$.73_d$	$.80_c$	$.67_d$

Note: Means with different subscripts are significantly different from one another (p <.01) by a Newman/Keuls Multiple Comparisons Test. Comparisons were only made within a given dependent measure. Consequently, significant differences on the meaning response variable were indexed by "a" and "b," while differences in latency were indexed by "c" and "d."

An alternative test of the reasoning that SE and NNE have similar deep structures would be to compare combined user comprehension on the two dialects. If SE and NNE do not differ on the deep structure level, at least as defined by the singular-plural distinction, then combined user comprehension of SE sentences should not differ significantly from such comprehension of NNE sentences. Inspection of combined user means indicated that comprehension of the dialects did not differ significantly on the meaning response variable (.83 for SE; .81 for NNE), but did differ on the latency measure (.70 for SE; .85 for NNE). Further analyses with the latency data showed, however, that when combined users required longer latencies for NNE sentences than for SE sentences, they did so only for the "means different" condition, and even this pattern was highly unstable.

One further result suggested by Table 2 is of theoretical interest. A significant dialect user main effort on the meaning response variable was found: SE users performed better than NNE users ($F = 9.7396$, $df = 1/36$, $p < .001$). The generality of this finding was restricted, however, by a significant dialect user by sentence form interaction ($F = 11.6787$, $df = 1/36$, $p < .001$). In a more detailed consideration of the pattern of interaction, Newman/Keuls Multiple comparisons tests indicated that SE users answered correctly significantly more often than NNE users with singular sentences ($p < .01$), but not with plural sentences. In short, the overall dialect user main effect difference was restricted to singular sentence form conditions across both dialects.

Discussion

Two explanations for the failure to find the hypothesized relationship between dialect of users and dialect of sentences appear plausible. First, the experimental task in the research by Baratz, which motivated the predictions that users would perform best when using sentences in their preferred dialect, was sentence repetition. This is a production task which focuses attention on the details of surface structure. By contrast, the task of matching sentences and pictures in terms of similarity of meaning is a comprehensive task; it focuses attention on overall sentence interpretation. Perhaps language behavior is sensitive to dialect variations only in production tasks and is not a relevant or important psychological variable in sentence comprehension.

An alternative explanation for the lack of dependence between dialect user and dialect found here involves the test sentences used. All sentences in the present study were extremely short and syntactically simple. It is possible that they did not provide an adequately difficult comprehension test of the hypothesized relationship between dialect of users and dialect of sentences. For example, consider the following sentences:

(1) The boy writes
(2) Duh boy wri"

(3) She was the girl who didn't go to school because she had no clothes to wear.

(4) That girl, she ain' go ta school 'cause she ain' got no clothes to wear.

Sentences (1) and (2) are test sentences from the present study, while (3) and (4) are sentences used by Baratz.[10] While (1) and (2) differ from each other by only one grammatical contrast (namely, the occurrence and location of the s-suffix). (3) and (4) differ from each other by seven such contrasts. One might ask whether the finding that dialect user comprehension did not vary as a function of dialect with sentences like (1) and (2) would have generality across sentences like (3) and (4). In the present study, it was reasoned that if SE and NNE sentences differed in only one grammatical respect, any behavioral differences which occurred could be unambiguously interpreted in terms of that single distinction. It could be the case that the short, syntactically simple sentences that resulted from such reasoning could have masked a relationship between dialect user and dialect which affects comprehension.

The finding that combined user comprehension of SE sentences did not differ significantly from such comprehension of NNE sentences may have occurred because the two dialects are functionally equivalent. And if this is true, it would follow that the dialects are similar on the deep structure level, since comprehension presupposes deep structure processing. However, in view of the fact that the present study considered only one grammatical distinction and that the above explanation is reasoned from a non-significant finding, this explanation should be regarded as highly tentative. Nevertheless, since the singular-plural distinction represented a particularly powerful test of the deep structure hypothesis,[11] if the dialects did differ on the deep structure level, one would certainly have expected that such differences would have been reflected in user comprehension behavior with that distinction. That such an expectation was not borne out provides at least preliminary behavioral support for the notion that SE and NNE have equivalent deep structures.

Finally, it was found that SE users responded correctly significantly more often than NNE users in the singular sentence conditions. It is important to understand the pattern of NNE user's errors in these conditions. When NNE users erred responding to "means different" conditions of singular sentences/plural pictures, they did so by pressing the "means same" button. Similarly, when NNE users erred responding to "means same" conditions of singular sentence/singular pictures, they did so by pressing the "means different" button. What seemed to have happened was that when NNE users erred with singular sentences, they did so by systematically constructing such sentences as plural.

There are two possible explanations for such behavior. First, a re-examination of the NNE version of the instructions revealed that the two verbs comprising the example sentences in the instructions began with [s] *(Duh girl(s) sweep* and *Duh boy(s) sit)*. Consequently, little phonetic difference occurred between the singular and plural NNE sentences. Compare the NNE singular forms *Duh girl swee"* and *Duh boy si"* with their corresponding plurals *Duh girls swee'* and *Duh boys si'*. Unless the noun plural [s] is elongated in the plural sentences, little, if any perceptual distinction can be made between the NNE singular and plural sentences which appeared in the NNE instructions. Unfortunately, a re-examination of the instruction tapes indicated that such elongation did not occur in the production of the example sentences, and consequently, both singular and plural sentence forms sounded virtually identical.

The second explanation involves the fact that in NNE grammar the present tense, singular-plural as marked by inflection can be approximated by the following rule: If a sentence contains any explicit, s-suffix, construe it as plural, if not, construe it as singular.[12] If NNE users applied this rule to the sentences which appeared in the NNE instructions, they would construe all of the sentences as plural because all of the example sentences in those instructions contained explicit, s-suffixes (See Table 1). If NNE users preceived both the singular and plural sentences in the NNE instructions as plural, then they probably approached the experiment proper expecting to find only plural NNE sentences. This expectation may have led to their perceiving most NNE sentences as plural. Insofar as this explanation is correct, it explains the pattern of NNE user errors with at least the NNE versions of singular sentences.

When NNE users responded to SE singular sentences, a somewhat different problem may have occurred. One phenomenon which has been shown to be common among such speakers is hypercorrection — i.e., the over-generalization of a grammatical regularity to inappropriate linguistic contexts. It seems quite probable that such over-generalization occurred in the present study. For example, notice that if the aforementioned rule for differentiating NNE singulars from plurals is indiscriminately applied to the SE sentences in this study, all such sentences would be construed as plural since all SE sentences contained explicit s-suffixes. This, coupled with the other suggestion that the NNE instructions could have caused some NNE users to expect only plural NNE sentences in the experimental task, would explain why singular sentences were particularly difficult for the NNE user population.

However, in terms of the key singular-plural grammatical contrast, no combined dialect user comprehension differences were found between SE and NNE sentences. If it is the case that dialect differences only affect dialect user encoding behavior, then inner-city language programs might do well to recognize this differential effect and to incorporate into language curricula teaching strategies that will be consistent with the behavior associated with both encoding and decoding tasks.

Notes

1. See, for example, William Labov *et al., A Study of the Non-standard English of Negro and Puerto Rican Speakers in New York City* (New York: Columbia University, 1968), vol. 1; Walter A. Wolfram, *A Sociolinguistic Description of Detroit Negro Speech* (Washington, D. C.: Center for Applied Linguistics, 1969); Ralph W. Fasold, *Some Grammatical Features of Negro Dialect,* Washington, D. C.: Center for Applied Linguistics, in press.
2. Wolfram, pp. 165–66; Fasold, p. 14.
3. Labov *et al.,* pp. 133–35; Wolfram pp. 35–39.
4. The linguistic position adopted in the present study is essentially that set forth by Noam Chomsky in *Aspects of the Theory of Syntax* (Cambridge: M.I.T. Press, 1966).
5. William Labov, "The Logic of Non-standard English," in *Language and Poverty: Perspectives on a Theme,* ed. Frederick Williams (Chicago: Markham Publishing Co., 1970), pp. 153–89.
6. The actual linguistic representation of the deep structure of sentences like *They're mine* would be much more complex than *They are mine,* but for present purposes the simplification will suffice.
7. Joan C. Baratz, "Teaching Reading in an Urban Negro School System," in *Teaching Black Children to Read,* eds. Joan C. Baratz and Roger W. Shuy (Washington, D.C.: Center for Applied Linguistics, 1969), pp. 92–116.
8. As with all writing systems, American English orthography is not sensitive to dialect variations. Thus NNE sentences can only be approximated with this system. The following procedures were used in the present study: (1) Where *d* replaced *th* in the word *the, duh* was the orthographic form used for NNE. (2) Where both the stop on a consonant in final word position and the *s*-suffix were missing from the same stem in NNE, double apostrophes were used to indicate the missing elements (*wri"* vs. *writes*). (3) Where only the stop was missing from a stem in NNE, a single apostrophe was used (*wri'* vs. *write*). In all three cases, such approximations should be construed as reflecting limitations in the writing system rather than in NNE sentences.
9. Since the deep structure issue necessitated speaking to a null hypothesis (*viz.,* NNE user comprehension of NNE sentences equals SE user comprehension of SE sentences), some protection was needed that should that null relationship occur, it would reflect a psychologically valid relationship between the NNE and SE user populations rather than mere chance expectation. To obtain some measure of protection, in addition to the independent variables (1), (2), (3), and (4), factors (5), (6), (7), and (8) were considered as assigned variables. This means they were treated as independent variables – i.e., they were removed as possible sources of error variance – although they were not manipulated per se. This procedure minimized the probability of obtaining any nonsignificant results. If the null hypothesis germane to the deep structure issue was found under such conditions, one could reason with some confidence that such a finding was not a function of chance. Subsequently, the assigned variables will only be considered if they interact with and thereby restrict the generality of the independent variables.
10. Baratz, pp. 102–3.
11. The difference between the implicit or zero marker which characterized the NNE singular sentences (e.g. *Duh boy wri"*) and the explicit *s*-suffix marker which characterized the SE singulars (e.g. *The boy writes*), defines an extreme contrast which seems to maximize the probability that behavioral differences will occur. If such differences do not occur in this case, it is unlikely that they will occur with other, less qualitatively divergent contrasts.
12. The actual role would be much more complex and context sensitive, but the above simplification will suffice here.

13

The Most Effective Language of Instruction for Beginning Reading: A Field Study

NANCY MODIANO

One of the major educational problems in America is to provide viable schooling for non-English-speaking children. Many educators think of the word *English* not as the classificatory term for a number of dialects, which it is, but as a very limited number of those dialects, the ones used by members of our dominant culture. Actually, the word "English" is a classificatory term referring to a great variety of dialects, ranging geographically across the earth and ranging socio-economically from those spoken by the elite to those used by the least advantaged. English encompasses dialects such as Queen's English, Harvard, and Standard American, which most Americans approximate in their speech, and dialects such as New Yorkese, Cockney, and a variety of Southeastern dialects spoken by the economically most impoverished elements of the U.S. population, black and white. This variety of language has given rise to one of the most explosive educational issues today, namely the education of all children who enter school with any mother tongue other than a so-called good dialect of English.

The research reported here deals with only one of the problems which revolve around this issue. I believe, however, that it has implications which extend to several other facets.

The investigation deals with a problem in reading, more specifically with the language of instruction for beginning reading for children of linguistic minorities. This question has wide application. There is hardly a country in the world which does not have sizeable linguistic minorities.

This study originated as a Ph.D. dissertation for New York University in 1966. Since then numerous speeches, articles, and a book have been based upon it.

Nancy Modiano of Catholic University in Washington, D.C., has done extensive fieldwork in applied anthropology in the United States and Mexico. An educational anthropologist, she was chairman of the committee on cognitive and linguistic studies of the Council on Anthropology and Education from 1969-71. In addition to numerous journal articles, she has written a book, *Indian Education in the Chiapas Highlands*.

Responses by educators and politicians who control schooling have tended to polarize around two positions. In some countries the vernacular is used for almost all formal schooling, with the national language being taught as a second language of relatively little importance. At the other extreme are countries such as France, Australia, Canada, and the United States, where the teaching of reading occurs almost exclusively in the national language. The research reported here was meant to determine which approach is most effective.

It was not possible to conduct such a comparative study in the United States because, in 1967 when the study was undertaken, there were almost no on-going programs in which children were being taught to read in any language but English. However, in Mexico, in the Chiapas Highlands near the Guatemalan border, there were several tribal areas which suited my purposes. These were Oxchuc, Zinacantán, and Chenalho. The residents of these three areas, descendants of the first Maya empire, live in rather close-knit farming communities. In Zinacantán and Chenalho the langauge is Tzotzil; in Oxchuc it is Tzeltal (both are closely related Maya-Quiche languages).

In each of these tribal areas some children attended federal or state schools in which all reading instruction was given in Spanish; this was one approach. Other children attended the schools of the National Indian Institute, where they began reading in Spanish only after they had learned to read in their own language and had acquired some oral Spanish vocabulary; this was the contrasting approach. The aim of all the schools, federal, state, and Indian institute, was to provide at least a primary education which would include mastery of oral Spanish, literacy in that language, basic arithmetic, and an awakening sense of nationalism.

Because of the differences in approach to literacy in the national language there were certain differences among teaching personnel. Institute teachers for the beginning classes had to be fluent in the local language; federal and state teachers did not. The institute teachers were recruited from among local Indians. When the institute schools were first opened in 1952 many of the teachers were barely literate themselves, but by the time of the field study the average amount of schooling had risen to six years. In the federal and state schools the teachers came from two groups. The older teachers tended to be local mestizos, members of the class which had exploited the Indians for centuries. Their relationships with the members of the hamlets they served tended to be strained. The other major group of federal and state teachers were recruited from recent normal school graduates, none of whom were local mestizos. Some of these latter teachers approached their work with missionizing zeal; others were all but immobilized by the appalling living conditions in which they found themselves (most were situated about a days' hike from the nearest road, food was often scarce, and the cold was often numbing). Regardless of their attitudes, none of the federal or state school teachers could speak the local language.

In the study, the all-Spanish approach of the federal and state schools was contrasted with the bilingual approach of the institute schools, which insisted upon literacy in the mother tongue and some oral Spanish prior to instruction in reading in the national language. Five schools per approach were tested in Oxchuc and in Chenalho, and three per approach in Zinacantán, for a total of thirteen per approach, or twenty-six in all. Within each tribal area, federal and state schools were paired as closely as possible with institute schools, using demographic data for the hamlets they served.

Whole schools were tested rather than particular grades or groups. This was done because, in the Highlands, Indian children are torn between attending school and working. Many try to do both, and this results in poor attendance. A child who has been enrolled for four years may have attended less than another whose parents have sent him daily for only one year. Also, some schools were too small to have more than one class, while others had as many as five, or over 250 children. Ages varied considerably within each class, due to competition with the demand for child labor and to the very late school entry of some youngsters.

Two principal measures were used to determine the approach with which children learned to read with greater comprehension in Spanish. The first measure was the proportion of students chosen by their teachers as being able to "understand what they read in Spanish." With combined probabilities the results strongly favored the bilingual Institute schools (probability .001). However, an argument could be raised that the teachers differed systematically in their interpretation of the phrase "able to understand what they read in Spanish."

The other principal measure used was a test of reading comprehension in the national language, Spanish. It was developed especially for the study, during a series of pilot experiments, since available tests contained little relevant to the local cultures. Two procedures were used to establish the validity of this test. One was its construction, for it used a format common to many popular reading comprehension tests but was based on material common to the lives of the children. The other procedure was correlational; children's scores on this test were compared to their scores on the comprehension section of the yearly achievement test, to their scores on an individualized test of reading comprehension based on materials originally developed for the local Indian population, and to their teachers' estimates of their ability to understand written Spanish. All of the resulting correlations were quite respectable according to the standards used to validate our own test of reading comprehension[1]

(r - .57, N-104; r - .65, N - 316; r - .49, N - 411). The internal reliability
    ach   ind   tchr
of the test was established by the split-half method (r - .97, N - 455).
                                                          tt

As was found in the analysis of the teachers' estimates of their pupils' ability to "understand what they read in Spanish," the children in the bilingual institute schools scored significantly higher on the reading comprehension test (probability .001). Instead of being more generous, it seems that the institute teachers, who originally selected the higher proportion, were more stringent in their evaluations.

Other measures also pointed up the efficacy of using the vernacular as a vehicle for the teaching of reading in the national language. Many more literate adults were produced by the institute schools in their twelve years of existence than by the federal and state schools which had been in existence for an average of twenty-six years (probability .001). The institute schools were also more effective in reaching the most resistant element of their local populations, the girls (combined probabilities .001).

Thus we see that reading comprehension in the national language was more effectively achieved when approached through the vernacular than when all instruction was given in the national language. Other studies have shown the same to be true in as diverse places as the Philippines, Ghana, India, and the Soviet Union. Why?

*   *   *

One reason lies in the nature of the reading act itself. We no longer question that it is impossible to comprehend something we read when we do not know the language in which it is written. Thus, we seldom attempt to teach reading to children who know no oral English at all. However, we seem less cognizant that ability to perceive both sounds and written symbols depends upon one's familiarity with them and upon one's ability to assign meaning to them. The very act of reading is dependent upon such perceptual ability; until a child can assign meaning to a written symbol he will have difficulty in even perceiving it. To read he must first receive a sensory impression of the graphic symbol — the letter, word, or phrase. He then selects aspects of his impression and organizes his response; he succeeds in this only when the final response has meaning to him. When the final response has generic meaning, such as the name of an object with which he is familiar, he does this with considerably greater facility than when the final response is the repetition of nonsense syllables learned by rote.

For precisely this reason there have been strong efforts to alter the content of some of our most widely distributed reading primers. Time and again the argument has been raised that inner-city children learn to read more slowly than their suburban peers because they cannot attach meaning to the stories they are expected to read nor to the bucolic illustrations accompanying them. The same problem, often in more severe form, is faced by non-English speaking children when we ask them to read what for them are a series of nonsense syllables, namely our own language.

Another crucial factor is attitudinal; this greatly influences the first factor, the perceptual. Although the primary purpose of language is communication, what a person communicates and how he communicates it are very much related to his personality and to his culture. The clothing we wear, the way we style our hair, and the language we speak all present us to the world. Through our language we tell others what we think, both about ourselves and the world around us, and with whom we identify. Our language is inexorably tied to our effective selves. What do we tell children when we say, "The language (or the dialect) you bring to school is unacceptable here"? What do we tell them when we say, "There is nothing here written in your language, so learn some foreign tongue"? Not only do we make the reading act far more confusing and difficult, but we also tell these children that a central part of their being is unacceptable to us.

Worse yet, it is at this point that we often drag a distortion of the Whorfian thesis into play; we do this both with non-English-speaking children and with some who speak any of the several nonprestigious dialects of English. The distortion is that all thought, or at least all formal operations, are dependent upon language. Bereiter and his colleagues best epitomize the extreme of this position when they state, as a rationale for training four-year-olds in the formal, structural aspects of Standard American that "culturally deprived children (those who have not mastered the grammar and vocabulary of Standard American) do not just think at an immature level; many of them do not think at all. That is, they do not show any of the mediating processes which we ordinarily identify with thinking." [2]

Whorf and Sapir, both linguists, were among the first to stress the wedding of language and thought and the inevitable influence of the one upon the other. They did not state, as has long been incorrectly attributed to them, that thought was entirely dependent upon language. Rather they showed a mutual dependency, especially in the case of classification, with thought and language shaping each other.[3] Much the same point of view was developed by Vygotsky.[4]

Thus, while we tend to remember and classify better that which we can label, we can always invent names or phrases for objects, thoughts, or mental constructions beyond our present language. This is true for even the most simple language or dialect spoken today, one with a bare two thousand elements. Indeed, if language were not modifiable it would never change or grow; the grammar of any particular dialect, including Standard American, is a side issue. A statement such as "Ah's gwan" is grammatically as complicated and communicates as much to speakers of its dialect as "I am going" does for speakers of Standard American English. Studies of thinking carried out with peasants in as diverse places as Liberia and Mexico have shown that neither grammar nor vocabulary are crucial factors in formal operations. Rather cultural expectations, personality, and the mastery of skills necessary for economic survival are all primary shapers of cognitive style, which includes skill in reading the natural and human environment, formal operations, and levels of abstraction.

Unlike Whorf, Sapir, and Vygotsky, Piaget has maintained all along that a thought must precede its description and that premature verbalization hampers the development of more mature thinking, at least with little children.[5]

But what has happened? We currently find that children who speak anything other than a prestigious dialect of English as their mother tongue also tend to reason concretely at ages when middle-class youngsters are building abstract castles in the air. Minority children tend to be exceptionally sharp at observing detail in their environment; they do not lose their ability to read people, nor do they cut themselves off from their feelings. None of these great cognitive strengths are rewarded in our schools nor are they tested by I.Q. examinations. These same children tend to avoid synthesizing and the manipulation of high-order abstraction; indeed they may reject such notions as unrealistic according to needs of their own lives. This is not a matter of bright or less bright; it is a matter of differences among cognitive styles. These children also tend to speak some dialect or language other than Standard American.

Two factors, minority-group children's language and their rejection of high-level abstractions are correlated, perhaps accidentally or perhaps due to some underlying commonality, but they do not have the causal relations generally attributed to them. The one does not cause the other; the use of nonprestigious English no more brings about the rejection of high-level abstractions than that rejection creates the nonprestigious dialect.

Despite this, people such as Bereiter, who have not lost their popularity, boldly assert that the rejection of high-level abstractions during the prepubescent years is due to a lack of mastery of a dialect associated with the dominant culture, be it Queen's English or Standard American. Others, like Martin Deutsch, then try to implement their philosophies,[6] in my opinion, to the great detriment of the children involved in their programs.

* * *

Another question raised by my study is that of staffing. Let us remember that in the institute schools, which were far more successful in teaching children to read with comprehension in the national language, the teachers differed systematically from those in the all-Spanish federal and state schools. The differences were primarily in two areas, in professional preparation and in familiarity with the local cultures.

As local Indians themselves, the institute teachers were completely cognizant of the language of their students and of the many nuances of their culture. Rough edges that existed in their relations with the hamlets they served were idiosyncratic, not due to their ignorance of the life around them. However, their professional preparation was sketchy. Spanish was a second language, and their ability to read and write in it varied from poor to only fair. These were the teachers who were more successful.

The federal and state teachers had better professional preparation. First, all knew Spanish as their mother tongue and read and wrote in it with ease. Second, most had received more formal schooling; many of them were normal school graduates, and some were eager to adapt their teaching techniques to the needs of their pupils. However, even the most dedicated could not make viable contacts with their pupils, so they were not as successful as their ill-schooled colleagues on the next hillside. What might this suggest for staffing, not only for Head Start, but also for elementary schools in non-middle-class areas?

* * *

To summarize, the conclusions which can be drawn from the field study reported here are as follows:

1. Children who do not speak the national language learn to read it with comprehension more efficiently if they first learn to read in their mother tongue;
2. Ability to communicate with one's students appears to outweigh language (content) or instructional methodology for successful teaching;
3. The more comfortable and less pressured people feel about learning a second language the faster they learn it.

These conclusions have broad implications for schooling in almost every country of the world. I reiterate: there is no causal relationship between the ability to reason abstractly and mastery of a dominant dialect. Children learn more efficiently if first taught to read in their mother tongue. It is imperative that programs which depend upon the mastery of a prestigious dialect or national language for the development of high-level abstractions be reevaluated.

Notes

1. J.B. Winer, *Statistical Principles in Experimental Design* (New York: McGraw-Hill Book Co., 1962), pp. 43–45.
2. Carl Bereiter *et al.*, "An Academically Oriented Pre-School for Culturally Deprived Children," in *Pre-School Education Today,* ed. F. M. Hechinger (Garden City, N.Y.: Doubleday and Co., 1966), p. 107.
3. Edward Sapir, *Language* (New York, Harcourt, Brace, and Co., 1921). Benjamin L. Whorf, "The Relation of Habitual Thought and Behavior to Language" in *Language, Thought and Reality: Selected Writings of Benjamin Lee Whorf,* ed. J.B. Carroll (New York: John Wiley and Sons, 1956).
4. Lew S. Vygotsky, trans. by E. Hanfman and G. Vakar, *Thought and Language* (Boston: M.I.T. Press, 1962). (Originally published 1934.)
5. Jean Piaget, trans. by M. Gabain, *The Language and Thought of the Child* (Cleveland: World Publishing Co., 1955).
6. Martin Deutsch, "Facilitating Development in the Pre-School Child: Social and Psychological Perspectives" in *Pre-School Education Today,* ed. F.M. Hechinger (Garden City, N.Y.: Doubleday and Co.), pp. 88–89.

PART THREE

Practical Application:
THE SCHOOL PROGRAM

In Puerto Rico when you apply [for a job], they ask you a lot of questions about yourself and your family, how much schooling you've had and where you come from. In New York, all they ask is, "Do you know English?"

— *La Vida,*
Oscar Lewis

14.

The Compelling Case for Bilingual Education

JEFFREY W. KOBRICK

In 1968 a Spanish-speaking community worker named Sister Francis Georgia, observing certain children "visibly roaming the streets" of Boston, conducted a door-to-door survey in a Puerto Rican section of the city. Of the 350 Spanish-speaking school-aged children she found, sixty-five percent had never registered in school; many others rarely attended or had dropped out. Armed with these facts, Sister went to the Boston School Department to seek help in locating and providing meaningful programs for Spanish-speaking children who were out of school. Skeptical, Boston school officials told her to produce the "warm bodies"; if she did, they said, "seats" would then be found.

At about the same time, leaders from Boston's poverty communities formed a "Task Force on Children out of School" to investigate the way the school system dealt with poor children generally. Among other things, the task force found that as many as half of Boston's estimated ten thousand Spanish-speaking school children were not in school. Between 1965 and 1969 only four Puerto Rican students graduated from Boston high schools.

Three years later, through the efforts of Sister Francis Georgia, community leader Alex Rodriguez, the Boston task force, and two key legislators, Education Committee Chairman Michael Daly and House Speaker David Bartley, Massachusetts, passed the nation's first comprehensive state bilingual education law, a summary of which appears at the end of this discussion.

The law declares that classes conducted exclusively in English are "inadequate" for the education of children whose native tongue is another

Reprinted from the *Saturday Review of Education* 55 (April 29, 1972): 54–57. Copyright 1972 Saturday Review, Inc.

Jeffrey W. Kobrick, staff attorney with the Boston Legal Assistance Project, was formerly an attorney at the Center for Law and Education at Harvard University. The following selection is a result of his interest in educational issues affecting poor and minority children.

language and that bilingual education programs are necessary "to ensure equal educational opportunity to every child." Massachusetts thus became the first state to *require* school districts to provide bilingual programs for children whose first language is not English. (Other states including New York, California, Illinois, and Texas have laws *permitting* local school districts to provide bilingual programs.) The law calls for the use of both a child's native language and English as mediums of instruction and for the teaching of history and culture associated with a child's native language. It authorizes state expenditures of up to four million dollars a year to help districts meet any extra costs of bilingual programs.

The Massachusetts law is a carefully constructed and innovative piece of legislation that hopefully will stimulate legislative efforts elsewhere. Indeed, because the federal Bilingual Education Act has been so underfunded – "Congress has been appropriating drops," notes Senator Walter Mondale, "when showers or even downpours are needed" – there is a critical need for state legislation and funding in areas where there are substantial numbers of Puerto Rican, Chicano, Indian, and other non-English-speaking children. The U.S. Office of Education estimates that five million children attending public schools "speak a language other than English in their homes and neighborhoods." And increasing evidence reveals the almost total failure of our monolingual, monocultural school systems to provide for these children's educational needs.

In New York City alone, 250,000 Puerto Rican children attend the public schools. The estimated dropout (or "pushout") rate for these students has been put as high as eighty-five percent. Of those who survive to the eighth grade, sixty percent are three to five years below reading level. Nor is the plight of thousands of Puerto Rican children any better in the schools of Bridgeport, Chicago, Philadelphia, Newark, Hoboken, or Paterson. In "The Losers," a report on Puerto Rican education in those cities, Richard Margolis writes: "Relatively speaking, the longer a Puerto Rican child attends public school, the less he learns."

Between two and three million Spanish-speaking children attend school in five Southwestern states where, as Stan Steiner shows in *La Raza: The Mexican Americans,* the schools serve only to "de-educate" any child who happens not to be middle class. More than a third of the Spanish-speaking children in New Mexico's schools are in the first grade, and over half of those in grades above the first are two years or more overage for their grade level. One Texas school board required "Spanish-surname" children to spend three years in the first grade until a federal court stopped the practice. Chicanos are still put into classes for the mentally retarded on the basis of intelligence tests administered only in English; again, federal courts are in the process of abolishing this form of discrimination. The average number of school years completed by the Chicano in the Southwest is 7.1 years.

Statistics relating to the education of the more than two hundred thousand Indian children in public or Bureau of Indian Affairs schools are equally dismal. In 1960, sixty percent of adult Indians had less than an eighth-grade education. Today the Indian dropout rate is more than twice the national average and in some school districts is eighty or ninety percent. In an all-Indian public elementary school near Ponca City, Oklahoma, eighty-seven percent of the children have dropped out by the sixth grade. In Minneapolis, where some ten thousand Indians live, the Indian dropout rate is more than sixty percent. In Washington, Muckleshoot children are automatically retained an extra year in first grade; and the Nook-Sack Indians automatically are placed in slow-learner classes.

One reason schools are failing in their responsibility to these children is that they offer only one curriculum, only one way of doing things, designed to meet the needs of only one group of children. If a child does not fit the mold, so much the worse for him. It is the child who is different, hence deficient; it is the child who must change to meet the needs of the school.

During the first four years of life, a child acquires the sounds, the grammar, and the basic vocabulary of whatever language he hears around him. For many children this language is Spanish or Cree or Chinese or Greek. Seventy-three percent of all Navajo children entering the first grade speak Navajo but little or no English. Yet when they arrive at school, they find not only that English is the language in which all subjects are taught but that English dominates the entire school life. Children cannot understand or make themselves understood even in the most basic situations. There are schools where a child cannot go to the bathroom without asking in English. One little boy, after being rebuffed repeatedly for failure to speak in English, finally said in Spanish: "If you don't let me go to the bathroom, maybe I piss on your feet."

The effects of this treatment on a child are immediate and deep. Language, and the culture it carries, is at the core of a youngster's concept of himself. For a young child especially, as Theodore Andersson and Mildred Boyer point out, "Language carries all the meanings and overtones of home, family, and love; it is the instrument of his thinking and feeling, his gateway to the world." We all love to be addressed, as George Sánchez says, *en la lengua que mamamos* ("in the language we suckled"). And so when a child enters a school that appears to reject the only words he can use, "He is adversely affected in every aspect of his being."

With English the sole medium of instruction, the child is asked to carry an impossible burden at a time when he can barely understand or speak, let alone read or write, the language. Children are immediately retarded in their schoolwork. For many the situation becomes hopeless, and they drop out of school. In other cases, believing the school system offers no meaningful program, parents may fail to send their children to school at all.

Schools seem unmoved by these results. At any rate, the possibility of hiring some teachers who share a child's culture and could teach him in a language he can understand does not occur to them. Since the curriculum is in English, the child must sink or swim in English.

The injustice goes further: Having insisted that a child learn English, schools make little or no constructive effort to help the child do so. Instead schools assume, or expect, that any child in America will "pick it up" without any help from the school. Alma Bagu tells this story about a little Puerto Rican girl's day in school in New York:

Sitting in a classroom and staring at words on a blackboard that were to me as foreign as Egyptian hieroglyphics is one of my early recollections of school. The teacher had come up to my desk and bent over, putting her face close to mine. "My name is Mrs. Newman," she said, as if the exaggerated mouthing of her words would make me understand their meaning. I nodded "yes" because I felt that was what she wanted me to do. But she just threw up her hands in despair and touched her fingers to her head to signify to the class I was dense. From that day on school became an ordeal I was forced to endure.

Like most of the people teaching Spanish-speaking or Indian children, Mrs. Newman presumably did not know the child's language. Yet she treated a five- or six-year-old as "dense" for the crime of not knowing hers.

The variety and perversity of the abuses committed against children are unending. In New York it is not unknown for teachers to lecture Puerto Rican students on how rude it is to speak a "strange" language in the presence of those who do not understand it. In the Southwest, where it is widely believed that a child's native language itself "holds him back," children are threatened, shamed, and punished for speaking the only language they know. Stan Steiner tells of children forced to kneel in the playground and beg forgiveness for speaking a Spanish word or having to write "I will not speak Spanish in school" five hundred times on the blackboard. One teacher makes her children drop a penny in a bowl for every Spanish word they use. "It works!" she says. "They come from poor families, you know."

These are not the isolated acts of a few callous teachers. America's intolerance of diversity is reflected in an ethnocentric educational system designed to "Americanize" foreigners or those who are seen as culturally different. America is the great melting pot, and, as one writer recently stated it, "If you don't want to melt, you had better get out of the pot." The ill-disguised contempt for a child's language is part of a broader distaste for the child himself and the culture he represents. Children who are culturally different are said to be culturally "deprived." Their language and culture are seen as "disadvantages." The children must be "re-oriented," "remodeled," "retooled" if they are to succeed in school.

Messages are sent home insisting that parents speak English in the home or warning of the perils of "all-starch diets" (which means rice and beans). Children are preached middle-class maxims about health and cleanliness. The master curriculum for California's migrant schools prescribes "English cultural games," "English culture, music, and song," "English concept of arithmetic"; nowhere is there mention of the Indo-Hispanic contributions to the history and culture of the Southwest. When Robert Kennedy visited an Indian school, the only book available on Indian history was about the rape of a white woman by Delawares. Even a child's *name* is not his own: Carlos becomes Charles; María, Mary.

Humiliated for their language and values, forced to endure the teaching of a culture that is unrelated to the realities of their lives, it is no wonder that children withdraw mentally, then physically, from school. "School is the enemy," said a Ponca Indian testifying before Congress. "It strikes at the roots of existence of an Indian student."

Far from accomplishing its professed aim of integrating minorities into the "mainstream," the monolingual, monocultural school system has succeeded only in denying whole generations of children an education and condemning them to lives of poverty and despair. There is no more tragic example of the fruits of such policies than that of the Cherokees.

In the nineteenth century, before they were "detribalized," the Cherokees had their own highly regarded bilingual school system and bilingual newspaper. Ninety percent were literate in their own language, and Oklahoma Cherokees had a higher English literacy level than native English-speakers in either Texas or Arkansas. Today, after seventy years of white control, the Cherokee dropout rate in the public schools runs as high as seventy-five percent. The median number of school years completed by the adult Cherokee is 5.5. Ninety percent of the Cherokee families in Adair County, Oklahoma, are on welfare.

Obviously, no particular "program," not even a bilingual one, can be expected to cure all this. The remark of the 1928 Meriam Report on Indian education holds true today: "The most fundamental need in Indian education is a change in point of view."

Bilingual-bicultural education is perhaps the greatest educational priority today in bilingual communities. Its aim is to include children, not exclude them. It is neither a "remedial" program, nor does it seek to "compensate" children for their supposed "deficiencies." It views such children as *advantaged,* not disadvantaged, and seeks to develop bilingualism as a precious asset rather than to stigmatize it as a defect. The very fact of the adoption of a program recognizing a child's language and culture may help to change the way the school views the child. It may help to teach us that diversity is to be enjoyed and valued rather than feared or suspected.

There are also strong arguments supporting the pedagogical soundness of bilingual education. Experts the world over stress the importance of allowing a child to begin his schooling in the language he understands best. Such a policy makes it more likely that a child's first experience with school will be a positive rather than a negative one. Moreover, as John Dewey and others have said, language is one of the principal tools through which children learn problem-solving skills in crucial early years. Policies that frustrate a child's native language development can cause permanent harm by literally jamming the only intellectual channel available to him when he arrives at school. Those who would concentrate on teaching a child English overlook the fact that it takes time for a child unfamiliar with the language to achieve a proficiency in it even approaching that of a child raised in an English-speaking home. In the meantime, struggling to understand other academic subjects, children fall hopelessly behind. In a bilingual program, by contrast, two languages are used as mediums of instruction; a child is thus enabled to study academic subjects in his own language at the same time he is learning English. Bilingual programs teach children to read their own language and to understand, speak, read, and write English (in that order). Language is oral. It is *"speech* before it is reading or writing." When a child enters school already speaking and understanding a language, he is ready to learn to read and write it. A program that prematurely forces English on a child can guarantee his eventual illiteracy in that language.

The "English-only" approach also misses the prime opportunity to teach a child to read his own language. Recent experience indicates that development of literacy in one's native language actually enhances the ability to learn English. When the Navajos evaluated their own bilingual school at Rough Rock, Arizona, they found that the children were more proficient in both languages than they would have been "if you tried to stuff English down the throat of a child who can't understand what you're talking about." Nancy Modiano reports similar results in a highly controlled experiment with Indian children in Chiapas, Mexico. (See Chapter 13 of this book.)

In addition to facilitating the learning of English, bilingual education has other benefits. It helps to correct what Bruce Gaarder, former chief of the U.S. Office of Education's modern language section, has called "an absurdity which passeth understanding." More than one billion dollars a year are spent on foreign language instruction. "Yet virtually no part of it, no cent, ever goes to maintain the native language competence which already exists in American children." Bilingual education also allows English-speakers to learn a second language far more effectively than they could in a foreign language program, because their classmates are native speakers. And it develops and enhances children's intellectual capabilities. Bertha Treviño found that in the Nye School, outside Laredo, Texas, both Spanish- and English-speaking children learned mathematics better bilingually than they did when taught in English alone. In Montreal, children who were educated bilingually scored higher on both verbal and nonverbal intelligence tests and "appeared to have a more diversified set of mental abilities" than their monolingual peers.

Despite the promise of bilingual education, however, only a handful of programs were in operation in the United States during the 1950s and 60s. In fact, prior to 1968, twenty-one states, including California, New York, Pennsylvania, and Texas, had laws requiring that all public school instruction be in English. In seven states, including Texas, a teacher risked criminal penalties or the revocation of his license if he taught bilingually.

In the late 1960s the Chicanos in the Southwest and other groups mounted a widespread campaign for bilingual, bicultural education. In 1967 Senator Ralph Yarborough of Texas introduced a bilingual education bill in Congress, which finally passed, in modified form, as an amendment to Title VII of the Elementary and Secondary Education Act of 1965.

The psychological impact of the federal Bilingual Education Act, a landmark in our history, cannot be overestimated. It reversed a fifty-year-old "one-language" policy and committed the moral force of the national government to meeting "the . . . educational needs of the large numbers of children of limited English-speaking ability in the United States." The act provided financial assistance to local educational agencies for, among other things: "1) bilingual educational programs; 2) programs designed to impart to students a knowledge of the history and culture associated with their languages; 3) efforts to establish closer cooperation between the school and the home."

This commitment by the federal government has slowly influenced states and local communities. Since 1968 eleven states have passed laws permitting local school districts to provide bilingual instruction and, as stated earlier, one state, Massachusetts, has required school districts to provide bilingual education programs (although participation by the children is voluntary).

Nevertheless, even today very few children enjoy the "luxury" of bilingual education. Title VII has become a highly selective program in 1972 serving only eighty-eight thousand of an estimated five million non-English-speaking children. The problem rests primarily with the funding structure of Title VII, which has proved singularly unable to stimulate comparable state and local efforts. The federal act, for example, pays the entire cost of the programs it supports. But since Title VII is grossly underfunded, the federal programs necessarily remain limited. If a local government wishes to institute additional bilingual programs, it must appropriate money from local funds. There is no provision for sharing costs across levels. Thus each level of government becomes reluctant to support a comprehensive bilingual program because it fears it alone will bear the possibly large costs of the program. If, however, costs were shared among the different levels of government — federal, state, and local — each agency might be willing to contribute more.

The Massachusetts legislation provides a needed innovation in this respect. The law requires school districts to offer bilingual programs but provides for state reimbursement of that portion of the cost that *exceeds* the district's average per pupil cost. For example, if a district's annual expenditure per child is eight hundred dollars and the cost to offer bilingual education is one thousand dollars, the district will be reimbursed two hundred dollars. The philosophy of the Massachusetts law is that a local school district has an obligation to spend at least as much for the education of a bilingual child as it does for the education of any other child. The funding formula thus allows state money to go much further than if the state alone bore the cost. By redirecting money from the regular program to a program that better serves the needs of the non-English-speaking child, scarce resources are put to much more productive use.

The appeal here, however, is not to expediency. Many children in this affluent land are being denied their fundamental right to equal education opportunity. To the needs of these children society must respond, and now.

The Massachusetts Statute

Every school district is required to take an annual census of all school-aged children of "limited English-speaking ability" and to classify them according to their dominant language. Whenever there are twenty or more children who share the same native language, the district must provide a bilingual program. A separate program must be provided for each language group.

The statute calls for the teaching of academic subjects both in a child's native language and in English; for instruction in reading and writing the native language, and in understanding, speaking, reading, and writing English; and for inclusion of the history and culture associated with a child's native language as an integral part of the program.

Although the school district's obligation to provide a bilingual program is mandatory, participation by the children and their parents is voluntary. Any parent whose child has been enrolled in a program has a right to prompt notice of such enrollment (in two languages), a right to visit his child's classes and to confer with school officials, and, finally, a right to *withdraw* his child from the program.

Parent Involvement

Parents are afforded the right to "maximum practical involvement" in the "planning, development, and evaluation" of the programs serving their children. Parents, along with bilingual teachers, bilingual teachers' aides, and representatives of community groups, also have the right to participate in policy-making and implementation of the law at the state level.

Bilingual Teachers

The statute creates a new state certification procedure for bilingual teachers that softens some of the previous rigidities and repeals a former U.S. citizenship requirement (which still exists in thirty states). It also allows bilingual teachers who have met some, but not all, of the certification requirements for teachers to serve provisionally and to count two years of provisional service toward a three-year tenure requirement.

State Reimbursement

The bilingual statute provides for state reimbursement to local school districts for that portion of the cost of a bilingual education program that "exceeds" the district's average per pupil cost. Additional costs not covered under the bilingual statute are eligible for reimbursement under the general aid to education statute. Although the program is "transitional" — a student's *right* to participate lasts only three years — any individual school district is allowed to go beyond this minimum, and programs that are "permitted" by the statute are reimbursed on the same basis as those that are "required." If a program gains support in a particular community, it is entirely possible that it could be extended into a full bilingual program.

The English-Speaking

The major weakness of the statute is that it is *silent* on whether English-speaking children may be enrolled in bilingual programs and thus does not contain adequate safeguards against the isolation of minority children in such programs. Bilingual education can be of great benefit to English- as well as non-English-speaking children, and provision for the enrollment of English speakers should be made. The *Harvard Journal on Legislation* has recently published a revised version of this statute, which provides for the enrollment of English-speaking children in the bilingual program.

15.

Poverty Children and Reading Curriculum Reform: A Broad Perspective

CARL L. ROSEN

Millions of young Americans continue to confront educational disaster as a result of school failure associated with reading underachievement. However, no other group of pupils represent a greater crisis and challenge to public education than do children from diverse poverty environments who, partially as a result of difficulties in reading, are being systematically and continuously recycled back into the same life of privation and segregation as their parents and grandparents before them. The comments and reports of massive reading retardation and school underachievement of these children are abundant.[3, 4, 13, 18, 26] Over ten million children from rural and urban poverty in thousands of towns, villages, settlements and urban ghettos across the nation — black, white, Mexican-American, Puerto Rican, Indian, and others — are in schools that are not providing them appropriate educational experiences.

This chapter is concerned with those children who, because of their racial, ethnic, linguistic, and social-class circumstances are all too often unsatisfactorily educated by a system that is not responsive to their needs. This discussion is predicated on the assumption that American society and its institutions can, through change and modernity, make massive contributions to the betterment of the human condition. The opinions expressed here might seem strong, but they represent the firm conviction that our public educational system can work. Middle-class America must, however, be willing to make the admissions and amends that are critical prerequisites to all citizens obtaining the freedom and opportunity so often sloganized in this society.

Reprinted from *Educational Technology* 10 (May 1970): 38–45.

Carl L. Rosen of the Educational Child Study Center in the College of Education at Kent State University has specialized in reading disabilities and is the author of numerous journal articles on minority children and reading. He has taught elementary grades and remedial reading, directed a Title I Reading Center, and consulted throughout the Southeast and Southwest. Thus he brings practical experience to his university teaching and writing.

This discussion will review the traditional in education, analyze the present, and offer some considerations for future educational curriculum reforms which appear to be relevant to this topic. Within this context it should be pointed out that the difficulty is not in refraining from criticism but in being neglectful of one's conscience and shame. It is indeed less hazardous to be loyal or silent regarding respected and hallowed public institutions than it is to be critical. The former behaviors should not necessarily be considered a greater sign of loyalty and responsibility than the latter, in spite of the ominous tenor of our times to the contrary.

The Tradition

The traditional public school has for generations perceived itself as a type of provider of a so-called free school with a common educational curriculum.[10] This type of school places the major burden of responsibility for achievement upon children, their families, and their environment. If the child is willing and able to avail himself of these opportunities, he can, through educational success, so the thinking goes, move into the "good life." By catching hold of this "educational life-preserver," the child of poverty is considered to have been given an *opportunity* to change his circumstances. The opportunity offered by this school requires that the poverty student break from his subculture and adjust his appearance, language, and behaviors to the social customs and expectations of the school, which are presented to him as being both superior to and more desirable than those of his family and community.

In this manner, many poor children have indeed been able, partially through such schools — sometimes in spite of them — to achieve an economically and socially superior status to that of their parents. Today some are still succeeding through such a process in improving their material standing in society. However, questions can be raised as to the price paid by such individuals and the effects of various forms of assimilation and acculturation on people and eventually on society.[19] Today, however, the majority of poverty children, crowded into ghetto slum schools in large urban areas or attending schools in rural poverty sections of the United States, have an infinitely more difficult state of affairs in operation. The far different past legacy of these people and the increasingly mechanistic, depersonalized, and insensitive racist society perpetuates a poverty caste for people who are only a few generations removed from slavery and violent suppression.

The schools of many such children maintain educational curricula that are unilaterally decided upon and adopted via state departments of education and school district central offices. Typically universal for all

children in a community, regardless of their special backgrounds or circumstances, various educational courses of study are prepared and sequenced
by textbook publishers for the national market. Billions of dollars are
spent on the purchase of textbooks which are rigidly and single-mindedly
utilized as standard curricula. As a result, schools today continue to confuse teaching in these programs with learning as they zealously devote
their entire day attempting to get young people through textbooks via
guides, schedules, and routines.

The term "achievement," commonly used to denote the outcomes
of such "textbook teaching," is typically measured by a mixture of arbitrary teacher judgments in the various subject areas and intermittently
conducted, mass-standardized testing. Despite the expenses involved in
such testing, little use if any is made of test results for teaching or self-
study purposes. In the case of assessing reading growth and abilities, few
teachers in slum schools and, for that matter, in most schools, are skilled
in observing and measuring the reading growth and needs of their pupils.
Reading instructional approaches are all too often based exclusively upon
single orientations to reading as reflected in commercially published programs. These materials are forced on the children according to a rigid
schedule, regardless of whether they are prepared for such an experience
or sufficiently fluent and masterful enough to move on to more difficult
and advanced sequences. Little knowledge of reading as a process is
apparent.

This system of *covering* textbook materials almost always seems to
necessitate the need to eliminate, suppress, manage, and control much of
what constitutes healthy, natural child behavior. Activity, movement, talking and use of natural language, pupil interaction, play, curiosity, and
special interests must become secondary to the unknowing teacher's daily
schedule of textbook consumption. Based on such notions as maintaining
class order, discipline, and teaching self-control, which some of these
schools associate with patriotism and Godliness, many teachers and prin-
cipals frequently and sometimes crudely and brutally commit grotesquely
insensitive acts. The motives of such people can range from confused and
misconceived, good-intentioned paternalism to bigoted attitudes of racial
and cultural superiority that often mask their need to dominate, master,
and control other human beings. In various ways and in too many schools,
children are thus forced and habituated to be silent, to remain seated,
and to attend to and be interested in only that which the teacher wishes
them to deal with and is *on the schedule*. Behaviors divergent from expectations are perceived as being signs of basically inferior home environments
or manifestations of immaturity or maladjustment, lately even signs of
cerebral dysfunction. Consistent discipline and ordered and structured

school days are often confused by educators with regimentation, conformity, and sometimes brutal suppression of the individual child's needs. The typical school sees poverty children as requiring the latter version of discipline.

Teachers operating in the center of activity try to serve a heavy educational fare from various teachers' manuals, textbooks, and workbooks in the different subjects. Like priestesses, they ritualistically attempt to present the contents of these materials and like efficiency experts they sometimes learn to manage and control conditions conducive to bringing children through these materials in the allocated time. While little of what they teach seems to be learned, they too often continue to provide reading instruction around the exclusive use of basal readings with little if any divergence, creative inclusion, or individualized attention to children's personal needs. These practices constitute serious misuse of such materials. The consequences of such practices universally contribute to underachievement and disinterest among the children and feelings of hopelessness among teachers. Very soon these experiences lead to convictions regarding minority children's inabilities to learn that result in even *further* underachievement.

A number of basal reading programs literally blanket the nation's schools today. Many school workers have come to perceive these materials as carrying built-in assurances of linguistic, contextual, and sequential infallibility. The world of basal readers is often white, neat, clean, neutral, orderly, and surburban. Many questions are being raised regarding the suitability of such content for black, Puerto Rican, Mexican-American, and Indian children in our society. The linguistic style of basal readers, while difficult to categorize in any manner in the earlier stages of such programs, becomes middle-class English as the readability increases. The possibility that various groups of poverty children might have other conceptual and linguistic styles is discounted by simply and prejudiciously considering such children to be linguistically and cognitively immature or crippled,[14, 28] since they are silent or imperfect in their use of standard English in the classroom.

Introduced to the white man's or Gringo's school in such a fashion and to the process of reading in as rigid, unrealistic, and inconsistent a way as this, it is small wonder that poverty children seem to massively underachieve under present conditions. To explain away this situation, some schools find it more convenient to deplore the home conditions of the children, which are judged by school standards and labeled as crippling or "deprived." Rather than objectively and dispassionately analyzing their own inadequate professional performance, some schools continue to displace responsibility, or grandly attempt to improve educational conditions in their own manner by launching all-out assaults on the behavior, customs, attitudes, language, beliefs, and habits of minority children, assuming that these variables are phenomena interfering with learning.

In the shock over being obviously unable to succeed with poverty children, teachers sometimes bear down upon them even more heavily. Inability of the students to read with comprehension in increasingly more advanced textbooks, as well as disinterest of the older students in a frequently irrelevant and absurdly unreal curriculum (along with growing student harassment, resentment, and aggressive behavior toward these school conditions), results in strongly suppressive forms of discipline quite common in many schools today. Physical manhandling, bullying, haranguing, and brow-beating young people into conforming and listening, even forcing verbal and written responses to their own notions of honor, patriotism, freedom, and gratefulness through effort and responsibility for the educational opportunity offered by the school, are no doubt major contributions to the contempt, anger, and rejection of many of these values among young people today. The insight and understanding of students, frequently superior to many of the school workers who are bullying them, often result in their self-separation from the school, its type of people, and the values that hold society together.

Little patience or tolerance is shown for the courageous teacher or principal who significantly attempts to question and modify educational conditions. Just as obedience is expected of pupils and students, so too is subservience to hierarchy, conformity, and loyalty to the system expected of its employees. Strong-line establishment biases tend to permeate educational leadership, which often tragically shows little, if any, commitment, compassion, or understanding and sensitivity to the problems of the poor. Operating sometimes with cynical contempt for democratic concepts of leadership or utter ignorance of the nature of the school as a public institution, many administrators are able to perpetuate themselves by using minority peoples and financial resources to present a facade of community representation, minority participation, and school modernization.

Schools and colleges of education have been training centers for school workers of every type. Perhaps no other nation in the world views the role of training its teachers, administrators, and specialists for their public educational system with as low a regard as does the U.S. The school or college of education is typically an "academic leper colony"[6] in the parent college or university under which it operates. Despised, ridiculed, or otherwise treated with contemptuous disdain by other departments and faculties, the school of education is all too often a grossly exaggerated facsimile of the very conditions existing in public schools. From the stereotyped, encrusted, and rigidly segmented teacher-training programs to the dreary and often mediocre staffs, the typical school of education frequently presents the routinized model and humdrum, unimaginative atmosphere that is so ingrained a pattern of public education. In this milieu teachers are trained and then certified to malpractice elsewhere. Restraint, neutrality, objectivity, and scholarly pursuit, certainly worthy and vital virtues in any profession, are all too often used as shams for a lack of values and commitment as well as disinterest in the real world outside the college classroom.[37] Few of the great challenges, the forgotten ideals, the lost and unfulfilled dreams, or the critical and growingly tragic consequences of decades of injustice are held up for future teachers, administrators, and specialists to ponder over. Instead, many schools of education continue to graduate workers who not only are unable to educate the new middle-class child for a totally different world, but also produce individuals who are tragically unsuited, unskilled, and hence unable to meaningfully educate poverty children for whom such maleducation results in an even greater personal loss.

In spite of years of providing methods courses in the teaching of reading, the overwhelming bulk of teachers who either teach reading or require students to read textbooks in their field manifest a profound lack of even basic notions pertaining to such experiences. One problem is that for years reading courses were either not required or, as is more common today, inadequately taught. Overfilled college classes, inexperienced or mediocre faculty, isolation of instruction from relevant experiences with children, as well as other inadequate instructional procedures have contributed toward the maintenance of ignorance regarding reading instruction among teachers, administrators, and specialists. Indeed, many reading specialists, both at the college and public school level, can be found who make few if any contributions given their superficial professional training. Very few in the field of reading have committed themselves to studying and contributing to the improvement of educational opportunities for poverty children. Even less interest for these issues is shown by university administrators particularly in periods of scarcity of federal funds.

The "Great Society" Years

The civil rights movement in the 1950s set into motion a period that subsequently was to result in a unique era of federal activity in education. As a result of initial thinking in the Kennedy Administration, the mid-sixties began with a manifestation of commitment typified by a legislative program for a "War on Poverty." The Economic Opportunity Act, the Elementary and Secondary Education Act, and the National

Defense Education Act launched a series of activities in education, among other areas, that in its scope and turbulence left few educators and institutions untouched. The vestiges and remnants of this short-lived period, with its widespread programs and activities, the momentum of which left the educational establishment reeling, can be found almost everywhere today. Some are picking at the fragments and debris of these past projects and programs, attempting to develop and circulate more comprehensive and systematic assessments. This section will comment on this era.

In the last several years, hundreds of millions of dollars of federal money, along with large contributions from various private foundations, have been turned over to diverse groups and institutions for so-called innovative programs and projects in education. Individuals of every age group, from pre-school to high-school dropout, adult jobless, and illiterate, were target populations for various projects. Diverse workers, including public school teachers and administrators, college and university personnel, and other community residents, participated in various ways in projects throughout the nation. Designed with the major intent of contributing to the improvement of education for urban black children and young adults, federal funding to a lesser degree was provided for various programs involving Mexican-American, Puerto Rican, and Indian children as well. Broad in geographic scope as well as in the diverse special fields included, activities ranged from specific attempts to provide educational services for poverty children, such as Title I remedial reading programs, to more multi-faceted programs such as Job Corps, Head Start, Youth Corps, and VISTA volunteers. Disciplines such as science, mathematics, and social studies were included, both in omnibus programs and specific projects. Training institutes for teachers in many of these disciplines were funded for summer sessions and occasionally for a full year. Dropout prevention, Upward Bound, and talent preservation programs aimed at correcting variously hypothesized conditions affecting young people were operationalized. Projects were developed both within public educational institutions and outside such structures. Some programs involved reciprocal and cooperative endeavors between various institutions. Workers from many disciplines allied to education, such as medicine, dentistry, sociology, and psychology, were variously involved, and aides, tutors, and volunteers were utilized as well.

An awareness of the somewhat flawed beginnings of this era has already contributed to a partial understanding of what has happened as a result. It appears, according to one report[24] to which this entire section is indebted, that this was a period of dominance characterized by a professional class of individuals who, with missionary zeal and certainly well-intentioned motivation, apparently confused their desire for rapid change and their self-righteous assertions of what should be done for and about poor minority people, with the possession of information both as to what the basic questions were and the methodology for their solution. Interacting in this "mix" was an executive and a legislative branch of government that often seemed more concerned with action, not planning; with operations, not clearly defined goals; and with structures, not functions. Apparently the consuming motivation was the need for visible action, not the need for careful designing of such programs nor the inclusion of conditions necessary for the objective assessment of results. The untested assumptions of the reformers, along with the less-than-altruistic motivation of the Administration during these years, seems to have resulted in various educational projects and programs, many of which might be considered lofty and naive, and quite a few, sloppy and irrelevant.

Earlier conditions were so poor, however, that few programs of this era were complete failures. Many were far from the successes they were promised to be, in spite of the grandiose and heady publicity that invariably seemed to precede their inception. Partial results from some programs and projects are becoming available. Evaluations of projects such as Higher Horizons, Upward Bound, and Head Start have provided preliminary data which indicate that reform and change resulting from various local enterprises were far from total successes.[20,27,34,36] Many variables and outcomes which should have been studied were not always included, and definitive data are far from easily available; but the information suggests that reform in education, based on these lines of thinking, will be far more difficult to realize than many assume. Underestimating or not accounting for difficulties, suggesting results more positive and immediate than were probable under the circumstances, attempting to legislate and purchase educational change, working from the limited knowledge available and being unaware of these limits because of false self-assuredness, and ignoring the need to explore many alternatives, to include in decision-making participation of minority peoples − all of these eventually led to the unfortunate conditions and less than outstanding results characterizing the events of the period.

Many forms of dysfunction prevailed. In some geographic areas, mimeographed lists of "canned" objectives were made available that could conveniently be copied and included in quickly drawn-up project proposals. Institutions began to acquire and nurture a class of professional project writers who were skilled in putting proposals "together" with less than direct concern with what specific groups of children required. Massive expenditures for the typical types of educational equipment and materials were made with few attempts to purchase materials on the basis of their suitability and appropriateness for poverty children or the availability of staff for their effective use. Moneys and educational equipment purchased for ghetto schools found their way into more affluent schools. Remedial reading programs funded primarily for poverty children often systematically eliminated such children from eligibility for services on the basis of absurdly arbitrary and technically fallacious criteria. Many remedial programs dealing with poverty children today continue to utilize approaches that require serious reappraisal. Much of the funding for various educational projects was funneled into salaries and positions for middle-class, white professionals. Some public institutions used government projects to unabashedly further their own needs and goals, which were not always directly or indirectly related to the education of poverty children.

These internal contradictions had a negative impact on such activities. A method for soliciting innovation without a valid set of original premises from a population of potential educational "innovators" who, more often than not, had demonstrated their past inability to deal openly and effectively with such problems, and a federal bureaucracy unready to administer such a massive program resulted in something close to a grotesque parody of the ghetto "hustle." Smooth operators, grabbing off chunks of the action with urbane, sophisticated aplomb were the order of the day. A new class of "hustler" became the casual commuter to and from Washington, D.C., and these conditions persist.

Much should be learned from these events and the mistakes made. A single theoretical orientation regarding the educational needs of the poor was uniformly adhered to and well suited to the opportunity structure of the reformers and their institutions. To place the blame for reading underachievement upon the child and his environment neatly fits the theoretical biases and needs of these reformers. To label and stereotype masses of children was all too useful in identifying target populations for project proposals. There were too many children, too little time, and far too many who wanted to ride the "gravy train" for such considerations. Gradually, the people for whom all of this was originally planned seemed to fade from concern. These conditions also persist today.

Beginning with the grandest of promises, the bureaucracies always overpredict results. By avoiding an open and objective analysis of other theoretical alternatives, by sidestepping vital issues pertaining to the participation of the poor in such planning, and by not being willing or able to see the contradictions and incompatibility of such behaviors, the conditions for failure are built in from the onset. The final misfortune of the period is the failure to derive information, objectively and empirically, from the careful internal analysis of specifics within various programs and projects. Funding is frequently provided with little detailed prior requirements pertaining to their scientific assessment. "Great Society," "War on Poverty," or "Right-to-Read" — the results tend all to be the same.

Considerations For Reform

Today random activity and uncertainty prevail, as confused and somewhat desperate school workers face new and more intensive pressures. Often unable to emotionally or intellectually face the realities of race, ethnicity, and social class, with little commitment often to anything but staying in the job and maintaining the kind of school system which had seemed satisfactory in the past, too many school administrators continue to hopelessly separate the poor, and sometimes the affluent as well, from their antiquated educational institutions. Many of these administrators look backward with nostalgia to that era when fanfare and rhetoric were an adequate enough smokescreen to obscure their inability to make realistic and meaningful changes of direct benefit to minority children of poverty circumstances. A good deal of their thinking regarding how to cope with this educational crisis continues to be based upon the need for increasing financial inputs to their schools through massive governmental support without recognition of the need for programs so that such funds will be specifically utilized to intensify the influence of education relative to the needs of poverty children.[10] The spectacle of the same people, continuing to call for federal funding, with no evidence of making their institutions more responsive to the needs of various poor children, is a sign of the critical nature of conditions today. Funding continues to be based on shallow promises.

This discussion does not presume to be able in some way to articulate the exact nature of procedures that must be undertaken to right the wrongs that our society has committed, and therefore, reform our educational system overnight. An attempt, however, will be made in this final section to present a series of considerations believed to be part of what is necessary to understand and hence plan for the reform of our educational institutions.

Cultural Bias and Racism

With well over two hundred years of history, most white, middle-class Americans take pride in the shift our country has made from an emerging but weak democracy in a world of powerful authoritarian states to the most technologically advanced industrial nation in the world. This position, however, has not come without its price. Our country quite early in the process pushed aside or ignored many of the earlier dreams and hopes for a just society and worthwhile life for all of its people. Our dramatic economic growth has come about through the thoughtless exploitation of peoples and natural resources, and the neglect of basic human values.

After generations of subjugation and suppression of minority peoples in our society — blacks, Mexican-Americans, Indians, and others — we are being told that we are a racist society, that we have in fact suppressed and subjugated these people, and that now they are preparing to free themselves from such conditions. In striving for this state, they do not ask but rather put our society on notice that they will obtain the necessary powers to do so. They are talking of political, economic, social, and psychological power to "be" and "become" a people first and eventually contribute, for the first time, as equals in our society.[9] That the United States is not quite as open, free, just, and equal a society to all its peoples as we have been educated to believe comes as a shockingly disloyal and perhaps untrue statement to most Americans. However, if people who are shocked by such possibilities would be willing and open-minded enough to observe their own environments, it would be a simple matter to note the deeply imbedded nature of prejudice, bigotry, and bias that pervade the attitudes and practices of many Americans. The imbeddedness of such behaviors regarding issues dealing with race, ethnicity, culture, language, and social class is all-pervasive. Our public schools tend to be but a reflection of such a society. The workers who contribute to the functions of such social structures carry their biases with them into their schools and classrooms. Poverty children who do not achieve in such schools are seen as deficient and deprived of a culture and language; hence as unable to learn. Schools exhibiting such cultural biases are seen by many middle-class people as valiant defenders of proper educational procedures. It is quite common to hear school personnel reason that these children have crippling environments[35] and that they, therefore, must be changed from what they are, as a result of their backgrounds, to what we think they ought to be. Our society must recognize these issues and the vicious circle that ineffective education perpetuates from generation to generation among the poor.

An Alternative Hypothesis

The deficiency-deprivation model has dominated both thinking and practice in the area of educating minority children from poverty environments for some time. On the basis of universally observed underachievement in reading, which seems to have critical consequences in all subsequent academic performance, such children have been said to be in one degree or another, linguistically, cognitively, and intellectually deprived and disadvantaged. Thus, educational strategies of a remedial or compensatory nature have been continuously applied to these children.

Research has been published in which observed differences are noted between minority children and middle-class children in various psychometrically determined characteristics. [7, 11, 33] Some commentary seems to be in order regarding such studies; one criticism might be that these differences might be more a reflection of the cultural bias of the measuring instruments used than manifestations of so-called deprivations or deficiencies. Stated differently, one linguist pointed out that while one group of researchers was measuring how well children mastered environmental tasks — not of their own environment — another group might very well ask how these children have learned and mastered tasks related to their own culture, language, and environment.[2] The practice of generalizing from observations of cultural differences to hypothetical environmental causes of such differences without collecting data to support these generalizations seems also to be narrow and unscientific. Indeed, the exclusive focus on the children's home environments as a cause of poor test performance or on genetic factors rather than on the middle-class biases of the test instruments and researchers themselves[8] suggests reasoning that is not without the element of bias. Generalizations regarding the influences of heredity and environment on such test performance may or may not be true or part of the truth. It is more likely that answers will be equivocal. The responsibility for verifying or refuting such assumptions, however, rests upon the scientist who must first collect and then account for data. Suggesting, in addition, that such measured differences imply discarding the notion of equal development of minority children through equal educational opportunity is somewhat premature in light of questions raised pertaining to the validity of such studies.

A growing number of observers are questioning the deprivation-deficiency model and are suggesting careful study of alternative hypotheses — one being that of cultural differences — as an explanation for the school underachievement of minority children.[3, 16] The model of cultural differences suggests that a conflict of cultures might be a useful alternative explanation for the educational underachievement of poverty children. A number of linguists for example, have reported studies and observations of black children's language system.[1, 12, 30, 31, 32] Evidence seems to point to the existence of a well-ordered and highly structured nonstandard dialect of English which differs from standard English in terms of the sound system, grammar, and vocabulary. In the view of several of these linguists,[3, 32] such differences create an "interference effect" in learning to read for some black children whose vernacular is this dialect rather than standard English. An instrument designed for assessing such dialectal differences has been reported in the literature.[2] It has also been noted that linguistic differences are of some importance in the reading underachievement of various groups of Spanish- and Indian-speaking children, whose vernacular is a language other than English.[16,29] Many other so-called bilingual children might be experiencing difficulties in reading associated with this phenomenon, as well as cross-cultural interference in the psycho-social domains.

Most American schools, apparently assuming that all children should speak standard English as they enter school, introduce all children to reading in English, regardless of what dialect or other language happens to be spoken at home. The so-called interference effect resulting from this type of procedure, in terms of learning to read, as well as communicating with teachers and learning in other subjects, could be critical. Requiring children to read in a language they do not speak or understand seems indefensible. A few studies are available dealing with the vernacular teaching of reading with populations of Indian and Puerto Rican pupils.[21,23] The results of these studies strongly support the value of introducing pupils to reading first in their mother tongue. It would seem important for a series of studies to be conducted with differing populations of black children to explore the influence of introducing various children to reading first in "Black English" on subsequent growth in reading abilities. The latter approach could prove to be more appropriate for certain of these children rather than typical remedial programs. The timing of which approach should come first for different children is a major research issue. Regional differences in language styles within subgroups further complicates these issues.

Broader implications than bilingual and/or bidialectal teaching of reading and language instruction might be consistent with the model of cultural differences. It would seem that linguistic differences, whether they be dialectal or involve a language other than English, might better be thought of as possible reflections of subcultural differences that require a new look at both the context in which learning takes place — the teacher, school, and format of instruction, as well as the content of instruction, the subjects, topics, and sequencing that children will be encountering. It would seem that a bicultural learning experience requires uniquely oriented schools, specially trained teachers, and content developed specifically for various minority children of poverty backgrounds. This appears to be a consideration of some importance.[5,15,22] The realization of such a goal calls for massive changes in current thinking.

Generalizations so often applied to black, Mexican-American, or Indian children — their inability to attend, their lack of interest, application, and motivation — might be considered in this context more an effect of unsuitable and inappropriate school learning conditions than a direct cause of the overly stereotyped factors of home neglect, family disorganization, and neighborhood decay. The implications of the model of differences are thus such that perhaps rather than remaking and remodeling minority children of poverty into an image of what the middle class sees as necessary for learning, a new school, teacher, and curriculum are in order. This school must be attuned to *their* environment, which has its own reality and integrity independent of middle-class society. Minority subcultures are complex, distinct, and functional for poverty children. Value judgments about them depend on who is looking at what, and from which side of the fence. Since few whites are effective in a black ghetto and few Gringos are effective in a Spanish ghetto, focusing a school in such a manner on the nature of its community and people indeed requires a somewhat different makeup of leaders, teachers, curriculum, and community participants. Such a school need not be seen as an impossible goal.

Reforming the Educational Establishment

The professional educator need not always consider himself a mere creature of society and its prejudices. He can strive toward becoming an educational leader and agent of change in his community and institution. While many structures in the educational system continue to provide rewards for personal and professional conformity, while many still demand loyalty and subservience reminiscent of other forms of government than democracy, still others are striving toward democratization and modernity. A growing number of leaders, although still too few, are becoming aware of the changes needed in American institutions if the country and way of life are to move forward. Schools must be shaped by leaders and the community to become more responsive through focusing on *people;* not on forms and structures.

The bottled-up feelings of powerlessness and hopelessness of poverty people might demand a form of catharsis other than that obtainable through institutionalized change, if this is not forthcoming. Leaders and specialists in education can begin the process, however, by analyzing their practices and procedures against a number of new criteria. Their prejudices, biases, ethnocentrism, and misunderstandings have made them ineffective in having a direct and significant influence on educational matters dealing with minority poverty children. Immediate steps, therefore, should be taken to turn to minority people for decision-making over the destinies of their children when they are in the majority and participatory representation when in the minority.[9] The contradictions between community representation in schools and leadership positions and American notions of democracy and self-determination should no longer be permitted to go unrecognized and unrepaired.

A new form of leadership is long overdue. Educational institutions with encrusted traditions and neutral or nonexistent value systems which inhibit creative talent must be reformed. Circular behaviors resulting from underlying paternalistic patterns must be identified, and leaders who perpetuate them must be helped to find less sensitive situations. The forces operating on all workers must be identified, and conditions must be established which will permit interracial, interethnic, and interprofessional communications. Color, ethnicity, and social class are life realities — they cannot be overlooked, denied, hidden, suppressed, or otherwise toyed with by leaders of the future.

Modern and more objective systems must be considered for the recognition and training of new leaders in education, representative of all people in this society. Interdisciplinary activities with community participation are necessary so that doors are opened to the development of different and more creative types of leaders. Their training must result in a break from authoritarian models and the misuse of institutionalized power. People of minority and poverty backgrounds must be trained as leaders to operate in environments to which they are sensitive. They must be given the freedom to create conditions that will result in achievement for their children. Trainees from diverse backgrounds should interact and together learn to define problems, coordinate resources, facilitate change processes, and solve problems so as to remake education for poverty children, eventually remaking education for all. A new bidialectal, bilingual, and bicultural emphasis requires leadership that is aware and open to all the realities of minority status and life in American society.

Civilizing Public Education

Crucial to all human learning and direction is the need for children to be in an environment sensitive and concerned with values and ideals that first begin with enhancing their own life conditions as individuals. A massed society, with sprawling slums, suburbs, and a rampaging technology has created a school in its very image. Separated from the people and its community by decades of promulgating its omnipotence and infallibility — such schools have been dealing with children as if they were analogous to raw materials which are pounded, beaten, molded, and shaped into products to be consumed by society, rather than human beings who should be learning to become free citizens in a democracy. Reform will require getting back to basics that have long since passed us by.

A regimented, conformity-oriented, and brain-washing school must be considered as running counter to the values of a democracy whose form of government is based on the assumption of an educated citizenry. Schooling for too many children and young people in our society is a grim experience. Teachers themselves reward children by freeing them from having to be in their classrooms or from assigned work. The frequent triumph of educational technology over human needs in our schools, the reverence for textbooks, equipment, and devices, and the way children are scheduled into classes and mechanically programmed — must be reversed if some relevant degree of civilization is to return to our schools.

Prudence, responsibility, spontaneity, creativity, eagerness to learn, pride in scholarly accomplishment, quest for a contributing way of life in one's society, and pride in one's people are not middle-class values; they are human needs.[17] Our schools do violence to such needs by over-ordering, managing, and controlling human beings. In this regard one might consider whether the reported underachievement in reading and other school subjects of many young people might possibly be an artifact of over-organized environments rather than manifest behavior.

Reforming the Training of Teachers

Exciting possibilities await the schools of education fortunate enough to have leaders with vision to plan and prepare in the present for the public schools of the future. To achieve these possibilities, an energetic, flexible, and sophisticated group of professionals and lay people are required. Interdisciplinary counseling and participation are necessary for the development of new models for teacher training. Emphasis on the recognition and development of tough, alert, sensitive, questioning, skilled, and resourceful young people must be maintained. The stultifying and banal segmenting of methods classes away from the realities of the community must be reconsidered, as individuals are helped to develop into teachers who can maximize learning opportunities for young children. Skilled in an understanding of the nature of language and the conditions necessary to enhance learning and intellect by means of language, these new teachers should be able to explore more creative and individualized approaches toward the development of pupils who can communicate. It is necessary to train teachers to consider the learning of reading not as a separate discipline with its own unique technology but rather as a language experience and an outgrowth of relevant learning experiences. These new teachers should be skilled in basing reading instruction on both the communication skills and background of children with whom they will work. Beginning with strengthening understanding and pride for one's self and one's own people by using natural content that connects the school with children's real worlds, people, and linguistic styles, teachers might see readers develop as a matter of course. Children must be educated who can move easily from one dialect to another and who can communicate fluently in various language modalities. To do this, teachers must either come from or know the child's subculture so well that they are part of their students' world, and deeper understandings of the reading process must be developed.

These teachers must be skilled in helping children find out what they can do — their talents, abilities, and liabilities — by becoming sensitive observers of individual abilities, needs, and growth in all areas of child development. They must become facile in developing learning contexts that permit children to think about and solve problems for themselves. The new teachers must learn, as many teachers of the past have never learned, to completely subjugate curriculum, textbooks, equipment, and other media to the needs of the children whom they are guiding. They must also be capable of showing the children how to become masters of this technology, how to use such devices wisely, justly, and purposefully. The entire city should become a learning laboratory for children. The artificiality of the school as a learning facility must be recognized, and accounted for. All of these assumptions require scientific investigation.

Research and the Reform Movement

Research stands as the basis for moving toward the more useful questions and answers needed if educational reform is to be realized. In spite of the positive rhetoric associated so often with the values of research, school people frequently become intoxicated by the notion that some new reading program or kit of materials or programmed collection of reading skills will result in a solution for severe and complex educational ills. The history of reading instruction is a symbol of the muddled results that accrue from unsophisticated and enthusiastic faith in the search for panaceas. The research of the new period must maintain the critical spirit so necessary to separate the need for inquiry and the search for truth from the pressing social needs for action and immediate reform. The latter can be entered into in such a way that vital information can be forthcoming for the adjustment of such projects to their betterment. Practical changes in upgrading and maximizing innovative action programs can be realized through highly skilled and well-designed assessments and analyses. The search for truth through scientific method is a cumulative, long-term, and separate process that cannot be thoroughly mixed up with applied action-oriented research.

Correct answers to educational problems, however, must be based upon relevant questions raised by individuals who are not only scientifically trained but experientially suited to be sensitive to many of the issues and nuances involved. These researchers must be able to bring insights into experimental designs of multiple phenomena important to their questions. The research establishment, almost exclusively made up of people of middle-class backgrounds,[25] is often too predisposed, in general, to mainstream concerns to meet the requirements in the area of cross-cultural research. Immersed in middle-class characteristics and the instruments for their measurement, many workers continue to show insensitivity to the necessities of useful research with poverty children. A serious need exists for an all-out, but well-planned, national program for the recruitment, training, and placement in key positions of people in fields of research and development. American leadership, often overwhelmed with fears of controversy over racial issues, tends to seriously inhibit possibilities for research in these areas.

The almost universal reliance in reading research on the quantitative assessment of variables requiring qualitative differentiation, as well as the continuous pursuit of the accumulation of research articles around theoretical approaches, suggests that much of current research in reading is possibly make-believe science-making. Greater attention must be paid in the future to the development of theoretical models of reading, the deeper exploration of the reading process itself, the careful study of changes in reading maturity at key points in a child's learning cycle, and the investigation of interacting influences of learning environment with a child's characteristics, as well as to the development of more sensitive techniques for observing reading growth and needs. Also important is the need to identify hypothesized differences in minority children, to explore the effects of adjusting schools to such differences, and to assess the results of such changes for the purposes of developing a new but differentiated model of public education for these children.

Conclusion

A Frankensteinian, massed, technological society has resulted in an educational system that appears to be unable to humanely educate young children. Its mechanical efficiency is a mark of its ineffectiveness. The system is particularly inappropriate for minority children from poverty backgrounds. In this system, the educational establishment develops all too frequently into a managerial class which seems to be more concerned with perpetuating its opportunity structure than with providing leadership in moving its institutions into more effective and responsive postures for educating human beings. The ordering, controlling and manipulating of the destinies of children about whom little is known and in some cases little care is evidenced should no longer be tolerated in our country.

Educational leaders, therefore, must make many far-reaching decisions in an unprecedented, increasingly chaotic environment, where social, political, and international issues are sometimes settled in the streets rather than around conference tables or in the voting booth. While a democracy cannot afford to permit any individual or group to unilaterally nullify legally established and legitimate institutions and leaders, it cannot afford to ignore the conditions basic to such events. The old cliches of law and order, which almost every American stands behind, can no longer be hauled out conveniently to suppress the fears and aspirations of people. The history of mankind has well demonstrated this.

Major changes are in order in United States society. Chief among them is the need to reaffirm our basic commitment to justice, equality, and opportunity for all. The schools of the United States should take the first steps in moving toward these goals by realizing major reforms in their operations. Some of the considerations underlying such changes have been briefly discussed here. A major question which remains at this point is, *will there be enough time?*

References

1. Bailey, B., "Toward a New Perspective in Negro English Dialectology," *American Speech 40* (1967): 171–77.
2. Baratz, Joan C., "A Bi-Dialectal Task for Determining Language Proficiency in Economically Disadvantaged Negro Children," *Child Development 40* (September 1969): 889–901.
3. Baratz, Joan C., "Teaching Reading in an Urban Negro School System," in *Teaching Black Children to Read,* ed. J. Baratz and R. Shuy (Washington, D.C.: Center for Applied Linguistics, 1969), pp. 92–116.
4. Barton, Allen, "Social Class and Instructional Procedures in the Process of Learning to Read," in *Twelfth Yearbook,* National Reading Conference, ed. C.Y. Melton and R.C. Staiger (Milwaukee: The NRC, Inc., 1962).
5. Bell, Paul, "The Bilingual School," in *Reading and Inquiry,* ed. J.A. Figurel, Proceedings of the International Reading Association 10 (1965): 271–74.
6. Bernstein, Abraham, *The Education of Urban Populations* (New York: Random House, 1967), p. 67.
7. Bernstein, Basil, "Language and Social Class," *British Journal Sociology 11* (1960): 271–76.
8. Burton, Jean L., "Intelligence and Intelligence Testing," in *Perspectives in the Education of Disadvantaged Children: A Multidisciplinary Approach,* ed. M. Cowles (Cleveland: World Publishing Co., 1967), pp. 97–125.
9. Carmichael, Stokeley and Charles V. Hamilton, *Black Power: The Politics of Liberation in America* (New York: Vintage Books, 1967), pp. 1–98.
10. Coleman, James, "The Concept of Equality of Opportunity," *Harvard Educational Review 38* (Winter 1968): 7–22.
11. Deutsch, Martin, "The Role of Social Class in Language Development and Cognition," *American Journal of Orthopsychiatry 35*: 24–35.
12. Dillard, J.L., "Negro Children's Dialect in the Inner City," *Florida Foreign Language Reporter 2* (1967): 7–10.
13. Flanagan, John C. *et al., The American High School Student* (Pittsburgh: Project Talent, University of Pittsburgh, 1964.)
14. Frost, J.L., "Developing Literacy in Disadvantaged Children," in *Issues and Innovations in the Teaching of Reading,* ed. J.L. Frost (Glenview, Ill.: Scott-Foresman & Co., 1967), pp. 264–74.
15. Gaarder, Bruce A., "Organization of the Bilingual School," *Journal of Social Issues 23* (April 1967): 110–20.

16. Goodman, Kenneth, "Let's Dump the Uptight Model in English," *Elementary School Journal 70* (October 1969): 1–13.
17. Goodman, Paul, *Compulsory Mis-Education and the Community of Scholars* (New York: Vintage Books, 1962).
18. "Harlem Youth Opportunities Unlimited," in *Youth in the Ghetto* (New York: HARYOU, Inc., 1964).
19. Howe, Harold II, "Cowboys, Indians and American Education," in *Papers of the National Conference on Educational Opportunities for Mexican-Americans* (Austin, Texas: Southwest Educational Development Laboratory, April 1968).
20. Hunt, David E. and Robert H. Hardt, "The Effect of Upward Bound Programs on the Attitudes, Motivation and Academic Achievement of Negro Students," *Journal of Social Issues 25* (Summer, 1969): 117–29.
21. Kauffman, Maurice, "Will Instruction in Reading Spanish Affect Ability in Reading English?" *Journal of Reading 11* (April 1968): 521–27.
22. Mermelstein, Mariluz and Bernard Fox, "The Sands Project," *High Points 47* (March 1965): 5–10.
23. Modiano, Nancy, "National or Mother Language in Beginning Reading: A Comparative Study," *Research in the Teaching of English 2* (Spring 1968): 32–43.
24. Moynihan, Daniel P., *Maximum Feasible Misunderstanding: Community Action in the War on Poverty* (New York: The Free Press, 1969).
25. Moynihan, Daniel P., "Sources of Resistance to the Coleman Report," *Harvard Educational Review 38* (Winter 1968): 23–36.
26. Mugge, Robert H., "Education and AFDC," *Welfare in Review 2* (January 1964): 1–14.
27. Raph, Jane B., "Language Characteristics of Culturally Disadvantaged Children: Review and Implications," in *Perspectives in the Education of Disadvantaged Children,* ed. M. Cowles (Cleveland: World Book Co., 1967), pp. 183–208.
28. Rosen, Carl L. and Philip D. Ortego, "Language and Reading Problems of Spanish-Speaking Children in the Southwest," *Journal of Reading Behavior 1* (Winter 1969): 51–70.
29. Shuy, Roger W., "A Linguistic Background for Developing Beginning Reading Materials for Black Children," in *Teaching Black Children to Read,* ed. J.C. Baratz and R.W. Shuy (Washington, D.C.: Center for Applied Linguistics, 1969), pp. 117–37.
30. Stewart, W., "Continuity and Change in American Negro Dialects," *Florida Foreign Language Reporter 6* (1968): 11–26.
31. Stewart, W., "On the Use of Negro Dialect in the Teaching of Reading," in *Teaching Black Children to Read,* ed. J.C. Baratz and R.W. Shuy (Washington, D.C.: Center for Applied Linguistics, 1969), pp. 156–219.
32. Stodolsky, S.S. and G. Lesser, "Learning Patterns of Disadvantaged," *Harvard Educational Review 37* (Fall 1967): 546–93.
33. "A Study of Head Start," *Phi Delta Kappan 50* (June 1969), p. 591 (excerpted from *The New Republic*).
34. U.S. Commission on Civil Rights, *Racial Isolation in the Public Schools,* vol. 1 (Washington, D.C.: U.S. Government Printing Office, 1967), pp. 115–40.
35. U.S. Dept. of Health, Education and Welfare, *The First Year of Title I ESEA: The States Report* (Washington, D.C.: U.S. Government Printing Office, 1966), p. vii.
36. Wrightstone, Wayne J. et. al., *Evaluation of the Higher Horizons Program for Underprivileged Children* (New York: Bureau of Educational Research, Board of Education of City of New York, 1964.)
37. Zinn, Howard, "The Case for Radical Change," *Saturday Review 52* (October 18, 1969): 81–82, 94.

16

When Should Standard English Be Taught to Speakers of Nonstandard Negro Dialect?

KENNETH R. JOHNSON

Many culturally disadvantaged black students speak a variety of English that linguists have labeled "nonstandard Negro dialect." The problem for the schools in the language arts program, obviously, is to teach these students standard English. All educators agree that this is one of the primary goals — perhaps, the most important goal — of the total instructional program. Educators do not unanimously agree, however, on *when* to teach standard English to disadvantaged black students who speak nonstandard Negro dialect. Stated another way, educators are not sure about the age group or grade level at which to expect these students to acquire standard English.

Currently, there is a lively controversy on this issue. Some educators feel that standard English should be taught to disadvantaged black children as soon as they enter kindergarten. Other educators feel that instruction should be delayed until the intermediate grades of elementary school. Still others feel that standard English should not be taught to disadvantaged black students until they reach adolescence or the secondary grades.

The purpose of this chapter is to discuss the question of when (specifically, at what age group or grade level) to teach standard English to disadvantaged black children who speak nonstandard Negro dialect. The study will pertain to three age groups or grade levels: students from the ages of five to eight who are in the primary grades, students from the ages of nine to eleven who are in the intermediate grades, and students from the ages of twelve to eighteen who are in the secondary grades. The discussion will point out the reasons standard English should not be taught to disadvantaged black children who speak nonstandard Negro dialect prior to adolescence or the secondary grades. Many educators

Adapted from *Language Learning* 20, no. 1 (1970): 15–30.

Kenneth R. Johnson of the University of Illinois at Chicago Circle is interested in both the sociocultural and the linguistic aspects of teaching the disadvantaged bidialectal student. In addition to journal articles, he has published a book entitled *Teaching the Culturally Disadvantaged*.

will disagree with this recommendation, because they feel that delaying instruction in standard English will penalize black students and deprive them of learning an important skill. The discussion here, however, will point out why these students cannot be expected to learn — and, more importantly, to use — standard English until they reach adolescence or the secondary grades.

Nonstandard Negro dialect systematically differs from standard English in its phonology and grammar. Some of the ways it differs phonologically are: speakers often omit certain phonemes of standard English (initial voiced [th]; medial voiced and voiceless [th]; final voiced and voiceless [th]; medial [v]; final [b], [d], [g], [k], [p], and [t]; [r] and [l]); distinction is not made between [i] and [e] before nasals; and syllables of words are "assimilated." Some of the ways it differs grammatically are: the final plural morpheme is often omitted if another word in the sentence denotes the plural *(I got three ball);* the possessive morpheme is often omitted *(The boy hat was lost);* the "double subject" and the double negative is used; the agreement morpheme is omitted from third person singular present tense verbs *(She go to the store in the morning);* the past tense form of an irregular verb and its present participle form are reversed *(I done my work; I have did my work);* the copular verb in present or present progressive tense is omitted *(I busy; I writing a letter).* Not all disadvantaged black children have every phonological feature of nonstandard Negro dialect in their speech. As a population, however, certain deviations occur in the speech of disadvantaged blacks with such frequency that the aggregate of these deviations from standard English comprise the variety of English labeled nonstandard Negro dialect.

The existence of nonstandard Negro dialect has been recognized only recently. Educators, at the urging of linguists, have only lately understood that many black children speak a variety of English that *systematically* differs from standard English. Educators have long recognized that the language of disadvantaged black children contains many phonological and grammatical deviations from standard English. These deviations were looked upon as just "errors." The language arts program consisted of helping these black children eliminate the errors from their speech and replace them with "correct" standard English patterns. The assumption that the speech of disadvantaged black students was full of errors, instead of being a variety of English that systematically differed from standard English, resulted in an instructional approach that, in its simplest form, told students "don't say it like that, say it like this." This approach has been demonstrably ineffective. Few disadvantaged black students taught in this way learned to speak standard English, and if they did it was not until they reached adolescence or the secondary grades.

Since the discovery of the fact that nonstandard Negro dialect systematically differs from and interferes with standard English, the above approach has been strongly criticized. A different approach is needed to teach standard English to disadvantaged black children. Because the phonological and grammatic subsystems of nonstandard Negro dialect systematically interfere with standard English much like the interference between a foreign language and English, a second language approach has been suggested as the instructional approach to take for teaching standard English to many black students.

Basically, a second language approach: (1) helps the students understand that there is a difference between their variety of English and standard English (without the usual accompanying stigma that is attached to the difference); (2) helps the students hear the standard sound or pattern; (3) requires the students to discriminate between the sound or pattern of their dialect and the sound or pattern of standard English that is in interference or conflict; (4) requires the students to reproduce the standard sound or pattern (notice, reproduction of the standard sound or pattern occurs after three previous steps; the traditional language arts program jumps from recognition of a difference — step one — to reproduction — step four); and finally (5) the students are given *oral* drill to help them establish the standard sound or pattern in their speech.

The second language approach is likely to be the successful approach to follow in teaching standard English to disadvantaged black children, and its advantages will not be debated here. This discussion, however, will attempt to determine whether or not the second language approach is one of the factors to consider in determining the age group or grade level at which to teach standard English.

The Primary Grades

As stated before, some educators feel that standard English should be taught to disadvantaged black children who speak nonstandard Negro dialect as soon as these children enter kindergarten. This point of view implies expectations that these children can actually learn and come to use standard English in time — certainly before they reach adolescence or the secondary grades. This assumption becomes questionable when the language development and language environment of disadvantaged black children are examined.

Like all children, disadvantaged black children come to kindergarten knowing the basic phonological and grammatical features of the variety of English spoken in their particular cultural environment. In other words, they know the basic features of nonstandard Negro dialect, because this is the variety of English spoken in their primary culture, the disadvantaged black subculture. In this subculture, nonstandard Negro dialect is used by the children's families, friends, neighbors, ministers, and black merchants. Almost everyone with whom they come into face-to-face contact uses nonstandard Negro dialect: the nature of our segregated society insures that young disadvantaged black children (and also older disadvantaged black children) have few opportunities to communicate with speakers of standard English. Thus, the language these children come to school speaking is nonstandard Negro dialect.

But although they speak this dialect, they don't know it perfectly. Like all children, black kindergarten and primary children are struggling to master the variety of English spoken in their particular primary cultural environment. It is unreasonable to expect them to learn to speak another dialect of English so closely related to nonstandard Negro dialect that many of the differences, or conflict points, cannot be perceived by them.

Because of this trouble in perceiving conflict points, second language techniques are difficult to use with young disadvantaged black children. As pointed out above, this approach requires the learners to hear the standard sound or pattern, discriminate the standard from the nonstandard sound or pattern, then reproduce the standard sound or pattern. This is a difficult task for young disadvantaged black children. For example, these children say *wif, mouf,* and *paf* for *with, mouth,* and *path.* Hearing the difference between final [f] and final voiceless [th] is difficult. Thus it is clear why these children have trouble when attempting to do a second language type audio-discrimination drill such as determining which pronunciation is given twice in the following series: *wif, wif, with; mouth, mouf, mouth; paf, path, paf.* As another example: nonstandard Negro dialect eliminates certain consonant sounds at the ends of words, and it is very difficult for young disadvantaged black children to distinguish the difference between their pronunciation of words without end consonant sounds and the standard pronunciation of these words. If these kinds of distinctions between conflict points cannot be made, second language techniques do not work. But young black children are neither comfortable enough in their own dialect nor far enough developed in their maturation for us to expect second language techniques to be successful with them.

It is often pointed out that young children learn a second language more easily than adults, and this argument is often used to support the teaching of standard English to disadvantaged black children who speak nonstandard Negro dialect. There are two false assumptions on which this argument is based. First, the argument assumes that learning a second dialect of a language is just as easy or no more difficult than learning another language; since children do learn other languages, then black children should be able to learn another dialect of English. Learning another dialect of English, however, is more difficult for young black children than learning another language; that is, it is more difficult than learning another language in an ideal setting. This leads into the second false assumption on which the argument is based. Young children do learn, surprisingly easily, another language when they begin to live and must function in a cultural environment where another language is spoken and is demanded of them for social and cultural acceptance and for communication. Under these conditions, children do learn another language more easily than adults. Disadvantaged black children, however, do not have the opportunity to live and function in a cultural environment where standard English is spoken. Our segregated society prevents this. Furthermore, the segregated environment in which black children live offers little opportunity for standard English to be reinforced in their cultural environment. This has been implied, of course, throughout this discussion: it is unreasonable to expect black children to learn a variety of English they contact only at school and which is not reinforced in their primary cultural environment.

Thus, the argument that disadvantaged black children should be able to learn standard English as easily as other children learn a second language breaks down on two counts: learning a second *dialect* in a school setting is more difficult for these children than learning a second language is for other children; and black children are not a part of a cultural environment where standard English is used and where the communication demands of the environment require and reinforce standard English.

Perhaps another reason children learn second languages is the joy of learning something new. Black children, however, already speak English, although not standard English. They can understand standard English, even if they don't speak it. (They do not, however, understand it perfectly, and some linguists and educators feel this is a tremendous handicap to these children in school.) Learning a second dialect is not novel enough to generate the kind of enjoyment children may have in learning an entirely different language.

Some educators are quick to point out that television reinforces standard English in the cultural environment of disadvantaged black children. (Not so with the radio, however — most blacks listen to "soul" stations, and the announcers on these stations often use nonstandard Negro dialect, or include in their speech many features of it.) This is partially a valid observation. That is, television does reinforce standard English, but it reinforces only the *understanding* of standard English, not the *speaking* of standard English. If it did reinforce speaking standard English, black children would be speaking standard English. (They, too, spend many hours watching television.)

The main reason disadvantaged black children don't learn to speak standard English by listening to television is that television is not an instructional situation. Announcers don't point out to their black listeners that the speech pattern about to be used contains a phoneme lacking in the listeners' dialect or includes the copula in a particular sentence where the listeners' dialect omits it. In other words, television announcing does not present its language in a second language approach; or, more importantly, in an instructional mode.

Finally, there is a question of need, or motivation, and this is the most crucial reason for not teaching primary black children standard English. What reason can possibly be given to primary disadvantaged black children, five to eight years old, to convince and motivate them to learn standard English? The teacher can't tell them they need to know a "better" variety of English. Even if this was true — and it is not — it wouldn't impress these primary children. The teacher can't point out to them that they need to learn standard English so they can go to college or get a better job. Their main concern, like that of most children, is play. Also, these children are "present oriented." The fact that they will need standard English for their future adult lives is ridiculous to point out at their young age. Thus, disadvantaged black children don't recognize a need for standard English, and without this recognition they lack the motivation to learn it.

For all of these reasons then, standard English should not be taught to primary-grade-level disadvantaged black children who speak nonstandard Negro dialect, and they cannot be expected to learn it. Instead, the language arts program for these children should concentrate on other things.

The most important activity that should be conducted in the primary grades is to encourage black children to use their own nonstandard Negro dialect. They should be given many opportunities to use their dialect and helped to develop it. The usual practice — particularly in the later primary grades — is to "correct" black children into standard English when they use their dialect. By the time they leave the primary grades, they have a reputation for being "nonverbal," because they have not been encouraged to use their own dialect, and when they did, they were often corrected. Too much correction turned off speech. The way to avoid correction is to either speak standard English (which they cannot do), or to be quiet (which too many choose to do).

A second emphasis of the primary language arts program — especially in kindergarten and first grade — should be to help black children increase their ability to understand standard English. They come to school with this ability, but they should be given many activities in the school setting to extend their ability to understand this dialect. Standard English is the language of the school — the language of instruction — and it is vitally important that disadvantaged black children develop the ability to understand it, even if they do not, or cannot, develop the ability to speak it.

Another emphasis of the primary language arts program for disadvantaged black children is expansion of vocabulary. These children come to school lacking much of the vocabulary the school expects, and on which instruction is based.

A lack of vocabulary reflects another deficiency: *a deficiency in those concepts on which the curriculum is based.* Thus the primary language arts program should concentrate on helping these children develop those concepts necessary for achievement. The reason disadvantaged black children lack these concepts is that they have not acquired the experiences in their cultural background which generate these concepts (or the vocabulary which labels these concepts).

This is not to say that disadvantaged black children are deficient in concepts, as many educators assume. These children acquire many concepts from their cultural experience. The trouble is, the curriculum is not based on the conceptual development acquired from a disadvantaged black subcultural experience. Instead, the curriculum is based on those concepts acquired from a middle-class dominant cultural experience. Thus, disadvantaged black children are given compensatory programs (programs which compensate for the lack of experiences which produce the concepts on which the curriculum is based).

But there is another way to educate these children. The school can use their disadvantaged background as a readiness for learning. In other words, the curriculum can be based on the concepts derived from their experience. Not enough research has been done to determine what the conceptual development of disadvantaged black children is. Research that is done usually reveals what they lack when compared to middle-class children, not what they have. Until we know what they have, the present kinds of compensatory education programs must be retained. That is, we must continue to try to give disadvantaged black children the concepts they lack so they can fit into the existing middle-class oriented curriculum, instead of altering the curriculum to fit their conceptual development. The point is, these children may not be *deficient* but *different,* and this is a distinction that many educators have not recognized.

This discussion has focused on one aspect of the language arts program for disadvantaged black children: the problem of teaching them standard English. An equally important aspect of the language arts program is reading. In line with the recommendation to delay teaching disadvantaged black children to speak standard English, it follows that the teaching of reading, too, should be delayed. It is unreasonable to expect disadvantaged black children to read a variety of English they do not speak. This, perhaps, is the main reason that many of these children don't learn to read well. The other alternative is to teach disadvantaged black children to read in their dialect first, then transfer them at a later date into reading standard English. This approach is being recommended by an increasing number of linguists and educators.

The Intermediate Grades

The reasons primary disadvantaged black children should not be taught standard English are also applicable to disadvantaged black children in the intermediate grades. These children have mastered their dialect: unlike their primary-grade counterparts, they are not struggling to learn the dialect of their primary cultural group. Still, it is unreasonable to expect them to learn standard English. For the same reasons as for primary disadvantaged black children, second language techniques are difficult to use with intermediate children; also, standard English is not reinforced in their linguistic-cultural environment. The main reason, however, that intermediate disadvantaged black children do not learn standard English is that they do not see a need to learn it. They lack motivation. Again, there is no way these children can be convinced that they need to learn standard English.

Intermediate children do not yet understand the social, vocational, or academic significance of dialect differences. They do not really need standard English in their cultural environment, and they do not participate in situations requiring standard English. Thus, they do not need it, and they are unlikely to learn it without a recognized need or the situational demands to learn standard English.

The language program for intermediate disadvantaged black children should be an extension of the language program for their primary counterparts. They should be further encouraged to use their dialect; they should be given many listening activities to extend the development of their ability to understand standard English; their vocabulary should be increased. In addition, children in the later intermediate grades — when they reach the age of ten or eleven — should be given activities that point out differences in language systems. (They should be taught that there are varieties of English, and no value judgment should accompany this teaching.) They should begin to receive instruction in hearing the difference between standard English and their nonstandard Negro dialect, and they should begin audio-discrimination activities which help them to distinguish between sounds and patterns of standard English and non-standard Negro dialect. This program follows the first three steps of the second language approach — or rationale — outlined above; however, it stops short of having intermediate-grade-level children reproduce standard English.

In short, the language program for disadvantaged black children who speak nonstandard Negro dialect should lay the foundation for the time when they will be taught to speak standard English — and that time is in the secondary grades.

The Secondary Grades

During the ages of twelve to eighteen years old, children become aware of differences in the kinds of English spoken by different groups. Also, during this period children become aware of the social significance of the differences between varieties of English spoken. They realize that standard English has more prestige than other varieties of English, and they recognize that standard English is the language to be used in certain kinds of situations. Further, during the secondary grades disadvantaged black children can be shown the need for learning standard English. Specifically, they can be helped to understand that standard English is the dialect for further education, and that it is the dialect which can broaden vocational opportunities. The recognition of these factors is necessary before these students can be motivated to learn standard English.

The main reason that this recognition does not occur until adolescence is that prior to this age level, black children have few opportunities to come into contact in face-to-face communication relationships with speakers of standard English, and they are not faced with situations that require the use of standard English. As they reach adolescence and later, however, their social sphere and their communication needs are broadened. They are made aware, by this broadening, of their deficiency in speaking standard English. Thus, at this time it is possible to motivate them to learn standard English.

Furthermore, during the secondary grades second language techniques can be used successfully. Secondary-grade-level students are no longer learning to speak nonstandard Negro dialect, and their maturation level is advanced to the stage that they can detect the subtle differences between their dialect and standard English.

Standard English, however, must be taught as an alternate dialect to be used in appropriate situations. At this writing, the language program attempts to teach standard English to these students as a replacement dialect. This has not — and will not — work. These students will not replace their nonstandard functional dialect with a dialect that is nonfunctional or dysfunctional as long as they have to live and function in their primary cultural environment, where their nonstandard dialect is spoken. They need the standard dialect only when they move outside their primary cultural environment and attempt to function in the dominant cultural environment. This does not occur until the secondary grades, or after they leave the secondary grades.

Linguist William Labov has hypothesized that language acquisition occurs in the following stages:

1. Zero to five years old — basic grammar learned.
2. Five to twelve years old — local dialect of primary culture learned.
3. Twelve to fourteen years old — children learn the social significance of their dialect; they come into more and more contact with others.
4. Fourteen years old — children attempt to approximate standard dialect.
5. Fifteen years old — the consistent standard dialect acquired (not acquired by lower-class).
6. Full range of language acquired in early adulthood.

A comparison of Labov's stages of language acquisition and the recommendations made here reveals a consistency. Specifically, Labov's stages indicate that children do not recognize a difference in their dialect and the standard dialect (that they don't know the social significance of their dialect) until they reach adolescence (twelve to fourteen years old), and that they do not begin to approximate the standard dialect until they are around fourteen years old. If these are the natural stages of language development, the recommendations made here are consistent with them and do not conflict with them. In other words, what is recommended here is that the language program for disadvantaged black children follow and conform to the natural stages of language acquisition as proposed by Labov.

Ironically, at this time (that is, the time they *can* learn standard English) many black children acquire an awareness that may prevent them from learning standard English. Specifically, they (1) may not believe that they will have the opportunity to use standard English, and (2) they may not want to learn standard English because it is "white folks' talk." Many black people have lost hope in the assimilation process. They feel that they will never be included in the mainstream of American society. Also, many young black people do not set their academic and vocational aspirations high, because they feel they have little chance of attainment. In terms of learning standard English, this means that they don't really believe that they will need it — they don't believe they will have the opportunity to function in a standard English-speaking environment. This attitude will surely dull their motivation to learn standard English, and motivation is the essential ingredient in successfully learning to speak the dialect.

In addition, many black secondary students do not want to learn standard English because they feel that in doing so they compromise their own identity. William Labov has termed this phenomenon "functional interference." There is, in the black population, an increasing pride in anything that is identifiably black and a rejection of anything that is identifiably white. Many black people — especially the young — are reluctant to give up the identity label of black English or even to acquire, in addition to their black English, standard English. It is ironic, then, that at the very time it seems ideal to teach black students standard English, they may refuse to learn it.

This entire discussion has been based on the assumption that our society and its schools will remain segregated. If black children were integrated into the dominant middle-class society, or were to attend schools with standard English speaking middle-class children, the considerations taken up here would be irrelevant. Black children would learn standard English because they would have the opportunity to function in an environment in which standard English was operable. They would learn standard English from their standard English-speaking peers. Likewise, if nonstandard Negro dialect, perpetuated by continued segregation, were to become a legitimate variety of English to which the dominant culture assigned the same prestige value as it did to standard English, the schools would not have to teach black children standard English. But since neither of these possibilities is likely to occur in the near future, the schools must continue to teach disadvantaged black students standard English as a second dialect. The time to do this is when these children reach adolescence and the secondary grades.

17.

Mexican-Americans in School:
English and Spanish Programs

THOMAS P. CARTER

There is widespread confusion about the objectives, techniques, content, and organization of school programs involving foreign languages. The basic distinction between foreign or second language teaching and bilingual school programs is rarely understood by school practitioners.

A foreign or second language program involves the introduction of a language new to students into a classroom where it is to be learned essentially for its own sake. In a bilingual program, two languages are used as media of instruction (carriers of curricular content). English as a Second Language (ESL), Foreign Languages in the Elementary Schools (FLES), or any other program to teach a new language to whatever group of children at any level, are second or foreign language instruction programs. A school would not be defined as bilingual merely because two language are taught in it (for example, Spanish to English speakers and English to Spanish speakers). Besides second (or foreign) language projects in the Southwest, new projects to teach native Spanish speakers in Spanish are gaining popularity. These projects can be classified according to the nature of the content taught and according to objectives. If those content areas traditionally associated with foreign language teaching are taught — for example, the language's grammar, pronunciation, spelling, drama, literature, business correspondence, and so forth — it is a "language program." If other content is taught — for example, world history, biology, arithmetic, algebra, and so forth — it is a "bilingual program."

Reprinted from *Mexican Americans in School: A History of Educational Neglect* by Thomas P. Carter (New York: The College Entrance Examination Board, 1970). Copyright© 1970 by the College Entrance Examination Board.

Thomas P. Carter of the departments of Education and Sociology at the University of Texas at El Paso, has concentrated on the problems of minority groups, especially of Mexican-Americans in the southwestern United States. A consultant to many commissions and organizations, he has published journal articles, monographs, and several books, including *Preparing Teachers for Mexican-American Children* and *School Discrimination: The Mexican-American Case.*

Chart 17.1

English and Spanish Language Programs in Southwestern Schools

Type	Program	Content	Objectives
PROGRAMS TO TEACH NEW LANGUAGE			
A. Spanish for English speakers	**1.** Foreign Languages in the Elementary Schools (FLES)	**1.** Hispanic culture	**1.** Competency Knowledge of Hispanic culture
	2. Traditional Spanish language program	**2.** Hispanic culture	**2.** Competency Knowledge of Hispanic Culture
B. English for Spanish speakers	**1.** English as a Second Language (ESL)	**1.** United States culture	**1.** Competency Knowledge of United States culture
	2. Regular school program	**2.** United States culture as represented in standard curriculum	**2.** Acculturation
PROGRAMS TO TEACH NATIVE LANGUAGE			
C. English for English speakers	**1.** Regular school program	**1.** United States culture as represented in standard curriculum	**1.** Competency Knowledge of native culture Enculturation
D. Spanish for Spanish speakers	**1.** Hispanic culture	**1.** Hispanic culture	**1.** Fluency Knowledge of Hispanic and Mexican culture Pride in antecedents Enhanced self-image
	2. Bridge	**2.** Hispanic culture as bridge to United States culture "Universal" or "fair" culture United States culture	**2.** Fluency Knowledge of both cultures Biculturism Acculturation

The table depicts graphically the status of language programs in Southwestern schools for native speakers of Spanish and of English. All such programs involve two major objectives: (1) competency in listening, speaking, reading, and writing the second language; and (2) knowledge of the culture the language carries (art, literature, history, great men, great events, and so forth). In addition to these two major objectives, given programs state or imply other goals as indicated.

Three "normal" or common types of programs are depicted on Chart 17.1. The types described as "English for English speakers" (C-1) and "English for Spanish speakers" (B-2) are the standard school approaches. In these, both Spanish- and English-speaking children are presented the regular school curriculum carried in the English language. The objective is to make both linguistic and ethnic groups competent in English and carriers of the dominant culture. "Spanish for English speakers" (A-1, 2) is a very common foreign language program in the Southwest. Its teaching approach varies tremendously from the older grammar emphasis to more modern audiolingual techniques.

The most common special (compensatory) language program is some variant of teaching English as a "new" language to Spanish speakers (B-1). The ESL program represents a departure from regular school efforts. It usually provides more intensive and structured exposure and employs techniques associated with the audiolingual approaches. However, the content changes little regarding United States culture: the objective continues to be bringing the child into American culture.

The use of the ESL approach and the audiolingual technique are still considered by many schoolmen to be unproved and experimental. For example, the Texas Education Agency cites the Pharr-San Juan-Alamo Independent School District's program as an "innovation project": "Non-English speaking children aged 10-16 were afforded extended instructional oral English, reading and writing, and advanced reading materials. A major aspect of the program was the use of special audio-visual materials, such as filmstrips and other visual aids."[1] California and other states consider what appear to be rather standard ESL programs as innovative. One might think that the audiolingual approach would be well established by this time, but it is still considered experimental by many schoolmen and its use is nowhere near as widespread as would be expected.

The *Miami Linguistic Reader*,[2] with its recommended activities, is being used apparently quite successfully as a method of teaching English and reading to Spanish monolinguals, and as a regular reader for the general population. The system was well thought of by all interviewees for this study who were actually using it. From observation of classroom situations and interviews of teachers, it appears that: (1) children project themselves into the content and characters; (2) the organization of the small instructional groups encourages children's spontaneity and naturalness; (3) teachers understand and can use the linguistic approach as exemplified in this series; and (4) teachers seem quite comfortable with the system as explained in the manual.

The Miami series is based on a set of carefully constructed premises. Paramount among these is ". . . that the child must have aural-oral control over the material he is expected to read." In other words, the child must know and attach meaning to the English he later reads. Robinett elaborates this point:

The *introductory* [readiness] *unit* preceding the introduction of formal reading, and the oral language activities surrounding the reading, attempt to provide systematic, meaningful oral practice on the basic features of American English. The linguistic content for oral mastery is structured in its presentation, taking into account contrasts within the English language system and contrasts between English and Spanish. In the ordering of the linguistic content, less concern has been shown for the "logical" sequences and manipulation typical of materials produced under the direction of linguists, and more concern has been shown for the communication aspects of the language experience and the relevance of the language to the content of the pupil's reading materials.[3]

Children appear to comprehend and communicate in the words and phrases later encountered in the reader. If this series is successful, as it appears to be, in teaching oral English before written English, it has overcome one of the principal and most common failings of other systems. Most systems reverse the procedure, expecting the child to read and understand a language he does not speak or understand. It is of course possible that the apparent success of this system is merely a placebo effect. Regardless of this possibility, which can be inherent in the introduction of any new curriculum, the series does seem to exemplify what can be accomplished by serious application of theory to educational practice.

Unfortunately, teachers almost invariably report more success than do more objective evaluators. On the basis of district reports, the ESL program in California was judged to be "generally successful": "On the average, students who could speak no English before the program gained a reading and sight vocabulary approximating an average second grade English-speaking child."[4] The program lasted about five months. More concrete evidence, based on teachers' ratings, tests, and so forth, indicate that schools undertaking "English for non-English speaking" Title I projects as a primary, secondary, or "other" activity during 1965-66 showed "substantial progress" in two percent, "some progress" in twenty-five percent, and "little progress" in fifty-five percent of the classes. Approximately eighteen percent of the schools did not specify their progress.[5]

Great variation exists among programs of English as a second language. A few classes observed quite adequately utilized modern audio-lingual techniques and so forth, but many relied almost exclusively on traditional grammar approaches. A few districts use sophisticated electronic language laboratories, yet many fail to take advantage of the most rudimentary mechanical or electric teaching aids. The variations in materials are great. In summary: (1) if the audiolingual method is to be used, a massive inservice teacher-training program is essential; (2) few language laboratories observed during this study were being operated to maximum efficiency; and (3) often the teachers observed were poor language models because of their own nonstandard, sometimes accented, speech.

The other infrequently encountered but significant "new" language program is the teaching of Spanish to Spanish speakers. Such programs share the two major objectives, language competency and knowledge of culture, common to all language programs. Some are based on the premise that a sound grounding in Spanish will provide a "bridge" to speed the learning of English (D-2). According to Guerra, one aspect of such programs is "to establish psychological rapport between teacher and learner in order to begin English instruction using Spanish as the familiar frame of reference; that is, Spanish as a bridge to learn English."[6] All the contemporary language programs to teach Spanish to Spanish speakers are meant to provide a bridge to English, but they differ in their stress on Hispanic culture and their priority of objectives. "Hispanic culture" programs (D-1) appear to have as an overriding objective the promotion of the youngster's pride in his "Mexicanness" and Hispanic cultural tradition. The emphasis is intended to remedy the child's assumed negative self-concept and to "develop a positive sense of identity." This strategy is compensatory in the sense that it glorifies a culture in order to enhance the child's ego function and to improve his self-image.

The program in Tucson's Pueblo High School appears to be a good example of this strategy: for the four high school years, "attention is given to the basic skills of speaking, reading and writing [of Spanish]. Equal, if not even greater, emphasis is given to helping the student develop a more positive self-concept through the study of his rich Spanish and Mexican cultural heritage."[7] Tucson's experimenters are exuberant over the success of their program. How successful such projects will be in facilitating English language learning and in instilling pride in things Hispanic is not known, but the principal of a Pueblo, Colorado, elementary school was described as giving the following subjective evaluation of a program to instill pride:

She was delighted with the progress already evident. Student attitudes and behavior had noticeably improved. The Mexican-American children carried themselves a bit more proudly. They got along better together. There was little or none of the name-calling that had been so prevalent before — calling which, though engaged in by Mexican-American children, was anti-Mexican in nature. The parents of these native speakers had reacted with enthusiasm to the new Spanish classes and the new spirit developing at Minnequa School . . . the last PTA function, a sort of Mexican fiesta, had been attended by more parents than ever before and there had been more parental cooperation in its planning and arranging.[8]

No objective data were found during this study to support such statements. Much criticism has been directed at such programs on the grounds that they may be divisive, that they idealize Mexican culture and society rather than validly portray them, and that the content is of little relevance to the poverty class of Mexican-American children (indeed the program at Pueblo was initiated for academically superior students). A great many questions concerning the objectives of programs like these must be considered.

The "bridge" programs (D-2) for teaching Spanish to Spanish speakers emphasize Spanish as a linguistic bridge to English but neither stress Hispanic cultural heritage nor use it as a vehicle to overcome any assumed negative self-concept. This kind of strategy might encourage individuals to find their identity within their own real social context. The Harlandale Independent School District in San Antonio is experimenting with programs that appear to be oriented this way. In one such program, four first grades in different schools were taught reading and writing in Spanish, as well as in English. The control first grades in each school received instruction in English only. A relatively short time, about an hour a day, was devoted to Spanish instruction. The students used reading materials created by specialists especially for them. The children were randomly selected for placement in the control and experimental sections, although there were some exceptions in the selection process. Pryor, who was principal consultant to and evaluator of the project, stated:

Pre-tests and post-tests were used, as well as personal adjustment rating sheets, personal data sheets, attendance records, reports of observers, and indications of pupil and parental attitudes. The design was to determine to what extent the sections of the first grade were equal or different at the beginning of the school term and how much relative change had taken place at the end of the term. That is, it was the design to determine the relative status or position of the experimental [instructed in Spanish] section of the first grade among all the sections of the first grade in the same school and to determine the extent of change of relative status or position among the groups at the end of school.[9]

Pryor reported that in one of the four elementary schools, the first grade that was instructed in Spanish "clearly made more progress in practically every aspect of the measures than the sections which were taught in English only."[10] In the two other schools this was also true, but the degree of difference between the control and experimental classes was not nearly so pronounced. In the fourth school, no evidence to favor Spanish instruction was found. Pryor cautions that a multitude of variables are present that may bias the findings but suggests that enough success was demonstrated to warrant further experimentation. The closing words of Pryor's report are: "The pupils in the bilingual [Spanish] sections of all four schools could speak, read, and write in two languages at the end of the first grade. This in itself might be considered a justification for the program."[11] This final point deserves the serious consideration of educators.

Programs to teach Spanish to Spanish speakers are now enthusiastically advocated by many linguistic scientists, social scientists, educators, and by a large percentage of Mexican-American leaders. We have seen state legislatures abolish laws prohibiting instruction in languages other than English, federal legislation provides limited funds for experimental programs in non-English instruction, and a widespread movement to teach in children's own vernacular is gaining momentum and influence among educators generally. In spite of the numerous possible benefits of such programs to the child and to the nation, a note of caution must be interjected. Conservative or prejudiced school boards or educators could favor programs to teach Mexican-American children in Spanish. Classes in Spanish for Spanish speakers could be used to justify present or future segregation of the group: if it is best to teach such children in Spanish, it could also be argued that it is most efficient to isolate them from those taught in English. "Spanish speaker" suggests Mexican-American to most educators, and all children with Spanish surnames or dark faces could be "encouraged" to learn their "native tongue," regardless of the status of the language in their homes or their ability to use it. Given only two polar choices, ethnic segregation with instruction in Spanish or desegregation without it, this author would choose the latter as most beneficial to the child and society. Many will violently disagree.

In considering any of the programs mentioned in this brief survey it must be remembered that the existence of functioning special programs for Mexican-American children can make a bad situation even worse. If programs exist, regardless of their quality or effectiveness, the school perceives itself as making a supreme effort to aid Mexican-American children. Any subsequent failure of the child is then seen as even more the responsibility or fault of the home environment. It could be argued that after all the school is expending x number of dollars in the kinds of special programs advocated by educational authorities, that it is doing its best, and that now it's up to the parents and children. Special programs must not be allowed to act to the detriment of Mexican-American children by encouraging self-satisfaction on the part of institutions and discouraging their further self-analysis and modification.

Notes

1. Texas Education Agency, Division of Compensatory Education, *Activities and Services Stated in Project Proposals, Annual Evaluation Report, Special Programs for Educationally Deprived Children under Title I of ESEA, 1965–66,* vol. 1. (Austin, Texas: 1966), p. 124.
2. This language series, which includes teacher's manuals, seatwork books, sequenced language and reading drill charts, supplementary activities, and audio-visual materials, has been published by D.C. Heath and Company (Lexington, Mass.) since 1965.
3. Ralph R. Robinett, *A "Linguistic" Approach to Beginning Reading for Bilingual Children* (Boston: D.C. Heath and Co., 1966), p. 3.
4. California State Department of Education, *Types and Percentages of ESA Title I Activities, Annual Report, 1965–66, Evaluation of ESEA Title I Projects of California Schools* (Sacramento: California State Department of Education, 1966), p. 522.
5. Ibid., pp. F3, F21, F41.
6. Manuel N. Guerra, *Language Instruction of Inter-Group Relations: An Analysis of Language Instruction (Spanish and English) to Spanish-Speaking Learners in California Public Schools, in Relation to the Search for Better Inter-Group Relations* (Sacramento: California State Department of Education, June 1967), p. 2.
7. National Education Association, Department of Rural Education, *The Invisible Minority . . . Pero No Vencibles: Report of the NEA-Tucson Survey on the Teaching of Spanish to the Spanish-Speaking.* (Washington, D.C.: U.S. Government Printing Office, 1966), pp. 22–23.
8. Ibid., p. 22.
9. Guy C. Pryor, "Evaluation of the Bilingual Project of Harlandale Independent School District, San Antonio, Texas," mimeographed (San Antonio: Harlandale Independent School District, June 1967), p. 62.
10. Ibid.
11. Ibid.

18.

The Role and Function of the Native Teacher

RICHARD C. BEDFORD

Surely everyone concerned with teaching language is now quite aware that the shift away from the once-dominant translation method to the aural-oral approach has made new, quite different, and in many ways greater demands on students. However, another, less-apparent effect of this shift characterizing language teaching for at least two decades has certainly been to impose a very high valuation on the ability of the teacher to speak the language he teaches. And this might seem a mere ponderous and tautological statement of the obvious were it not for certain ramifications yet given only scant attention.

Looking at the matter more clearly, we find that even the extremely slow and impeded penetration of the aural-oral approach in certain parts of the world is, in fact, attributable to the new high valuation on teacher aural-oral fluency. That is, many teachers of very limited aural-oral fluency — and paradoxically even those who might otherwise have favored it — have felt it necessary to resist self-defensively. The aural-oral approach may quite readily be seen as a threat, since it makes demands for aural-oral fluency which many teachers not only do not have but have no way to acquire.

Yet, by no means all of the resistance has been in self-defense of lack of fluency. Much of it is traceable to the fact the aural-oral approach has radically changed teaching patterns and classroom atmosphere. Bluntly, the teacher accepting this newer approach must work much harder. The teacher's performance has to be a very active one, for he

Reprinted from *Language Learning* 18, nos. 3 & 4 (1968): 199–210.

Richard C. Bedford of Doshisha University in Japan has worked with bilingual programs in Japan, Indonesia, Alaska, and the continental United States. In addition to numerous journal articles, he has published a book entitled *English Experienced*.

has to sustain a brisk pace in intensive pattern practice in order to develop the hypnotic rhythm necessary for automatization of student response. Speech, as distinguished from writing standing on the page, ever-ready for repeated analysis, is transient.

And not only is language teaching no longer so leisurely a process as it was in the era of the translation method, but the relationship between teacher and student has changed accordingly. In short, the new approach has demanded a new type of teacher and new psycho-social relations, for the teacher implementing the aural-oral approach has had to engage his students in a continuous exchange. No longer a mere bucket-filler, the active teacher — via the pattern practice which characterizes the aural-oral approach — maintains a continuous dialogue with his students. Ever alert to all aspects of the highly transient sound stream, the teacher has no time in speaking to muse, speculate, and consider. It might be argued that if nothing else the aural-oral approach has demanded the ability to respond faster, to think on one's feet as it were. And that demand has perhaps been even greater on the teacher than on the students. Moreover, every aspect of the teacher's spoken performance is under continual student scrutiny, for he is the model to be mimicked. He must be consistent in the midst of the impermanence of the spoken word. In short, the teacher is less the somewhat distant adjudicator of translation days than the constant sparring partner.

Understandably, the brisk pace and the closer contact with students has been resented by many veteran teachers, who see these changes as an annoying imposition, a disturbing encroachment on long-familiar, comfortable patterns of operation and relationship. The effectiveness of their opposition may in part be traced, of course, to the fact that in many societies deference to age and stamina has placed older and frequently less-fluent teachers in the most influential positions. Failing to block adoption of the aural-oral approach, many have been able to shift their activities exclusively to literature. This has left the teaching of speaking — widely regarded as a chore — to defenseless younger staff members, who somehow have had to bear the consequent revelation of their own limited fluency.

Not only has this acquisition by default forced attention on the fluency of the younger and often only slightly more fluent staff member, but introduction of the new approach has greatly increased the demand for foreign "teachers." In fact, the doctrine of usage — a cardinal tenet often applied without serious regard for the equally important consideration of levels of usage — and the consequent acceptance of the native speaker as ultimate authority, have provided convenient justification for the hiring of any and virtually every foreigner. Indeed, having one's own native English speaker — whether he has minimal teaching credentials or is no more than a semi-articulate native speaker — has become a status symbol for many schools abroad. Not only is the foreign presence necessary to sustain the reputation of the school, but, in many places — as in Japan and Hong Kong — where competition among schools is cutthroat, it is an indispensable lure for increasing enrollments. Thus, a sizable army of native speakers of the target language — the biggest contingent of which is probably English-speaking — has marched around the globe to take up teaching posts. And while the Fulbright Commission and the Peace Corps have, in supplying native English speakers, undoubtedly offered budgetary relief to schools in many countries, they have probably whetted the appetite for native English-speaking teachers.

Whatever the qualifications of the foreigners who have arrived on the teaching scene abroad, however, the fact is that the native teacher who strongly advocates the aural-oral approach has too often found himself in a curious position. That is, ardently propagandizing for the approach and the need for native speakers of the target language, he has too often further undercut his own status. Moreover, since he usually bears the largest teaching burden, he is often blamed for the widespread lack of student fluency — despite the fact such inadequacy may be clearly traceable to a raft of other causes out of his control. Unable to become a native speaker of the target language, which is what he is really if illogically being blamed for, he may be considered a faulty and inadequate substitute, even a tolerated necessary evil. And perhaps the unkindest cut of all is the fact that students, in their cruel youthful innocence, are sometimes quite unsubtle in favoring foreigners. Openly asserting they are being cheated when denied opportunity to study under the native speaker of the target language, they frequently grant only grudging acceptance to native teachers.

Thus, in many places we find that, although apologized for and apologizing, the overworked native teacher is nevertheless frustrated at the position of makeshift and second best he is accorded. He is often uneasy about his role in the teaching process, confused as to his function. And, since his feelings of frustration can color the native teacher's relationship with foreign staff members as well as with his students, this uneasiness and confusion may be seen as the most significant ramification of the shift to the aural-oral approach. Our attention is drawn, therefore, to a consideration of ways to eliminate the native teacher's sense of inadequacy.

As a start, we suggest that instead of merely trying to do what his foreign colleague is equipped to do much better, the native teacher can accept and advocate the need for a reasonable division of labor. Indeed, while teaching with foreigners in a cooperative setting, he can recognize that such a division may provide some salutary limits on the province of those foreigners with less than minimal teaching qualifications. And, in assessing his own strength, the native teacher will find that the one asset he has, which the foreign teacher rarely can match, is his fluency in his students' native language.

Admittedly, his ability to explain in the native language is often regarded as something less than an asset abroad, where earlier and now out-dated proscriptions against use of the native language in pursuit of the target language are still rigidly upheld. But, as that fluency does allow him to explain a great deal more — and that a great deal more efficiently — than the foreigner can, the native teacher's use of the students' native language is certainly defensible. Of course, this is not to say that students should be encouraged to believe that language learning is a process of finding exact equivalents, as may be the case in arithmetic, let us say. In fact, they should be made to recognize that such equivalents are impossible, since language usage demands situational interpretation, and speakers of two different languages will, of course, interpret the same situation quite differently. At a recent lecture a quite confident and enthusiastic advocate of the "Direct Method" suggested that *glare* and *stare* could easily be distinguished for foreign students by merely demonstrating the two by appropriate facial expressions. It did not seem to occur to the lecturer that the situation in which either one of the expressions would be used acceptably while the other would be excluded could differ considerably. Moreover, the *glare* is not only situational, but the facial expression he had labeled *glare* could be interpreted as something quite different — demonic power or resolute heroism, let us say — by those from another cultural background. On the other hand, any foreign observer who has noted the Japanese tendency to stare without apparent feeling of embarrassment would have wondered about the possibility of a common understanding of the significance *stare* might have for our lecturer and his audience. Indeed, as Whorf and others have implied, the characteristic interpretation of experience, peculiar to its native users and distinguishing them from others, is related to language and cultural difference. For instance, the notion of what *child* is varies considerably as the level of sophistication required of children varies considerably from culture to culture. The twelve-to-fourteen-year-old American girl child going on a date inevitably seems impossibly monstrous to most of the Indonesian or Arab students I have taught.

The effectiveness of much explanation, then, will be proportional to the realization that just as everything cannot be learned without explanation, so also it is true that everything cannot be explained. Very often, of course, the native teacher will, in confronting some aspect of usage in the target language, find that there is no comparable concept available to him in the native language. My attempts to convey the idea of *self-sufficient, self-reliant, self-confident* and other self-plus-adjective combinations have revealed to me that the concept of *self* — on which all of these terms depend, of course — is quite different for those from other than English-speaking cultures. Moreover, I had no more luck in the conveyance when I enlisted the services of a colleague who natively spoke my students' language, although, interestingly enough, he had recourse to Buddhist terminology in his attempt to provide them with a term of even vaguely comparable meaning. Many of us have also discovered, of course, that to convey the meaning of *love,* in the English romantic sense, to a Japanese is about as frustrating as to render fully in English the meaning of the Japanese *shibui.* And, although the native teacher must exercise some discretion, by pointing up those contrasts in experience and values he can force student attention on what would not be thought of or would not be said in their native language. The native teacher can take an English word, such as *privacy* or *casual,* for instance, and try to defuse it of the associations or selfishness, ingratitude, irresponsibility, or even of morbidity it may have for his students. By presenting the differing associations it may have with family, with a house, or with a particular piece of land, the native teacher may sensitize his students to the fact that there can be various ideas about the *self.*

Thus, rather than attempt to do the impossible — to give equivalents as was done under that translation method now largely discredited — the native teacher can try to convey some sense of why it is impossible. For example, he is best equipped to explain to his students that since all peoples are not raised to believe in the virtue of humble restraint, the immediate acceptance of a proffered gift and the immediate opening of it as well as the open expression of gratitude for it reflect a set of social values quite different from those with which his students are familiar. Similarly, the native teacher in societies organized along essentially tribal or clan lines should be able to make his students hesitate to assume that the failure of all members of a family to express gratitude to the benefactor of one family member indicates that foreigners are boorishly discourteous.

Moreover, the native teacher need not be overly concerned with the fact he is speaking *about* the target language and its speakers rather than speaking in the language — although many linguists still find that a cardinal sin. He should recognize instead that there is no way to convey meaning unless we know what is meaningful and how — if not why — it is meaningful to speakers of another language. The full truth of this was brought home to me quite unexpectedly recently, for I found that the denotative definition of the word *mother* as "female parent" is no less value laden than the vastly freighted connotation of the word, since both *female* and *parent* had quite different meanings both denotatively and connotatively for my Japanese students than I would have assigned them.

Admittedly, all of this would require that the native teacher know a great deal about both the language and the underlying values he shares with his students as well as those of speakers of the target language. But surely such a function will make more suitable demands on his bilingualism than the teaching of pronunciation and idiom, let us say, which can more reasonably be left to his foreign colleague.

Yet, this leads us to the second legitimate responsibility of the native teacher, as distinct from that of the foreign teacher and stemming from the native teacher's fluency in the students' language. That is, the native teacher is, in fact, in the best position to spot and discourage the common student resort to silent translation. Ignorant of the structures of the students' native language, a non-native teacher is likely to be unaware of the source of most student problems stemming from their silent translation, and their consequent erroneous imposition of structures of the native language on expression in the target language. To the native teacher, fluent in the students' native language, the source of error should be immediately apparent. His students' omission of articles can be readily anticipated by a teacher who natively speaks Slavic languages lacking articles. On the other hand, the statement, *Yes, I don't like ice cream,* which might seem to the foreign teacher a ridiculous student response to the question "Don't you like ice cream?" will be readily recognized by the native Japanese teacher as a mere translation by the student of a pattern required in his native language. In the native language he shares with them, and again making use of contrasts to show fundamental structural differences as well as underlying differences of situational valuation, the native teacher can channel student attention so as to discourage such erroneous substitution of characteristic structures.

Unlike the outdated advocate of literal translation who encourages a hunt for equivalents, then, our native teacher focuses on differences between the two languages. That is, the native teacher can point out that a tentative attitude used for expression of some future possibility in the students' language is likely to seem either quite indecisive or even sly when translated directly into English. He might also be able to give students who speak a language lacking articles some realization of the subtle emotional toning possible through a shift from personal pronoun to article as when the English *Open your mouth* is changed to *Open the mouth.* Of course, he will have to do the job skillfully, since his students share the common feeling that anything unfamiliar and different is amusing or illogical. In employing this focus, therefore, he should attempt neither to defend nor to justify the structures of one language over those of another. Certainly the fact English lacks the very elaborate honorific system peculiar to Arabic, let us say, does not mean Americans lack a sense of status or that there are not levels of usage to be nicely calculated in terms of relative speaker-audience social level. The native teacher merely presents differences and does not evaluate. And here it might be pointed out that the tendency of some native teachers, upon returning from training abroad, to take a patronizing or even somewhat derogatory attitude toward peculiarities of their native language, along with other aspects of their culture, can alienate students from language learning.

A native teacher who focuses on linguo-cultural differences can, in fact, also make a major contribution to the cooperative teaching effort. That is, by apprising the unaware foreigner that the source of a particular problem lies in the students' resort to silent translation and substitution of structures, the native teacher can increase the foreigner's understanding and, ultimately, improve his teaching. At the same time, by this rationalization of the division of labor, the native teacher can help insure best use of the foreigner with less-than-minimal teaching credentials.

In fact, it is in his day-to-day cooperative relationship with the foreign teacher that a third function of the native teacher can emerge. And although perhaps somewhat less obviously derived from his fluency in his native language, this function may also be traced to that source. That is, perhaps the most important function of the native speaker is to serve as a living example of the possibility of learning the target language. Unlike the foreigner, the native teacher realizes the enormous differences which distinguish the structures and underlying attitudes of the native language from those of the target language. Unlike the foreigner, whose ignorance of their language is quite apparent to the students, the native teacher has shared their learning experience, has personally known the many painful difficulties and how often they seem insurmountable. Only the speaker of a language de-emphasizing personal pronouns can appreciate the annoyance which English sex-linked pronoun usage can represent; only the person speaking a language having fairly consistent sound-spelling patterns can really know the agonies which lie in wait — in the form of the text of an English textbook — even for students under the aural-oral approach. Thus, many students enduring the frustrations and discouragements familiar to all who try to learn a foreign language can gain genuine reassurance, inspiration, and incentive from their observation of the native teacher's ability to converse with a foreigner in the language they are struggling, often desperately, to learn.

Obviously this function in particular can best be handled by the native teacher who is most fluent in the target language. And, as earlier noted, his limited fluency has been a frequent source of difficulty for the native teacher. Yet, the native teacher cannot afford to shrink from the opportunity to speak in the target language, despite his limited fluency. Realizing he is an example whose attitude as well as performance will inevitably be mimicked by his students, the native teacher surely will recognize that his own silence can only encourage their silence, despite his urging that they speak. Indeed, it can be said that the instruction and advice which the native teacher can impart as to how to learn the language will be effective to the degree to which his students find his experience and opinions validated by the visible and audible evidence of the fluency he has acquired through labors such as theirs.

Instead of retreating, therefore, even the native teacher of very limited fluency in the target language must seize every opportunity to converse with his foreign colleague, absorbing as much as he can to improve his recognition and encouraging correction so as to raise the level of his own production of the language. Persistent efforts will increase his own fluency as well as that general understanding of underlying values which he can pass on to his students. And, in making a greater effort to speak, following the native teacher's example, his students will also find their fluency increasing, of course.

Thus, by accepting a division of labor based on his strength, the native teacher can be suitably employed where he can best utilize his fluency while avoiding disastrous competition in areas where the foreigner has natural superiority. The too-common lack of confidence and sheer frustration of the native teacher can be eliminated if he will recognize and accept full responsibility for those functions for which he is best equipped. What now too frequently is an unpleasant three-way relationship between native teacher, students, and foreign teacher can be changed to one of fruitful cooperation and mutual profit.

19.

Reading Literature and Learning a Second Language

BRADFORD ARTHUR

Whereas pattern practice, transformational and substitution drills, conversations, and dialogues are all accepted parts of the standard fare for linguistically oriented ESL programs, literary texts as part of an ESL program are not to the taste of all teachers.[1] Those who have tried to use literature to help teach English as a second language have not always been successful. In the 1968 TESOL convention, the discussion of literature and second language teaching centered not on how literature should be used but on whether it should be included at all. Some of the teachers who have tried to use literature to teach language skills have published their grief. Many more have cried on the shoulders of their colleagues. Tales of success are few. And yet, a feeling persists that the study of literature should have considerable value for second language learning if only the right texts could be found, if only they could be used properly.

Literature in the schools must serve some useful purpose; it must be a means toward some end that the community or society considers important. Education is a process of preparation. Its ultimate objectives are to be realized outside the schoolyard. On the other hand, literature is valuable not only because it may be useful but also because the act of reading literature is, at least potentially, a pleasant experience. Literature is frequently read entirely for pleasure. Through the use of literature, a language-learning experience might become at the same time a source of immediate pleasure and satisfaction for the student. This possibility makes literature an appealing teaching device for ESL teachers.

Reprinted from *Language Learning* 18, nos. 3 & 4 (1968): pp. 199–210. An earlier version appeared in *Workpapers in English as a Second Language* (Los Angeles: University of California Press: 1968).

Bradford Arthur of the Department of English, University of California, Los Angeles, has specialized in English linguistics and the training of teachers of English as a second language. Among his publications is *Teaching English to English-Speaking Children,* a guide to the values of linguistics for English teachers.

But all too frequently the ESL teacher sees his class confused and bored by a story which he had anticipated would please them. Reading literature for pleasure and using literature for language learning seem frequently to be mutually incompatible experiences. If literature is to become a successful part of an ESL program, ways must be found to make literature both useful and enjoyable. More specifically, answers must be found to questions like the following. What is the nature of the enjoyment to be derived from reading literature? What ESL goals can literature usefully serve? Given answers to these first two questions, how can literature serve the ESL goals enumerated in the answer to the second question and at the same time be a source of the sort of enjoyment described in the answer to the first question? Finally, how can the theory developed through the first three questions be applied in an actual ESL classroom? Answers to these four questions are contained in the following discussion.

1. What is the nature of the enjoyment to be derived from reading literature?

It would be nonsensical to command a reader to enjoy the story he is reading. Enjoyment is beyond conscious control. You might, however, demand of yourself to read a few pages; to give yourself a chance to get into the story. So you read a few pages, and then, maybe, something happens: intellect and emotions become so concentrated on the story that for a time you lose awareness of your surroundings and of yourself existing outside the story. For a child, this experience may involve a total identification with some character in the story. An adult may experience the world created in the story without necessarily assuming a role in it. His experience is more intellectual than the child's but not necessarily less intense.

The act of reading literature, or better, the act of entering the world created in a particular work of literature, has been described with exceptional clarity and eloquence by Maurice Natanson:

To enter the world of *The Brothers Karamazov* requires a peculiar decision to suspend our ordinary believing in our own world. "Suspend" is an unhappy term here, but a further account of what is involved may overcome the difficulties. My decision to enter the world of Dostoevski's novel is essentially a resolve to set aside the ordinary flow of daily life, by attending only to the horizon given to me in the literary work. The real world, of course, continues to exist. Suspending my belief in it does not in any way involve denying it. Rather, in shifting the focus of my attending to another world, I bring into view the continuing awareness of my thinking, my anticipating, my remembering, my wondering. It is now the very structure of these activities of consciousness which becomes the object of my concern. I am not suggesting that reading a novel means becoming introspective about that reading. Just the opposite. There is an extrospective character to our attending to *The Brothers*.

But in that complex awareness we call reading, there is presented directly the continuing consciousness of the world we encounter. Our own world has not been negated or cancelled; it persists. But it continues as methodically out of play in order to make possible at each moment the literary microcosm.[2]

Natanson is describing a special sort of interaction that can occur between a book and its reader. This interaction certainly cannot be evoked by any randomly selected bit of prose. There is something special about the prose constituting Dostoevski's novel that makes the response possible. Nor is Natanson's response to the novel the inevitable response of every reader to *The Brothers Karamazov*. Another reader might find it impossible to "enter the world" of the novel even though he might very much want to do so. In order for this interaction to occur the book must be right and the reader must also be right in the sense that he must be in a frame of mind and in a situation where he is prepared and able to receive the book in the right way. The literary quality of writing is, at least in part, the quality of the reader's response.

To speak of literature simply as something contained in certain special books is misleading. A complete statement should center not simply on the book but on the special interaction between the book and the reader — what might be called the *literary experience*. Simply reading a book generally considered "good literature" does not necessarily mean engaging in a literary experience. Conversely, a literary experience may be produced by a book that would not generally be called literature.[3]

The immediate pleasure or satisfaction to be derived from reading or hearing literature is the pleasure derived from a special kind of emotional and intellectual involvement with the story, what is here called a literary experience. All literary experiences share certain characteristics. First, the reader cannot consciously induce a literary experience; it must, in a sense, happen to him. Second, a literary experience requires a story suitable for the reader and a reader willing and prepared to react to the story. Finally, a literary experience requires the reader's total intellectual and emotional involvement. The reader cannot at the same time be conscious of anything external to the story.

2. What ESL goals can literature usefully serve?

ESL teachers have generally agreed that literature can aid language learning in three different ways. First, literature helps build vocabulary. The vocabulary used in written English and especially in literature is many times larger than the vocabulary common in speech. If a student's training is limited to conversation practice and to other forms of drill designed primarily to improve his proficiency in spoken English, that student will not have an opportunity to hear, let alone to master, the majority of English words.

In addition to these differences in vocabulary, certain syntactic patterns occur more frequently in written than in spoken English. Any teacher who has taught composition to native speakers of English is aware of his students' tendency to switch to the passive voice when they pick up their pencils. Subordinate clauses also occur more frequently in written English. Some authors may use subordination within subordination so extensively that their sentences become all but unintelligible as spoken English. Such complexity of sentence structure presents far fewer problems for a reader, since he can go back over what he has read and try to make sense out of sentences that confused him the first time through. Certain stylistic word order inversions also occur exclusively or almost exclusively in written or literary English. A poet might write, "Into the valley of death rode the six hundred." But he would almost certainly say, "The six hundred rode into the valley of death."

Thus literature may serve in an ESL program by helping students to master the mechanics of vocabulary and grammar. But some teachers have used literature in a third way: to help students of English as a second language understand the societies in which English is spoken.[4] By reading the literature of the society, a student is able to get below the superficial artifacts and to grasp some of the deeper psychological forces that motivate behavior within the society. Characters in novels and stories behave according to the social norms of the author and his audience. We admire the bravery of Hemingway's heroes because we have been brought up in a society where that sort of bravery is praised. By reading a Hemingway novel, the foreign student may come to recognize, to understand, perhaps even to share this attitude toward bravery. Such understanding, often neglected in foreign language training, is ultimately as important as understanding the literal meaning of words and sentences in the new language.

3. **How then can stories and other forms of literature expand a student's understanding of vocabulary, sentence structure, and cultural assumptions and at the same time evoke in that student a literary experience?**

The answer given here is based on the following principle: *if literature is to provide a useful vehicle for the teaching of second language skills, it must first succeed as a literary experience.* After all, literature is not the only vehicle for introducing new vocabulary words, new sentence patterns, and a knowledge of culture. Expository, descriptive, factual prose could accomplish these same goals. Indeed, nonliterary prose would certainly accomplish these goals more effectively than literature that students face with dread or indifference. Literature has a place in the ESL program only if it teaches better than other forms of prose. Moreover, it seems probable that literature is only going to teach better if students are responding to the literature as literary experience rather than as a language-learning device. Consequently, what seems at first to be a desirable side benefit of using literature — the immediate pleasure that students may derive from a total involvement in the reading — turns out to be a necessary prerequisite for the use of literature.

Writers who have used literature for didactic ends have followed this same principle. They have realized that if their writing is to succeed as a philosophical, political, or moral statement, it must first succeed as literature, that is, as a literary experience. A boring play or story is not likely to teach anything. On the other hand, stories that succeed in fascinating or entertaining or arousing the emotions of an audience through a literary experience may also succeed in changing public opinion or arousing public indignation. Nineteenth century Americans despised the cruelties of Simon Legree and were touched by the gentleness and kindness of Uncle Tom. This same audience came more and more to question the morality of slavery. Americans in the mid-twentieth century read of the naiveté and stupidity of the ugly American, and many began to question the wisdom of American foreign policy in Asia.

If literature is to be used in a second language program, the goals to be achieved through the use of literature must be compatible with the reading of that literature for the literary experience. If the student cannot read the literature with total involvement and at the same time use the literature as an aid to language learning, then the use of literature should be abandoned. This conclusion seems natural; indeed, it seems inescapable, and yet it may lead to a dilemma.

What are some of the assumptions that an author makes about his audience? Obviously, among other things, he assumes that they will be able to understand the literal meaning of the words that he is using. To be sure, the reader may from time to time run across an unfamiliar word, but this should not slow him down. He should not have to keep running to the dictionary or to footnotes to find out what the story is all about. Such continual interruptions of the story prevent the reader from sustaining a total involvement in the story itself, and total involvement must be sustained if the story is to be a literary experience. The author also assumes that his reader will be able to understand the structure of sentences used in the story. The reader cannot sustain total involvement in the story if he must continually struggle with the mechanics of sentence structure. More subtle, but nonetheless important, are the assumptions that the author makes about his reader's understanding of culture. Unless the reader is aware of the cultural assumptions in a story, or perhaps more accurately, unless the reader is himself making these assumptions, he will misunderstand the story. The reader's ability to enter the world of the story will depend in part on his ability to perceive that world the way the author did.

In order to read a story with pleasure, to read it as literary experience, the reader must understand the literal meanings conveyed by words and sentence structures in addition to the cultural connotations of the words and of the actions and situations that those words describe. But if the reader understands the language of a story, then that story will be of no value to him as a language-learning device. A story won't teach vocabulary unless it uses words the reader doesn't already understand. Similarly, a story can teach sentence structure only if that story introduces sentence structures with which the reader is not familiar. Finally, literature increases knowledge of culture only if that literature provides examples of cultural assumptions unfamiliar to the reader. Using literature as part of a second language learning program would seem to reduce, perhaps even to preclude, the possibility that this literature will ever evoke a literary experience.

Even if this conflict of interests is not absolutely necessary, it certainly does frequently exist. Over and over again, ESL teachers complain of the frustrations encountered in trying to generate students' enthusiasm for the literature they are reading. Many teachers have abandoned the use of literature and have substituted forms of nonliterary, expository prose. Still other teachers have tried to resolve this dilemma by using various simplified texts of literary classics. Unfortunately, such texts frequently fail to preserve the literary value of the original.

This discussion has led to a pair of conclusions which, taken together, seem distressing. First, literature can be used to teach something else only if it first succeeds as literature, and second, literature as it is used in second language learning programs generally does not succeed as literature. Indeed, this failure seems due in part to the ESL goals which literature is being used to serve.

But the discussion so far has assumed that a reader understands a story only by drawing on a previous understanding of the words and sentence structures through which the story is told. Occasionally just the reverse occurs: an understanding of the story as a whole may precede an understanding of certain of the words or sentence structures used in that story. This is clearly true for young children listening to stories. After all, children are still learning their own language. They are not familiar with more than a small portion of the words in their language. They still find many complex sentence structures puzzling. And yet some linguistically rather sophisticated children's stories do evoke a literary experience for their listeners. The impressive body of children's literature in English attests to the existence of a demand which this writing meets.

Adults too may find a literary experience where they do not find complete verbal understanding. Any modern audience of a Shakespearian play is bound to lose some of the meaning couched in archaic words and sentence structures. Yet current enthusiasm for these plays has encouraged countless modern performances.

To receive a story as a literary experience without a complete understanding of the words and sentences in that story requires some other, nonverbal, clues to the meaning of the story. Such clues can be provided. The logic of the story provides an important clue to meaning. A puzzling word or sentence can often be understood from the context. If the story is accompanied by pictures, that context will be in part nonverbal. If the story is read aloud, the changes in tone of the reader's voice provide other clues to meaning. If the story is in any sense "acted out" with hand puppets, cartoon characters, or live actors, then, of course, numerous other visual clues to meaning are provided. But all of the nonverbal clues to meaning suggested here have one important element in common; all can be introduced without disrupting the story. In fact, they become part of the story, part of the literary experience.

Another way to provide a situation in which a literary experience can precede total verbal understanding would be to use stories with which the student is already familiar in his native language. The student would then be associating unfamiliar language with familiar meanings. This reverses the more usual situation in which a known language system is used to convey new information. A special characteristic of literary experiences makes this reversal possible. A literary experience is repeatable. A good story can be retold again and again. The literary experience may be intensified rather than diminished by this retelling.

In all of these ways an ESL teacher can encourage his students to receive English stories as literary experience. But will such stories also provide a language-learning experience? There are at least two important reasons for supposing that they will. First, stories received as literary experiences are repeatable. The value of a story that the second language learner is willing or anxious to hear over and over again is obvious. One of the most serious limitations on the length of a foreign language lesson is the fatigue or boredom that sets in after the student has been forced to repeat a lesson or to listen to this continual repetition. This sort of fatigue is perhaps the primary limiting factor on the length of language laboratory sessions. Stories that evoke a literary experience would provide a corpus of English sentences the student could listen to several times with sustained interest.

A second reason why a literary experience will also be language-learning experience is that the language of literature is memorable. The use of rhythm and rhyme by poets and by many prose writers as well makes their words and sentences easier to recall. Moreover people tend to remember best what interests them most deeply rather than what they are told to remember or are consciously trying to remember. The behavior of young children supports the truth of this statement. A child unable to remember his own address or telephone number may be able to recite verbatim long passages from several of his favorite storybooks.

4. **How, then, can a teacher encourage his students to experience a story as literature?**

Since the concern here is with a literary experience rather than with literature, an answer to the above question must consider all of the elements that go to make up that experience. Such elements include a literary text, various nonverbal accompaniments to that text (illustrations, sound effects, etc.), and an environment in which the literature is received. In order to encourage a literary experience the teacher must control the effect of all these elements on the student.

The Choice of Literary Text

The teacher must begin by finding a text than can evoke a literary response in his students. To do this he may have to look beyond the standard lists of literary classics. Literature, as the term has been used here, is not an absolute label attached to certain books. It describes any book capable of evoking a certain kind of response from readers, and books that elicit that response may vary from one group of readers to another. The teacher must search for clues as to what stories will evoke this response in his particular group of students. He might, for example, observe what books his students read in their own language or what TV programs they watch. It may be possible, especially with younger students, to record and translate stories that the students themselves have made up in their native language.

In any good ESL textbook, rigorous control is imposed on the rate at which new material is presented to the student. The same kind of control should exist when a second language is taught through literature. The student must not be overwhelmed by a story which includes many new vocabulary words and at the same time several new grammatical structures. If the story is used to teach grammar or vocabulary, certainly this same story should not present the student with new or unfamiliar cultural assumptions. Perhaps, at least in the earlier stages of language learning, the stories used to teach the student should be stories with which he is already familiar. Translations of popular stories from the student's native language into a reasonably simple English version may provide appropriate second language learning stories if the literary value of the story is not lost in the translation. Countries where English is an official second language (such as India, the Philippines, and various African nations) may produce a body of literature written in English. This literature allows the ESL teacher to introduce students from these countries to the English language without, at the same time, introducing British or American culture.

The Nonverbal Accompaniment to the Text

The number of nonverbal clues to meaning that accompany the story should be maximized. The story should have pictures and plenty of them, even if the students are adults. For children the story might also be accompanied by various sound effects. Ideally, the story should be read aloud by the teacher since the teacher's tone of voice provides another nonverbal aid to understanding. Literature has generally been introduced in an ESL program as an aid to teaching reading. Consequently, students have had little or no exposure to literature in English until they were well along in their mastery of the language. If literature is presented orally, it can be introduced at an earlier stage of language learning.

At the earliest stages of language learning, the pictures and other nonverbal clues should be complete enough to sustain the story line without any support at all from the words. Perhaps the story should be first introduced to the students as a completely nonverbal experience. The words would then be correlated with an experience that the student already understood rather than used to evoke understanding. Another related technique, which takes advantage of the repeatability of literature, would be to retell the same story several times gradually increasing the complexity of the language used.

The Reading Environment

The environment in which the literature is to be read should be made as relaxed and noncoercive as possible. If a student is forced to sit down and listen to a story in spite of any desires he may have to the contrary, he is not likely to respond appropriately to the story. The more relaxed and informal the situation in which the reading occurs, the more likely students will be to receive the story as a literary experience. Novels and other stories are not at their best when read or heard from behind a desk.

The teacher should minimize the amount of explanation that he gives to accompany the story. Ideally, the story should explain itself. Certainly the teacher should avoid interrupting the story to explain what is happening or to define words. A joke which has to be explained isn't funny. For the same reason, students are not going to respond to stories which are continually interrupted by explanations. A more effective way of defining new words would be to use the words in a context that makes the meaning clear. This context might include pictures as well as words.

The reading of a story should not be followed immediately by a test on the reading. Students who are aware of this impending test will be preparing for the test rather than enjoying the story. They will be concentrating on the wrong thing and consequently defeating the purpose of using the story.

* * *

All of these suggestions have been offered in the hope that ESL teachers will find some of them useful in their own teaching situations. But no general discussion can anticipate all of the specific problems that the individual teacher faces. The art of teaching is the art of creating, from available materials, a situation in which learning will occur. The point of this discussion has been to suggest some general guidelines for the effective use of literary texts in creating a language-learning situation. In particular this discussion proposes that rather than trying to make the reading of literature a conscious language-learning experience for the student, the teacher should concentrate his primary attention on presenting literature in such a way that it evokes a literary experience in the student. If this experience is thwarted or made secondary to some nonliterary goal, the inherent cultural and linguistic difficulties in literature will make literature an inappropriate source of second language learning material. If, however, students are presented with stories and encouraged to experience those stories as literature, without the imposition of other goals, the resulting literary experience will also be an effective language-learning experience and will provide a valuable supplement to pattern practice, substitution drills, and other language-learning devices.

Notes

1. This discussion is meant for teachers considering the use of literature in a second language teaching program. The recommendations made here should not be misapplied to another, different teaching situation: the teaching of British or American literature to students whose native language is not English. These two areas of teaching have totally different objectives. The ultimate objective of the teaching discussed in this paper is the mastery of the English language by non-native speakers. To expand these same non-native speakers' knowledge or appreciation of English literature is a worthy but different goal.
2. Maurice Natanson, *Literature, Philosophy, and the Social Sciences: Essays in Existentialism and Phenomenology* (The Hague: M. Nijhoff, 1962), pp. 96–97.

3. Both Dostoevski and dimestore novels can and do evoke the sort of literary experience described here. But the fact that a literary experience may be evoked by something less than "good literature" does not render the distinction between good and bad literature meaningless. What is called here a literary experience may, in fact, be a range of different but related experiences. Such differences might distinguish good from bad literature. Or perhaps the goodness of literature depends on the philosophical or moral content of the writing. Such concerns are centrally important for the teaching of literature but are not crucial for the use of literature in teaching English as a second language. (See n. 1 supra for further explanation of this distinction.)

4. For further discussion of literature as a vehicle for teaching British and American culture in an ESL program see: John F. Povey, "Literature in TESL Programs: the Language and the Culture," *TESOL Quarterly 1* (June 1967): 2.40–46; and Charles T. Scott, "Literature and the ESL Program," *The Modern Language Journal 48* (December 1964): 489–93, reprinted in *Teaching English as a Second Language,* ed. Harold B. Allen (New York: McGraw-Hill, 1965), pp. 292–99.

20

Language Drill and Young Children

Muriel Saville-Troike

Ƴ Linguists and educators have developed efficient methods of teaching English as a second language ·using various types of pattern drills. They have contended that language habits are best developed when students repeat phonological and grammatical structures as a group and as individuals. Instead of talking to students about language and teaching by translation, they have taught English by having students use the language in drills which have been structured to present new linguistic elements in an ordered sequence and to reinforce them through frequent practice.

In spite of the often-successful use of these language teaching methods with older children and adults for a quarter of a century, their application to early childhood education has not been completely accepted. There remains a feeling among some educators that young children "catch" a second language through exposure to others who speak it, and that structured language lessons violate some principles of "natural" growth and development. ⌡

It is quite true that a child who grows up with standard English spoken all around him usually speaks the language with sufficient fluency by first grade to permit communication with adults and peers in linguistic structures which are far more complex than those he will meet in the beginning reading material. But many children, including thousands of American Indians, do not fit this developmental pattern. They either do not hear English spoken by family and friends, or they are "exposed" to a nonstandard form of the language which may differ substantially from the variety which they will need in school. English is not a secure and uncon-

Reprinted from *English for American Indians* (Winter 1969), a newsletter of the Office of the Assistant Commissioner for Education, Bureau of Indian Affairs, Department of the Interior, Washington, D.C. Prepared by the Center for Applied Linguistics, Washington, D.C.

Muriel Saville-Troike of Georgetown University, Washington, D.C., has long been involved with the problems of bilingual education, especially with Navajo children. Formerly of the University of Texas, she has co-authored *A Handbook of Bilingual Education* with Rudolph C. Troike.

scious habit they bring to the new school environment; it is rather a foreign element to be conquered before further learning can take place.

In a few schools, this barrier to learning (to concept development) is never erected. When a teacher speaks the children's native language when they first enter the school situation, this foreign element is removed. Even when the native language is used only incidentally in a classroom, some immediate verbal communication is possible, and a rapport is established which is conducive to security and learning. When the native language is additionally used for instruction, concept development may be based on what the child has already learned and not wait until the time when English can be used.

Whether or not a bilingual program is immediately feasible in any particular classroom, English is an important component of instruction. Although beginning reading materials are now being developed in some American Indian languages, including Navajo and Hopi, and much learning can take place without textbooks if a teacher is creative, the acquisition of English is a prerequisite within the United States for higher education, and for social and economic mobility.

My own experiences in teaching English as a second language at both the kindergarten and university levels have convinced me that in a classroom situation a language is seldom caught by mere exposure, but requires a sequential and systematic presentation of structural elements for maximum effectiveness and efficiency with students of all ages. When provisions are made for different interest levels and attention spans, I believe language "drill" is compatible with the more informal curriculum of early childhood education. I would like to illustrate types of language activities which have been developed specifically for teaching the contrastive sounds of English to children in kindergarten, beginner, or first grade classrooms.

Carefully graded lessons to present English sentence structures are already available to most teachers. An early lesson for students with no knowledge of English might consist of the teacher holding up several objects in turn, saying "a _____" with each and having the children repeat each phrase. Individual children would then take turns selecting an object and saying "a _____." There is not enough information on the learning styles in different cultures to permit safe generalizations, but the following order provides a guideline for language activities: (1) recognition − the teacher provides a verbal model; (2) imitation − the group responds; (3) individual production.

During the free play period which follows such an elementary presentation, the objects introduced in the drill (e.g. doll, bead, peg, ball, truck, block) should be available to the children. The teacher and aide would encourage the children to identify the objects verbally during that time. Whenever possible, more than one object should be used to illustrate the range of meaning appropriate to each word. "Doll" includes rag doll, large doll, and small doll; "bead" includes square bead, red bead, yellow bead, and round bead. Further abstraction will be achieved as these objects are presented in pictures and then on small flash cards which can be used by pairs of children in some of the pattern practices and in response to the teacher in group activities. The subsequent lesson would expand these phrases to complete sentences, "This is a ____," and new words should be presented in structures of gradually increasing complexity.

Correct pronunciation should be a component of language instruction from the beginning so that faulty habits will not be practiced as English is acquired. Children who have learned some vocabulary items before entering school often still use their native sound system in producing them, so that this aspect of instruction benefits even those who may already be able to communicate in English. While most vocabulary development will occur when words are presented in carefully graded sentence patterns, many new words will be learned in pattern practices of the type suggested below — particularly if pictures and objects are available to illustrate each lesson. Their primary function, however, is to teach the recognition and production of sounds which are contrastive in English, but not in the language which is native to the children.

A pair of English sounds which is difficult for speakers of many American Indian languages such as Navajo, Papago, Alabama, Hopi, and Eskimo, is the /ϴ/ of *th*ing and the /d/ of *th*is.* A pattern requiring frequent use of /ϴ/ is "*Th*imble, *th*imble, who has the *th*imble," played as you do "Button, button, who has the button." You may then give the thimble (or any other article containing /ϴ/) to one child and have him say "*Th*ank you for the *th*imble." He chooses a child and passes the thimble on to him. The game continues until each child has had a chance to say "*Th*ank you for the *th*imble." This sound is reviewed daily during snack time if each child says "*Th*ank you" when he is served.

The sound /đ/ may be practiced by teaching the song "Here We Go Round the Mulberry Bush." Have the children act out all the verses which begin "*Th*is is *th*e way we ____." Individual children produce /đ/ in a game where one child is "it" and says "Do *th*is" as he performs some action. All of the children imitate him. If he says "Do *th*at," any child who imitates him is out.

---

* Slashes, as in /p/ and /b/, are used to indicate the basic sounds or phonemes of a language. These sounds contrast with other sounds in the language and make it possible to indicate differences in meaning in such words as, for instance, "pack" and "back" in English. In standard English orthography, phonemes are indicated in a variety of ways, e.g. /i/ is often indicated by the following spellings: f*i*t, w*o*men, s*y*stem, etc., and /f/ by *ph*oto, rou*gh*, sta*ff*, etc.

After both /ϴ/ and /đ/ can be produced, several patterns may be practiced in which they must be distinguished. Have several spools of different colored thread in front of the class. The children take turns saying "I *th*ink I want *th*e _____ *th*read," practicing color names as well as the sounds being drilled. You may also have a relay race. Give each team a thimble to pass to the next in line. As a child passes the thimble to the one behind him, he must say "*Th*is is a *th*imble." Once the children have learned the English labels for several objects containing /ϴ/ and /đ/, put these, or pictures of them, on a table in front of the class: Say "I'm *th*inking of some*th*ing *th*at's on *th*e table. What is it?" One child at a time answers, "I *th*ink it's *th*e _____," until the object is guessed. The child who names the object is then "it" and has others guess what he is thinking of. Phonological drill can also be incorporated into lessons for concept development. Discuss the meaning of the words "thick" and "thin." Then let children in turn point to a picture or object and say "*Th*e _____ is _____ (*th*ick or *th*in)." After attention has been called to shapes, put various objects in a bag. The children take turns reaching in without looking and guess what the object is by the way it feels. They should say "I *th*ink *th*is is a _____."

While individual and small group responses are often desirable, at times the entire class should repeat words after the teacher, whose pronunciation serves as a model. This can be made more interesting for young children by telling them about echoes and making such drill an "echo game." The children need not know the meanings of all the words to profit from such activity. A suggested list for /ϴ/ and /đ/ would be:

this	bathtub	bathe
thumb	mother	mouth
that	panther	lathe
thread	father	moth
they	birthday	smooth
think	feather	teeth

Voiced and voiceless stops do not contrast in many languages. To introduce /t/ and /d/, first, using your natural pronunciation, say the names of several pictures representing words that contain /t/ in the initial and final positions.* Then have the children repeat them as the picture is shown:

---

* The phonemes /t/ and /d/ between vowels in the middle of words are pronounced alike in many dialects of American English, and are different from /t/ and /d/ in initial and final position, e.g. *tot*ter, ba*tt*ed, *did*dle, etc.

toy	foot
telephone	meat
tree	plant
toe	cat
television	rat

Put the pictures in front of the class and let each child take a turn with the pointer, touching a picture and saying, "I am *t*ouching the _____." Then say the names of several pictured objects which contain /d/ and have the children repeat these after you:

duck	red
doe	wood
doll	hand
dish	bed
desk	salad

Make several colored deer, dogs, ducks, and donkeys from construction paper. As a child takes his turn he might say to another "*D*o you want a re*d* *d*uck?" The child who is asked answers either "Yes, I *d*o want a re*d* *d*uck," or "No, I *d*on't want a re*d* *d*uck.I want a green *d*og." The child who has chosen an animal then asks another "*D*o you want a blue *d*onkey?" Continue this game until all the animals have been chosen.

To help teach the distinction between /t/ and /d/, make a chart with two pockets and paste one picture illustrating a word beginning with /t/ over one pocket and one illustrating a word beginning with /d/ over the other. Paste pictures of objects whose names contain /t/ or /d/ on several flash cards and have the children sort them into the appropriate pockets. A dog, for instance, should be put in the pocket under the doll, and a cat under the picture of a television. If the children do not know all of the necessary labels, the teacher should supply them as each picture is selected. The same pictures of objects whose names contain /t/ and /d/ may be used to play "Take and Trade." The first child who is "it" says "I will *t*ake a (*t*ruck)." He holds it in front of the class. The next child says "I will *t*ake a (*t*elephone). Will you *t*rade your (*t*ruck) for my (*t*elephone)?" All children who have had a turn remain standing until the game is over so that the participants may have a chance to trade for any item already chosen. This game requires a more complex sentence pattern, and the children will require prompting a few times until it has been learned. A child who does not yet want to use English, but who wants to participate in such activities, should be allowed to have a turn, with the teacher providing the necessary language pattern.

Similar activities may be used for /k/ and /g/. In addition, words containing /k/ and /g/ should be said by the teacher. The children are instructed to clap or raise their hands when they hear /k/, but not /g/. If this is too difficult, first use words with /k/ and words with entirely dissimilar consonants, such as *man, floor,* and *green.* Then put a picture illustrating a word containing /k/ or /g/ on each rung of a ladder cut from construction paper. The children can "climb the ladder" by telling what is on each step, climbing up and down.

Minimal pairs are very useful for teaching the contrasts in English phonology once the concepts "same/different" have been taught with concrete objects and pictures. Without concern for meaning, the teacher should then ask "Are these words the same or different?"

> cat – cat
> cat – dog
> man – man
> girl – boy

When gross differences can be distinguished, drill may begin on those sounds which are contrastive in the children's native language, but in minimal English pairs, such as:

> man – tan
> car – far

Finally, minimal pairs should be presented which contain the English phonemes which are not contrastive in the native language, such as /k/ and /g/ for speakers of Eskimo and Hopi:

> cave – gave
> Kay – gay
> crew – grew
> cot – got
> came – game
> cab – gab
> coat – goat

These can be used in the following way:

> Teacher: cave – cave
> Children: same
> Teacher: cot – got
> Children: different

The contrast should be first introduced in the initial position in the word, where it can be heard most easily. Children who are reluctant to speak can clap when the words are different, raise their hands, or ring a bell.

The contrast of the voiceless stop /p/ and the voiced stop /b/ in English is a particular problem for speakers of Navajo. The Navajo stop /b/ is similar to the English unaspirated [p] in "spot," but can never occur in final position. The echo game can be used to give Navajo children practice in pronouncing /p/ in various environments:

pan	apple	soap
pen	happy	tap
pig	rapid	rap
Peter	staple	gap
pull	maple	cap
pretty	open	ship
pony	paper	cup

Put small articles with names containing /p/ in packages quickly made by wrapping them in newsprint. Children choose one and say "My *p*ackage has a _____ in it." The same type of practice can be done for the voiced stop /b/. Make a list of a few words showing /b/ in initial, medial and final positions and have the children repeat them. Then have each child put an object into a bag and show it to the class saying "My *b*ag has a _____ in it."

Both /f/ and /v/ are new speech sounds for Navajo children. They should first be presented in echo games with words to be repeated after the teacher. Then put pictures or objects containing /f/ in a bag for the "finding" game. The children take turns taking something from the bag and saying "I *f*ound a _____." For further practice, one child is blindfolded and touches another child who must say "*F*ee, *F*ie, *F*oe, *F*um." If the blindfolded child guesses the speaker, he can be "it" again. When /v/ is introduced, play a "visiting" game. The teacher says "Joe, who do you want to *v*isit?" Joe replies "I want to *v*isit Rose." He takes Rose's place in her chair and Rose is asked who she wants to visit. The game continues until many of the children have changed places.

The contrast between /f/ and /v/ can be practiced by cutting fish of different colors and attaching a paper clip to each. The children go fishing with a pole and magnet and say when they are successful, "I have a *(color)* fish."

Consonant clusters usually present a problem for children learning

English. An echo game may be used for both initial and final clusters. All of the following examples contain /s/, but others may be added:

stove	spool	stool
school	spider	spoon
sponge	stone	stack
sharks	sheets	maps
tacks	cats	barks
tents	hops	bats

Minimal pairs may be used in a "same/different" activity, as suggested above.

sale – scale
suit – scoot
soon – spoon
sake – steak
cider – spider
worse – works
toss – tops
loss – lots
bass – bats
toss – tossed

Vowels are harder than consonants for children to distinguish, and they should probably not be emphasized until the "drill" techniques have been established. English /ə/, as in cut, and /æ/, as in cat, are usually the most troublesome.

Say these words that contain /ə/ and have the children play the echo game and repeat them after you:

cut	but	hunt
shut	bunt	rut
mutt	fun	sun
putt	one	gun
run	nut	come

Repeat the preceding words along with several that do not contain the sound /ə/. Have the children raise their hands whenever they hear a word containing /ə/.

Next use words that contain both /a/, as in f*a*ther, and /ə/, as in m*o*ther, in the same manner:

cot	cut	mop
but	bond	bunt
pop	bun	box
fun	rot	hut
doll	hunt	got
nut	hop	one

Have the children repeat the following minimal pairs and then use them for a "same/different" drill:

cot – cut	dock – duck
lock – luck	doll – dull
not – nut	hot – hut
sock – suck	pop – pup
pot – putt	clock – cluck

Contrast /ə/ with /e/ in the same way in such words as b*u*t and b*e*t, and then make another chart with two pockets. A minimal pair, such as pictures representing "run" and "wren" should be pasted over the pockets. The children sort pictures as suggested for /t/ and /d/.

Cut shoes from colored paper and use a wooden doll bed. The children take turns choosing a pair of shoes and saying "I put the *(color)* shoes under the bed." This exercise may be combined with a lesson on prepositions and shoes may be put *on* the bed and *by* the bed as appropriate.

The vowel /æ/ may be introduced with an echo game:

band	cap	sand
map	pat	calf
rat	have	at
hat	lamp	hand
back	bag	van

Have pictures of a cat and several hats of different colors prepared for use on a flannel board. Each child chooses a hat, puts it on the cat, and says "I put a *(color)* hat on the cat." Then have the children color and cut out a hat, bat, or cat. Each child holds his picture in front of him and says "I'm a _____."

Let the children hear and feel the difference between /a/ and /æ/ by repeating these minimal pairs:

cot – cat	got – gat	spot – spat
pot – pat	hot – hat	not – gnat
rot – rat	tot – tat	cop – cap
mop – map	bond – band	bog – bag
bottle – battle		

Have pictures of a cot and several cats of different colors prepared for the flannel board. Each child chooses a cat, puts it on the cot, and says "I put a *(color)* cat on the cot." For additional practice with this vowel contrast, the children may stand or sit in a circle and throw a ball back and forth to one another, saying *"(Name), catch the ball,"* as they throw.

Certain types of activities will be more effective than others with different teachers and different groups of children. Those which are most effective should be adapted for introducing and reviewing other sounds.

Knowing which English phonemes require direct teaching is essential if a teacher is to be sensitive to the children's language errors and prepared to correct them. The problem areas may be predicted from a contrastive analysis of the native language and English. There are a few works providing information on contrastive features of English and American Indian languages, such as *English as a Second Language for Navajos: An Overview of Certain Cultural and Linguistic Factors* by Robert Young, and *A Teacher's Guide for Teaching English to Native Children of Alaska (Eskimo and Athapaskan)* edited by Donald H. Webster. Similar articles for other Indian languages would be very useful for teachers and those interested in the preparation of materials.

21

Priorities in Instituting the Teaching of English as a Second Language in a Southwest Texas School

Robbie Choate Cooksey

This is the history of a small step one Texas school took toward better education for Latin-American students who had been denied the equality of opportunity which is America's traditional promise. This simple story is told for the encouragement of other schools which must begin their journeys to educational equality at the same point. For this one began, as theirs must, from a point of almost total disregard of the second-language problems of a ninety percent Spanish-speaking student body in a district which at that time was still using instructional methods and texts identical to those of schools whose total school population were native speakers of English. It is possible that taking the first small step required more determination and singlehearted effort than will many of the miles yet to go.

To understand the sequence of steps taken, one must know the local conditions which dictated priorities. The following are elements of the local situation as I saw them after I had been in the district as supervisor for two years.

The teachers were not trained in second-language teaching. Faculty members laid the blame for the poor academic progress of Spanish-speaking students at the doors of their parents: "They'll never learn to speak English if they don't speak it at home!" This frequently-voiced suggestion for solving the language problem, offered with a straight face, registered a lack of training, an unawareness of the nature of language, and a necessary hardening of the heart toward the plight of the children. Hardening was necessary if a teacher was to return day after day to a defeating classroom.

As in many schools of this area, the faculty was marked by its num-

---

Reprinted from *Tesol Quarterly* 2 (September 1968): 181–86.

Robbie Choate Cooksey of Pan American University, Edinburg, Texas, is a pioneer in bilingual education in the Lower Rio Grande Valley in Texas. When the following study was written, she was supervisor of instruction in a Rio Grande Valley school district.

ber of nondegree teachers, its many teaching outside their fields of training, its many who had had no fresh college training for ten, fifteen, or twenty years, and its large annual turnover in staff. One or two teachers held membership in professional organizations other than the Texas State Teachers Association and the Classroom Teachers Association, both of which must be classified, on the local level, as being essentially politically oriented rather than curriculum-directed bodies. When I first came to the district, there was no local supervision and no inservice training program. The word was *laissez faire,* i.e., indifference coupled with and encouraged by administrative non-interference which both reflected and reinforced the prejudice existing between the socially and economically dominant Anglo minority and the Spanish-speaking majority. Truth, even when moderated by compassion, realistically spotlights these conditions of six years ago.

School statistics, compiled in the fall of 1965, reveal the damage done by language deficiencies, educational deprivation, and poverty — a syndrome of disability which seemed destined to perpetuate itself endlessly (see Table 21.1).

Table 21.1
System-Wide Data on Educational Disabilities
in Percentages by Grades

Grade	Percent Over-Age	Percent Below Grade	Percent Inadequate in English	Percent Spanish-Speaking
1	40	13	95	96
2	56	35	88	95
3	64	48	88	94
4	66	45	84	92
5	74	59	64	91
6	69	60	88	94
7	73	71	45	91
8	66	63	57	88
9	65	39	52	86
10	67	45	62	85
11	54	28	52	77
12	60	64	60	75

Note:
Column headings signify the following:
Grade — Current Grade Assignment
Over-Age — Percentage of children one year or more older than normal for assigned grade
Below Grade — Percentage of children testing one year or more below the assigned grade level in all English language skills
Inadequate in English — Percentage of children with deficiencies in English language skills so marked as to handicap their participation in class
Spanish-Speaking — Percentage of native speakers of Spanish

Such disturbing statistics, translated into the living faces of boys and girls defeated by their world, demanded action. Yet, there had to be first a very great desire to salvage the Latin-American child. There had to be a desire great enough to reckon the cost of, and be willing to pay for, possible failure; schools in this area of Texas are frequently the battle-ground for local political factions, and roots of bitter factionalism feed on the differences in culture and language. Because of that climate, school personnel who wish to remain in the district appear indifferent to local inequities while wearing the protective coloring of the dominant faction.

Realistic willingness to try for change was the first necessity. Following two years of probing into the depths of local failure, desire to effect change hardened into determination on my part as supervisor. Together with determination was the disturbing certainty of my inadequacy. Searching for possibilities of bringing education to our children, I began an intensive study of second-language teaching with a book salesman's gift copy of Nelson Brooks' *Language and Language Learning.*[1] References in Brooks led to other books; their footnotes and bibliographies led to others, and challenging possibilities began to appear. Without formal training or guide, my search was without plan; and, while persistent, it was not unlike the burrowing of a gopher crisscrossing his tunnels in the dark. The search could have been easier, but it could not have been more exciting or rewarding. Since its beginning four years ago, many books have joined Nelson Brooks on my shelves; but the first three which were studied — perhaps a curious trio — are treasured: English Language Services' *English This Way,* Book 3,[2] Robert Lado's *Linguistics Across Cultures,*[3] and the Boggs-Dixson *English Step by Step with Pictures.*[4]

While trying to learn the best theory and techniques of second-language teaching, I assessed the hazards of beginning a broad program of teaching English as a second language from preschool through grade twelve. My decision was that no program could get off the ground as long as the faculty maintained its defeatist attitude, complacency, and seeming contentment with a fourth-rate education for the Spanish-speaking child. Working under the assumption that the temporary defeat of the teachers was due in large part to lack of training and absence of challenge, I decided to begin an intensive teacher-training program, with changes in attitude as its first goal. I believed there could be no better way to initiate change in teacher attitude than to involve them in the joy of language discovery. In training meetings, I forced teachers to take their own language out of its category of unconscious habit. As they explored its complexity, rigidity, and flexibility, they gained respect for the grip it has on the user because of habit. The speech of five-year-olds demonstrated how native language is learned, as well as the firm grasp the child may have of both structure and sound before he attains school age. Specific structural patterns in English and Spanish were contrasted, using as illustrations errors heard daily in the school halls or encountered repeatedly in student compositions:

> *This peoples have move.*
> *He appreciated me to help him.*
> *He didn't had some pencils, too.*
> *Does she lives here?*
> *You like to study, isn't it?*
> *My father was content of the work.*
> *Bill asked whether can the old cars start.*
> *The govern was sick all more for a year.*

As teachers realized the reasons for a Spanish-speaker's making errors similar to these, they grew in tolerance; and the old solution, "They just need to speak English at home," was heard less frequently. The idea was emerging that language cannot be originated out of simple desire to communicate and that one can produce only what one has been taught.

After 1½ years of implementation, inservice training still remained the heart of the program. It was never a sophisticated type of inservice with "name" speakers or university teams imported as trainers. That was not possible. It was, simply, that as I learned, I taught. A prompt transfer of learning was attempted, usually in small group meetings by levels — primary, intermediate, or secondary — in an effort to give each what seemed immediately useful in both theory and methods. Also, as quickly as possible, the best of instructional materials and equipment was purchased, and a materials-and-training center was established where teachers could become acquainted with both before their placement in the classrooms.

Almost immediately following the earliest training, secondary language arts teachers began using tape recorders and headphones with commercially prepared tapes for English as a second language; intermediate teachers began using oral drills from *English This Way;* and primary teachers taught non-English-speaking five-year-olds for ninety minutes after school each day. The after-school classes were necessary because there was neither space nor teachers to hold classes during the regular day. Extended exposure to spoken English was provided in our community by showing free at night, during the regular term and in summer, standard movies in English rented for that purpose.

It would be foolish to state that all teachers applauded this program, all learned what was presented in inservice meetings, all tried new language techniques in their classes, all dropped cherished superiority illusions and displayed new warm regard for the Spanish speaker and his culture. It would be equally incorrect to state that the program of teaching

English as a second language did not lift off the ground. After the first year's four-month effort, response on the part of alert intellectual leaders and the faculty was encouragement enough to validate another year of training and trial.

As in the first four months, inservice training gave direction, cohesion, thrust, and heart to the effort, even as it expanded the teachers' understanding of second-language teaching. Phases of language theory and methods which were covered in this training included the intimate relationship between a culture and its language; a limited contrastive analysis of the sound, structure, and vocabulary systems of the two languages; oral drill techniques with practice and suggestions for their use in class, including methods for a judicious control of student origination of utterances beyond their point of training; some ideas for adapting to the needs of second-language learners the texts provided by the state, with emphasis on preparing sound and structure drills from selections in those texts; and good sequencing of the introduction of new structural elements. This last was particularly difficult for teachers to grasp because of the brevity of their training and the great gulps of new information they were force-fed in haste. Sequencing information offered the teachers was that which I obtained in a step-by-step comparison of the order in which new structures were introduced in five texts for students of English as a second language. Much of the success of this inservice program has to be credited to the new receptivity of most teachers, their continuing spirit of willingness, and their high interest. Of help also was the feeling abroad that our small district led this area in beginning to break through the second-language barrier to education, that it alone was definitely training teachers in second-language teaching, and that it had the only kindergarten through twelfth grade second-language program in the area.

Some success was measured in the classrooms. Administering locally prepared tests of oral language proficiency to all students in grades four through twelve proved that we needed more skill in making tests. However, they also seemed to provide enough valid results to justify our selecting some specific structures as instructional goals for grades four through six. After ninety-six days of instruction directed at these goals, our post-tests indicated that the pre-test disability of eighty-five percent had been cut to thirty-one percent. Informal teacher evaluation of the effectiveness of the entire program has been encouraging. The most obvious affirmative result, in my opinion, has been the disappearance of much of the attitude of complacency and defeatism, and replacement by fresh-blowing winds of enthusiasm, enterprise, and expectancy. Many successes seem suddenly possible and surely are possible any time an intelligent corps of teachers is informed and challenged.

Witness to the new spirit is an attempt by secondary English language arts teachers to write a curriculum guide which will actually try to reach each student at his exact level of language ability and bring him forward along the full continuum of language skills to a point of proficiency commensurate with his native ability. No one can fully appreciate the terrifying difficulties of writing such a guide if he has not had to try teaching English to the conglomeration of extreme language abilities and disabilities confronting the teacher of our secondary classes. At present, it seems that the guide will be as fresh and novel as is the effort. For there are no guides available to copy — none, that is, which provides guidance for teachers who have in one class students ranging from the completely non-English-speaking to native speakers of English whose proficiency with their language is far above that of their assigned grade level. That local teachers see the need for such a realistic guide, and will attempt to develop one, is indication that change is already inside the door.

In review, the priorities for instituting a program to teach English as a second language in this school were the priorities necessitated by the local social-political climate, the mood and competency level of the faculty, and the lack of language training on the part of the one instructional supervisor. Such local restrictions dictated this order of needs: (1) leadership concern so great as to sustain the effort of self-training and to reckon the need worthy of the risk involved in attempting a vigorous schoolwide program; (2) training and challenge for the teachers; (3) selection and procurement of the best materials and equipment; (4) decision as to extent of the attack, that is, how many students to teach and in what grades; (5) testing for disability, selecting objectives, teaching for change, and post-testing; (6) reappraisal of methods, materials, and inservice training; (7) maintenance of the high level of interest and effort necessary for a continuation of the program. If this last need can be met, despite the loss of key supervisory personnel and the influx of untrained new teachers, there is a possibility for full two-language competency for Latin-American students in this school and for their scholastic achievement in other fields — an achievement which has had to wait upon language development.

If the effort can be maintained, such success is possible. There remain, however, dangers to success in this area of Texas. There is danger in a rejection of personnel whose vision and drive forced a beginning. There is danger in a reascendancy of those on the school board who see in power the promise of return to the "Old South" idyll of a decade ago when Anglos, fat in their egos and bank accounts, sat comfortably on the stooped back of uneducated Latin poverty, whose fourth-rate education was guaranteed by prejudicial policies. There is danger in the Spanish-speaking citizen, with attention and energies totally engaged by his own rising expectations, permitting the replacement of concerned and aggressive educator-administrators by political administrators. There is a peculiar danger in the reappearance of the administrative lullaby of *laissez faire*. In the heat-soaked lethargy of the Southwest that song, like the high-frequency incessance of cicadas in the mesquite trees, drugs the mind and dulls the heart's resolve.

One reality forced itself to the front during the length of the program. It is the reality which prompted my writing of this account — the truth that a full solution, even to its own language problem, cannot be made by any one school district. The extreme mobility of school populations in this area of winter homes for migrant farm workers and the culture-language cohesion of the Latin-American people make necessary a coordinated, systematic, areawide attack, rising out of each local school. For one school to give realistic attention to the language needs of four levels of disability in its secondary English classes is good; but it is not enough. For one school to admit the inadequate training of its faculty and attempt to make up the deficit by specialized inservice programs is good; but it is not enough. Pupils move; teachers move. What is needed is not ideas endlessly discussed in area meetings, nor small spot experiments in scattered classrooms, but an admission that second-language teaching has been done effectively overseas for many years. For students who are here today and in the fields tomorrow is the answer high-level conferences carried on with detached placidity? Or regional elbowing for grants and promise of publicity while the season runs out in the classrooms? The thousands of students pouring out of our schools year after year, fully equipped for failure, demand the immediate bold implantation of established second-language techniques into classrooms manned by trained teachers, even if those teachers must be trained on the job and as they perform the job. This has been done in nations overseas who have seen their need. Why cannot it be done in America?

Notes

1. Nelson Brooks, *Language and Language Learning* (New York: Harcourt, Brace and World, 1960).
2. English Language Services, *English This Way* (New York: The Macmillan Company, 1963).
3. Robert Lado, *Linguistics Across Cultures* (Ann Arbor: University of Michigan Press, 1967).
4. Ralph S. Boggs and Robert J. Dixson, *English Step by Step with Pictures,* rev. ed. (New York: Simon and Schuster, Regents Edition, 1971).

22.

A Practical Reading Course for
the Slow Learner in High School

Beverly Ashton

Introduction

In many high schools across the country, little, if any, consideration has been given to the problems of bilingual and bidialectal students. These pupils either drop out as soon as possible or, if they do hang on from grade to grade, receive a diploma due to the kindness of sympathetic teachers or the need for classroom space. Very little has been written concerning the problems of non-native speakers at the secondary level. The following selection can serve as a basis for planning a practical program for use by teachers who wish to provide their students with some means of handling everyday problems which involve reading.

Frank Pialorsi

*   *   *

Educators are increasingly aware of the necessity for more effective classes for the slow learner, the unmotivated, and the deficient reader in the high schools. Most secondary teachers need no evidence to know that a definite problem exists.

As a former high school English teacher who taught slow learner English classes, I tried some of the materials available on the market which claimed a low reading but high interest level. These materials were designed for the high school student. A few were successful, but I found that many materials were still too difficult for these students to read, or had the same repetitious format of the elementary books. Some were just too expensive.

Reprinted from *English Journal* 60 (Jan. 1971): 97–101. Copyright© 1971 by the National Council of Teachers of English. Reprinted by permission of the publisher and Beverly Ashton.

Beverly Ashton has been a reading teacher consultant to the Garden City, Michigan, public schools since 1968. For years a teacher of secondary school English, she developed the program discussed here in actual classroom situations.

Teachers of a required subject, who see all students regardless of ability level, have the opportunity to prepare all students for life situations if they but have the proper materials. Perhaps it is up to them to develop such materials.

The following course was developed for students who were reaching sixteen, the age when they can legally drop out of school in Michigan. I was alarmed at the rate at which my classes were shrinking and felt something had to be done. Fortunately, my principal, Gerald C. Gould, encouraged his teachers to be innovative, so I looked for a class plan which would answer the several important needs of these slow learners. This meant that the course had to be:

1. practical enough to motivate the students,
2. challenging enough to maintain the interest of the students,
3. interesting enough to the students to make it desirable to read, and
4. realistic enough to "show it like it is," which would show these students, without preaching, how much they need a high school diploma.

This discussion describes a successful unit that evolved from these criteria. Whatever you call this unit — Budget Unit, Unit for Successful Living, English for Everyday Living, Practical Application of Reading and Mathematics — it seems to stimulate these slow learners.

The course was used with eleventh-grade students, but it was later incorporated into Garden City's high school phase elect English program and was used for both eleventh- and twelfth-graders. The teachers like it because it is versatile enough to enable them to branch out in several directions while they are using it. The administration likes it because it costs so little to use and the failure rate in this course is almost nonexistent. Businessmen like it because it is free advertising and it is to their advantage to have prospective buyers a little more knowledgeable in the use of money.

The course begins with each student's being required to purchase an inexpensive cardboard cover in which to put lined paper and the budget work sheet, all of which will be used as a notebook which he can keep after the class is over. The classroom should be stocked with catalogs from every department store, income tax forms and instructions, booklets on budgeting and methods of obtaining loans (which can be procured from a local bank), booklets about credit buying, and FHA rate schedules for house loans from a realtor. All of these are read by the students, and if the popularity of books is judged by the rate at which they disappear, these booklets are well liked.

Table 22.1
English for Everyday Living
Budget Unit Worksheet

NAME _____

INCOME	Year	Month	Week
Salary	$7,000.00	$583.33	$134.61
Deductions (Federal & State Tax Social Security)	Federal 1058.20 State 115.00 Soc. Soc. 336.00 1509.20	125.76	29.02
ACTUAL INCOME	$5,490.80	$457.56	$105.59
FIXED EXPENSES			
Savings	549.08	45.76	10.56
Life Insurance	240.00	16.00 - 10000 policy 4.00 - 2000 policy 20.00	4.62
Rent (Mortgage & Taxes)	1,500.00	125.00	28.85
Insurance (Car, house, etc.)	359.00	29.69	6.91
Installment Payments (Car, loans, furniture)	680.04	56.67	13.08
TOTAL FIXED EXPENSES	$3,329.12	$277.21	$ 64.02
TOTAL AVAILABLE FOR FLEXIBLE EXPENSES (actual income minus total fixed expenses)	$2,161.68	$180.35	$ 41.57

MONTHLY FLEXIBLE EXPENSES	Year	Month	Week
Food	780.00	65.00	15.00
House Operation (Gas, lights, phone, repair, etc.)	420.00	6.50 phone, 12.50 gas, 10.00 electricity, 3.50 water, 2.50 repair, 35.00 total	8.08
Transportation (Fuel, repair)	300.00	25.00	5.77
TOTAL FOOD, TRANSPORTATION AND HOUSE OPERATION	$1,500.00	$125.00	$ 28.85
TOTAL AVAILABLE FOR MISCELLANEOUS FLEXIBLE EXPENSES	$ 661.68	$ 55.35	$ 12.72
MISCELLANEOUS FLEXIBLE EXPENSES			
Clothing			
Medical, Dental			
Recreation			
Personal Care			
Gifts, Contributions			
Dues, Subscriptions	Union dues 81.60	6.80	1.57
Personal Allowances			
TOTAL MISCELLANEOUS FLEXIBLE EXPENSES			

All figures used in this discussion are appropriate only for the Detroit area. However, I have found that local merchants are very cooperative about providing them, so there is no problem about getting the figures for any area. It should be noted that the merchants are also cooperative about coming to speak to classes, so the amount of community involvement is up to the teacher.

The course revolves around a prepared work sheet containing certain postulated figures (see example, Table 22.1). It should start with an average salary which might be offered to the students in the local area when they graduate from high school. The key word here is *graduate,* as many jobs are not available unless the applicant has a high school diploma. In the Detroit area, salaries range from $3.05 an hour at one of the local food chains to $3.75 an hour (including the cost of living) at one of the automobile plants. A $7,000 beginning salary is fairly average. The student must now budget his money so that he can provide for himself and a nonworking wife, yet buy furniture for his apartment and eventually save for a home of his own. (The girls in the class are nonworking wives for this problem and must budget the money for their families.) A non-working wife is specified to show the students why it is so difficult to survive with only one salary when they first start out. Rather than wedding gifts, each student iş allowed $1,000 in cash, but that is his only asset. The students have no car, no furniture, no insurance — nothing. (It is interesting to ask them how they would spend the $1,000 before they begin the unit, and then ask them again after the unit is finished. This will convince them of the value of this unit, if nothing else has.)

First, compute the deductions together. This exercise gives the teacher a good opportunity to incorporate a federal income tax study, if she so desires. Next, make out W-2 forms (which can be obtained from the local Internal Revenue Bureau) for the students. They use these in learning how to fill out a 1040 tax form. Michigan has a state income tax ($1,200 is allowed for each dependent, then 2.5 percent of taxable income; for this problem we do not count other deductions), so this is considered in our calculations. Social security is figured at 4.8 percent.

After actual, or take-home, income is figured, certain facts must be given. Savings are 10 percent of take-home pay. Life insurance is $20 a month: $16 a month for a $10,000 policy for the husband and $4 a month for a $2,000 policy for the wife. Car insurance depends on the area in which the applicant lives, whether or not he has had driver's training, and how many tickets he has had. The figure $359 is standard for a boy of eighteen years of age, who lives in the suburbs of Detroit, has had driver's training, and has had several tickets. The food, house operation, and transportation are low-cost figures, and the food costs do not include cigarettes, soft drinks, or entertainment.

For rent and car installment payments, the students must cut ads from the local papers and paste them in their notebooks. Students who are familiar with various areas of the city can help the others to choose an adequate apartment. Some students who are knowledgeable about cars help the less knowledgeable in their selection of a car. The car is the only item that the student can buy on an installment plan until there has been a class discussion of the advantages and fallacies of credit buying.

The car should be purchased from one of the dealers' ads in order to take advantage of the financial arrangements. In Michigan, the dealer will charge 12 percent interest compounded annually. Most loans are issued for a three-year period; practically speaking, if the student buys a car for $1,500 (this is a figure ascertained from the current Detroit papers for a 1968 serviceable sedan), multiply 3 (the time) by .12 (the interest) which equals .36 (the total rate of interest). Then multiply $1,500 by .36, which equals $540, the interest for the loan. Add $1,500 and $540 and divide by the thirty-six months to get the monthly payment for the car, in this case $56.67. This is only approximate, but it is close enough to work with. All of these steps can be demonstrated on the blackboard. Later, if the teacher wishes, she can go into the discussion of charge accounts, and if the student has prior knowledge of annual interest, it is easier to point out the high cost of borrowing money.

The student must also take into consideration the deposits he must make to the telephone company, the gas company, and the security deposit for the apartment. Plan $25 for each of the utilities and a month's extra rent for the apartment. If the ad in the paper specifies that utilities are provided for in the cost of the rent, assume it means gas and water; therefor, the student can subtract this amount from the House Operation account.

Union dues can be planned on an average of $6.80 a month. If the students are to receive a salary as high as $7,000 a year when they have no experience, insist that they include the union dues.

The budget work sheet included here shows a typical first attempt by the students to budget their $7,000-a-year salary. This budget will not operate, as there is too little money left over for flexible miscellaneous expenses. It will have to be completely adjusted; the students must examine their values to ascertain what they can do without.

Each student may divide the total available for miscellaneous flexible expenses as he or she sees fit, as each student puts emphasis on different things — some students have been taught to tithe to their church, so must take this into consideration. Teach that the husband and wife each must have a personal allowance, no matter how little. And insist that they must have some recreation each month.

The students must buy furniture and equipment for their apartment. Remind them that they have nothing — no bed, no kitchen utensils, no linens. Using the catalogs in the classroom, or handbills or advertisements that they receive at home, they must buy all furniture on a systematic basis, paying cash for each from their savings, putting a picture of each item with the cost into their notebook in the order in which they'll buy them. Here it is useful to have the home economics teacher or a resource person from the local stores explain the advantages of buying good quality items versus the expense of having to replace cheaper quality goods in a shorter time. Still keep in mind that in some cases, the cheaper is the more economical in the long run.

Many discussions or courses of study can develop and result from this unit. Progression into a study of the financial effects of a baby would be a profitable course. The latest figure in the Detroit papers shows that the cost of a baby in 1971 is about $1,600.

A career unit also would be highly beneficial. If a career unit is included, then the salary each student will work with can be the starting salary for the job of his choice rather than the standard $7,000. An in-depth study of the effects of unwise credit buying would be worthwhile. This unit can also be expanded to a class of average or above-average students. The students could be required to get all figures themselves, and do a more thorough study of all the facets of this unit.

As for the notebook, require that pictures, want ads, and figures be kept for future reference. This activity has a sobering effect, a reminder of the financial facts of life. The notebook also forms a basis on which to mark if a letter grade has to be issued in the course.

This unit is an enjoyable one to teach. Many speakers, field trips, and reading materials can break up the time spent working with mathematics. It may come as a surprise to find that many students who were never good in arithmetic do very well when they are working with this unit, and many who refuse to read regular textbooks pore over the materials assembled in this classroom. Most encouraging, the students respond with enthusiasm as they learn practical lessons they can apply directly to their everyday lives.

Suggested Reading

Abrahams, Roger D. and Rudolph C. Troike, eds. *Language and Cultural Diversity in American Education*. Englewood Cliffs: Prentice-Hall, 1972.

Allen, Harold B. *Readings in Applied English Linguistics*. New York: Appleton Century Crofts, 1964.

_____ and Russell N. Campbell, eds. *Teaching English as a Second Language*. 2nd edition. New York, McGraw-Hill, 1972.

Anderson, Nels. "The Uses and Worth of Language," in *Studies in Multilingualism*, ed. Nels Anderson. Leiden, The Netherlands: E. J. Brill, 1969.

Andersson, Theodore and Mildred Boyer. *Bilingual Schooling in the United States*. 2 vols. Austin, Texas: Southwest Educational Development Laboratory, 1970.

Brooks, Nelson. *Language and Language Learning*. New York: Harcourt, Brace & World, 1964.

Burling, Robbins. *Man's Many Voices: Language in Its Cultural Context*. New York: Holt, Rinehart, and Winston, 1970.

Burma, John H. *Spanish-Speaking Groups in the United States*. Durham, N.C.: Duke University Press, 1954.

Carter, Thomas P. *Mexican Americans in School: A History of Educational Neglect*. New York: College Entrance Examination Board, 1970.

Cheyney, Arnold B. *Teaching Culturally Disadvantaged in the Elementary School*. Columbus, Ohio: Charles E. Merrill Books, Inc., 1967.

Chomsky, Noam. *Aspects of the Theory of Syntax*. Cambridge, Mass.: MIT Press, 1965.

Cordasco, Frances and Eugene Buschioni, *Puerto Rican Children in Mainland Schools*. Metuchen, N.J.: Scarecrow Press, Inc., 1968.

Duprey, Virginia H. *A Technique of a Minority-Bilingual Group*. New York: Macmillan Company, 1955.

Estes, Dwain M. and David Darling, eds. *Texas Conference for the Mexican-American: Improving Educational Opportunities*. San Antonio: Texas Education Agency, 1967.

Fagan, Edward R. *English and the Disadvantaged*. Scranton: International Textbook Company, 1967.

Fishman, J. A. *Readings in the Sociology of Language*. The Hague: Mouton, 1968.

Frost, Joe L. and Glen R. Hawkes, eds. *The Disadvantaged Child: Issues and Innovations*. Second edition. New York: Houghton Mifflin, 1970.

Gallarza, Ernesto, Herman Gallegos, and Julian Samora. *Mexican-Americans in the Southwest.* Santa Barbara: McNally & Loftin, 1970.

Garza, Hernán Solís. *Los Mexicanos del Norte.* Mexico City: Editorial Nuestro Tiempo, 1971.

Grebler, Leo, Joan W. Moore, and Ralph C. Guzman. *The Mexican-American People.* New York: The Free Press, 1970.

Hall, Edward T. *The Silent Language.* Greenwich, Conn.: Fawcett, 1959.

Heller, Celia. *Mexican-American Youth: Forgotten Youth at the Crossroads.* New York: Random House, 1966.

Helm, June, ed. *Spanish-Speaking People in the United States: Proceedings of the 1968 Annual Spring Meeting of the American Ethnological Society.* Seattle: University of Washington Press, 1970.

Hertzler, Joyce. *A Sociology of Language.* New York: Random House, 1965.

Johnson, Kenneth R. *Teaching the Culturally Disadvantaged.* Palo Alto: Scientific Research Associates, 1970.

Kelly, L. G., ed. *Description and Measurement of Bilingualism: An International Seminar.* Toronto: University of Toronto Press, 1969.

King, Paul E. "Bilingual Readiness in Primary Grades." Microfilm no. ED-17631. Bethesda, Maryland: Leasco Informational Products, Inc. for Educational Resources Information Center (ERIC), 1966.

Knowlton, Clark S. "Bilingualism: A Problem or an Asset?" Microfilm no. ED010744. Bethesda, Maryland: Leasco Informational Products, Inc. for Educational Resources Information Center (ERIC), 1965.

Labov, William. *The Study of Nonstandard English.* Washington, D.C.: Center for Applied Linguistics, 1969.

Lado, Robert. *Language Teaching.* New York: McGraw-Hill, 1964.

————. *Language Testing.* New York: McGraw-Hill, 1961.

————. *Linguistics Across Cultures.* Ann Arbor: University of Michigan, 1957.

Lambert, W. E. and G. R. Tucker. *Bilingual Education of Children: The St. Lambert Experiment.* Rowley, Mass.: Newbury House Publishers, 1972.

Lester, Mark, ed. *Readings in Applied Transformational Grammar.* New York: Holt, Rinehart and Winston, 1970.

Lorentin, Joseph O. and Shelley Umans. *Teaching the Disadvantaged.* New York: Teachers' College Press, 1966.

Mackey, William F. *Bilingual Education in a Binational School.* Rowley, Mass.: Newbury House Publishers, 1972.

————. *Bilingualism as a World Problem.* Montreal: Harvest House, 1967.

Manuel, Hershel. *Spanish-Speaking Children of the Southwest: Their Education and the Public Welfare.* Austin: University of Texas Press, 1965.

Menyuk, Paula. *Sentences Children Use.* Cambridge: MIT Press, 1969.

National Advisory Committee on Mexican-American Education. *The Mexican-American: Quest for Equality.* Washington: United States Office of Education, 1968.

National Council of Teachers of English. *Language Programs for the Disadvantaged: Report of the NCTE Task Force on Teaching English to the Disadvantaged.* Champaign, Ill.: National Council of Teachers of English, 1965.

Politzer, Robert L. *Linguistics and Applied Linguistics: Aims and Methods.* Philadelphia: The Center for Curriculum Development, 1972.

Saville, Muriel and Rudolph C. Troike. *A Handbook of Bilingual Education.* Washington, D.C.: Clearinghouse for Linguistics, 1970.

Stern, H. H. *Foreign Languages in Elementary Schools.* London: Oxford University Press, 1967.

Taylor, Marie E. "An Overview of Research on Bilingualism." Microfilm no. ED049876. Bethesda, Maryland: Leasco Informational Products, Inc. for Educational Resources Information Center (ERIC), 1970.

Turner, Paul R., ed. *Bilingualism in the Southwest.* Tucson: The University of Arizona Press, 1973.

United Kingdom Department of Education and Science. *Bilingualism in Education.* London: Her Majesty's Stationery Office, 1965.

United States Commission on Civil Rights. *Mexican American Education Study Report 1: Ethnic Isolation of Mexican Americans of the Public Schools of the Southwest.* Washington, D.C.: U.S. Government Printing Office, 1970.

Valencia, Atilano A. *Bilingual-Bicultural Education: A Perspective Model in Multicultural America.* Albuquerque: Southwestern Cooperative Educational Laboratory, Inc., 1969.

Zintz, Miles. *Education Across Cultures.* Dubuque, Iowa: Wm. C. Brown Book Co., 1963.